Law and Economics as Interdisciplinary Exchange

Law and economics is an established field of research and arguably one of the few examples of a successful interdisciplinary project. This book explores whether, or to what extent, that interdisciplinarity has, indeed, been a success. It provides insights on the foundations and methods, achievements and challenges of Law and Economics, at a time when both the continuing criticism of academic economics and the growth of empirical legal studies raise questions about the identity and possible further developments of the project.

Through a combination of reflections on long-term trends and detailed case studies, contributors to this volume analyze the institutional and epistemic character of Law and Economics, which develops through an exchange of concepts, models and practices between economics and legal scholarship. Inspired by insights from the philosophy of the social sciences, the book shows how concepts travel between legal scholarship and economics and change meanings when applied elsewhere, how economic theories and models inform, and transform, judicial practice, and it addresses whether the transfers of knowledge between economics and law are symmetrical exchanges between the two disciplines.

Péter Cserne, PhD, is Associate Professor in Law at the University of Northumbria, UK, and extramural fellow of Tilburg Law and Economics Centre (TILEC). He has held visiting positions at Columbia, Oxford and Toronto Universities and the Max Planck Institute for Comparative Private Law in Hamburg. A lawyer and economist by training, he has published widely on legal theory, economic analysis of law and contracts. He is the founder and convener of MetaLawEcon, an international academic network for research on the foundations of economic analysis of law.

Magdalena Małecka, PhD, is Marie Skłodowska-Curie Global Fellow (University of Helsinki and Stanford University). Her Marie Curie project is a philosophical analysis of the applications of the behavioral sciences to policy. Before starting the Marie Curie Fellowship, Magdalena was a postdoctoral researcher at TINT Centre for Philosophy of Social Science (University of Helsinki) and a Max Weber Postdoctoral Fellow at the European University Institute in Florence. While remaining affiliated with TINT, in February 2018 she joined the Institute for Advanced Studies at the Central European University in Budapest for five months as a Junior Core Fellow.

The Economics of Legal Relationships
Sponsored by Michigan State University College of Law
Series Editors:
Nicholas Mercuro,
Michigan State University College of Law
Michael D. Kaplowitz,
Michigan State University

Empirical Legal Analysis
Assessing the Performance of Legal Institutions
Edited by Yun-chien Chang

Predatory Pricing in Antitrust Law and Economics
Nicola Giocoli

The Role of Law in Sustaining Financial Markets
Edited by Niels Philipsen and Guangdong Xu

Law and Economics
Philosophical Issues and Fundamental Questions
Edited by Aristides N. Hatzis and Nicholas Mercuro

Public Procurement Policy
Edited by Gustavo Piga and Tünde Tatrai

Legal Origins and the Efficiency Dilemma
Nuno Garoupa, Carlos Gómez Ligüerre and Lela Mélon

Law and Economics of Public Procurement Reforms
Edited by Gustavo Piga and Tünde Tátrai

Law and Economics as Interdisciplinary Exchange
Philosophical, Methodological and Historical Perspectives
Péter Cserne and Magdalena Małecka

Extraterritoriality and International Bribery
A Collective Action Perspective
Branislav Hock

*The first three volumes listed earlier are published by and available from Elsevier

For a full list of titles in this series please visit www.routledge.com/The-Economics-of-Legal-Relationships/book-series/ELR

Law and Economics as Interdisciplinary Exchange

Philosophical, Methodological and Historical Perspectives

Edited by
Péter Cserne and Magdalena Małecka

Routledge
Taylor & Francis Group
LONDON AND NEW YORK

First published 2020
by Routledge
2 Park Square, Milton Park, Abingdon, Oxon OX14 4RN

and by Routledge
52 Vanderbilt Avenue, New York, NY 10017

Routledge is an imprint of the Taylor & Francis Group, an informa business

British Library Cataloguing-in-Publication Data
A catalogue record for this book is available from the British Library

Library of Congress Cataloging-in-Publication Data
Names: Law and economics: Theoretical and Practical Dimensions of Interdisciplinarity (Conference) (2017 : Helsingin yliopisto) | Cserne, Péter, editor. | Małecka, Magdalena, editor. | Helsingin yliopisto, host institution.
Title: Law and economics as interdisciplinary exchange : philosophical, methodological and historical perspectives / edited by Péter Cserne and Magdalena Malecka
Identifiers: LCCN 2019025826
Subjects: LCSH: Law and economics—Congresses.
Classification: LCC K487.E3 L3883 2017 | DDC 343.07—dc23
LC record available at https://lccn.loc.gov/2019025826

ISBN: 978-0-367-13505-8 (hbk)
ISBN: 978-0-429-02685-0 (ebk)

Typeset in Bembo
by Apex CoVantage, LLC

Contents

Contributors

Piotr Bystranowski, PhD candidate, Department of Legal Theory, Jagiellonian University

Péter Cserne, Associate Professor, University of Northumbria at Newcastle School of Law

Fabrizio Esposito, Postdoctoral Fellow, Edmond J. Safra Center for Ethics, University of Tel Aviv

Magdalena Małecka, Marie Skłodowska-Curie Fellow, Stanford University and University of Helsinki

Alain Marciano, Associate Professor, MRE and Université de Montpellier, Faculté d'économie

Patricia Marino, Professor, Department of Philosophy, University of Waterloo

Steven G. Medema, Research Professor, Duke University, Department of Economics

Stefano Solari, Associate Professor, Università di Padova, Department of Economics and Management

Aleksandar Stojanović, PhD candidate, Collegio Carlo Alberto and University of Ghent, Law Faculty

Giovanni Tuzet, Professor, Department of Law, Bocconi University (Milan)

Silvia Zorzetto, Associate Professor, Department of Legal Sciences, Università di Milano

Acknowledgments

Most chapters in this volume were originally presented during a two-day workshop entitled "Law and Economics: Theoretical and Practical Dimensions of Interdisciplinarity" at the University of Helsinki in November 2017. The workshop was a collaboration of TINT Centre for Philosophy of Social Science at the University of Helsinki and MetaLawEcon, an interdisciplinary academic network of focusing on foundational issues of Law and Economics. The effort of joining forces in discussing Law and Economics as an example of interdisciplinary exchange proved very rewarding, thought-provoking and stimulating. The book is a result of this collective intellectual endeavor.

The editors would like to thank Professor Uskali Mäki, the director of TINT, for his enthusiasm and support for organizing the workshop. We are also very grateful to Dr. Fabrizio Esposito for his involvement in the organization of the workshop. We thank all speakers of the workshop, both for presenting their insightful perspectives on the topic and for acting as commentators, as well as researchers from TINT and the Law Department of the University of Helsinki for commenting on the papers presented during the event, some of which are included in this volume.

Magdalena Małecka's work on this editorial project was supported by Academy of Finland grant no. 308682 and the Marie Skłodowska-Curie Fellowship for the project EPISTEMEBEHAVIOUR.

Introduction

Péter Cserne and Magdalena Małecka

Law and Economics is arguably one of the success stories of interdisciplinary research. The application of concepts and models of standard microeconomics to explain and evaluate legal rules, doctrines and institutions has led to the development of an academic field which seems well established both in an epistemic and an institutional sense. On the one hand, Law and Economics scholars share a common terminology and they believe in the great explanatory power of their models. On the other, they have formed associations, they publish in specialized journals and teach courses and entire specialized programs dedicated to the economic analysis of law.

Yet there are continuing and also nascent doubts about both the coherence and the future of Law and Economics as we know it. Is the behavioral model underlying standard Law and Economics limited or superseded by empirical findings and insights from cognitive psychology? Have efficiency and welfare maximization really managed to replace values such as justice and rights in evaluating laws? Are they still considered superior to other consequentialist evaluative standards such as innovation and growth? How are empirical or theoretical generalizations of economics relevant for and channeled into the core of legal discourse which typically focuses on the particularities of individual transactions and disputes? These and related questions have been addressed in a number of isolated meta-theoretical discourses about Law and Economics in recent years. The goal of this volume is to move this discussion forward.

Through a combination of general reflection on longer trends and detailed case studies on current developments, contributors to the volume analyze whether and in what sense Law and Economics is a successful interdisciplinary endeavor.

Inspired by insights from the philosophy of social sciences, the book shows how concepts travel between legal scholarship and economics, how they change meanings when applied elsewhere and how economic theories and models inform and transform judicial practice. It also asks whether the transfers of knowledge between economics and law are symmetrical exchanges between the two disciplines. In this way the volume provides new insights on the foundations and methods, achievements and challenges of Law and Economics, at a time when both the continuing challenges to academic economics and the growth of empirical legal studies raise questions about the identity and possible further developments of the project.

By analyzing the diverse aspects of interdisciplinarity, the ambition of this book is to open new perspectives on Law and Economics for both insiders and outsiders. To Law and Economics scholars, it provides inspiration and an opportunity for self-reflection. It can also be a valuable resource for scholars specializing in science studies, the philosophy of economics, the philosophy of social sciences, legal theory and the philosophy of law.

The title of the volume – *Law and Economics as Interdisciplinary Exchange: Philosophical, Methodological and Historical Perspectives* – serves as an organizing principle for the book, where various chapters discuss aspects and cases of how ideas, concepts, models and techniques are transferred and translated: from economics to law and back, from philosophy to policy, as well as from theory to applied work. As far as the analytical framework and conceptual tools are concerned, while the chapters are diverse, they are informed by (and so the volume as a whole relies on) the burgeoning literature on interdisciplinarity in the philosophy and sociology of science and in the methodological literature in legal theory. Some chapters discuss the interaction of law and economics from philosophical or meta-theoretical perspectives. Others explore these issues through case studies which provide in-depth analyses of interdisciplinary practice in theoretical or applied contexts, such as property rights, automobile accidents or consumer protection. In a few cases, the meta-reflection accompanies the discussion of examples. Taking inspiration from the literature on interdisciplinarity, the volume intends to raise the foundational questions in a coherent manner and in this way contribute to a better understanding of Law and Economics as interdisciplinary exchange.

★ ★ ★

Some of the most intriguing questions raised by the interdisciplinary character of Law and Economics concern the interplay of epistemic (or internal) and institutional (or external) factors. Economics has been sometimes characterized as imperialistic science. In our context, this suggests that an economic analysis of law, by imposing certain ways of analysis on law and without engaging with alternatives, such as doctrinal or other social scientific analyses of law, is asymmetrical. Such asymmetry may be problematic in either an epistemic or an institutional sense, insofar as it provides a rather limited understanding of law and/or it violates certain norms or values of academic practice. Put differently, if certain modes of analysis dominate Law and Economics, the question arises whether this is due to their inherent worth or the hard or soft institutional power of their proponents.

While we do not attempt to answer *this* question directly, the various chapters, organized in three parts, address three key issues which are pertinent for judging whether Law and Economics is indeed a successful interdisciplinary research project.

First, in what sense can we characterize Law and Economics as a scientific enterprise and how can we locate it within the broader set of possible interactions of the two disciplines? (Part I). Second, which transfers of concepts and methods from economics to legal scholarship have features of symmetric exchanges, and which are asymmetrical, and why? (Part II). Third, in which ways are different kinds of normative reasoning relevant for legal practice informed by economic theory, and what are the tensions between them? (Part III)

Péter Cserne and Piotr Bystranowski in Part I address the first issue. In Chapter 1 Cserne reflects on the types of knowledge various approaches to Law and Economics can produce. Taking into account both insights from the philosophy of science and the practice-relatedness of both economics and legal scholarship, the chapter suggests a typology of the most relevant interactions between the two disciplines – eight types of interdisciplinary exchanges that can feature under the general label of Law and Economics. Thus, Law and Economics is best seen as a plural and heterogeneous set of interdisciplinary exchanges, and while the same can be said about its parent disciplines as well, disagreements within economics and legal scholarship only partly determine the dynamics of Law and Economics as interdisciplinary exchange.

Piotr Bystranowski's Chapter 2 analyzes the ways in which proponents of Law and Economics employ Thomas Kuhn's philosophy of science in order to reflect on the scientific character (and superiority) of their approach. Bystranowski discusses two contexts in which these attempts are made: to justify the scientific status of Law and Economics and to provide an interpretation of the advent of Law and Economics, as well as the subsequent developments of the field. He argues that both attempts of theorizing inspired by Kuhn fail and suggests why this is the case.

Part II asks how methods and analytical tools are transferred between the economic and the legal fields. This transfer of ideas is not necessarily unidirectional. Attempts to employ economics in the study of law and to invoke law in the study of the economy lead to different challenges. This is well illustrated by the contributions of Alain Marciano and Steven G. Medema, Stefano Solari and Aleksandar Stojanović.

In Chapter 3 Alain Marciano and Steven G. Medema show that the application of economic theory to law at the very heart of the Law and Economics movement – the law school of the University of Chicago – was not as straightforward as the conventional histories of the movement suggest. The authors discuss the work of legal scholars in Chicago, Walter J. Blum and Harry Kalven, Jr., who, although immersed in economics and interacting with the main actors of the Law and Economics movement in the early 1950s, largely rejected economics as a possible and useful help for solving legal problems. Blum and Kalven believed that economics and law are grounded in fundamentally incompatible normative visions. Marciano and Medema identify this belief as one of the significant obstacles to the theoretical integration of the two disciplines.

Stefano Solari (Chapter 4) also analyses the incompatibility of law and economics as scientific disciplines, the interaction of which must lead to tensions in combining and exchanging their basic concepts. Solari pays attention to the different epistemologies underlying these two disciplines and argues that the application of standard economics to law results in oversimplifications and misunderstandings that also create challenges for legal practitioners. These claims and tensions are illustrated and discussed by the author on the basis of the notions of property rights employed in the two fields. Solari argues that they are conceptualized differently, almost radically so, in economics and in law.

Chapter 5 continues scrutinizing the case of economic analysis of property. Aleksandar Stojanović points out that even though this branch of Law and Economics is an exemplary contribution to the field, as well as to economic analysis, it has been recurrently criticized for the inability of its framework of transaction costs and property rights to account for crucial legal aspects of property. Stojanović notices that the discussion of this issue has brought a number of epistemological assumptions to the fore. His chapter adopts the standpoint of the philosophy of interdisciplinarity to evaluate the arguments of both sides of the debate and to suggests potential ways forward.

While single-minded wealth maximization has few adherents these days, Law and Economics faces a number of specific normative challenges stemming from the practical nature of law and the normative character of legal scholarship, as well as the reluctance of economists to directly and openly engage in normative reasoning. Is Law and Economics sufficiently well informed about the values that are involved in individual and collective practical decisions? What are the adequate ways for courts to invoke economic concepts and methods while engaged in value-based normative reasoning? The chapters authored by Patricia Marino, Fabrizio Esposito and Giovanni Tuzet and Silvia Zorzetto in Part III address these issues from three different angles.

In Chapter 6 Patricia Marino brings her work on value pluralism and moral reasoning to suggest that engagement with ethical theory allows for an analysis of issues concerning plural values in Law and Economics. She takes issue with a recent proposal by Eyal Zamir and Barak Medina, who attempt to incorporate deontological morality into Law and Economics. Even though Zamir and Medina intend to go beyond the consequentialist, efficiency-based reasoning in Law and Economics, Marino shows why their effort collapses into a version of consequentialism and why we should be concerned about this. Marino's analysis reveals why it has been so far a challenge for the Law and Economics movement to combine its framework with nonconsequentialist ethical theories and what could be done to overcome this theoretical impediment.

Fabrizio Esposito and Giovanni Tuzet (Chapter 7) propose another alternative to consequentialism: legal inferentialism. They argue that, as normative economics cannot provide us with consensual criteria as to which economic consequences should matter in legal practice, for instance whether lawyers should be concerned with consumer welfare or total welfare, economists should pay closer attention to the normative considerations embodied in legal practice itself. Within the methodological framework of legal inferentialism, which the authors develop, the value choices enshrined in legal reasoning allow the selection of economic consequences that matter from a legal point of view. They discuss this proposal on the basis of the legal sources of the EU Unfair Contract Terms Directive.

Silvia Zorzetto is also concerned about the impact of Law and Economics' framework on legal practice (Chapter 8). She analyzes transfers of neoclassical economic theories and concepts to judicial decisions and asks whether and to what extent judges in civil law systems are familiar with the Law and Economics approach, as well as whether they rely on it during adjudication. Zorzetto discusses the arguments formulated by Italian courts, mainly in contract and tort cases, and she shows that the influence of Law and Economics there is only apparent. Furthermore, she demonstrates that references to Law and Economics made by Italian judges are often superficial; the economic concepts change their meaning when applied in court and serve to dress up rulings decided on a purely equitable basis rather than on economic criteria or models.

Part I

Searching for the right "paradigm"

1 Knowledge claims in Law and Economics

Gaps and bridges between theoretical and practical rationality

Péter Cserne

The interdisciplinary character of Law and Economics raises many meta-theoretical questions for both participants and observers. The aim of this chapter is to address some of these questions. With reference to some key insights from the philosophy of science on interdisciplinarity and through a number of examples, this chapter reflects on the types of knowledge various approaches to Law and Economics (L&E) can produce. While this topic lies at the crossroads of different ways of doing research in both parent disciplines of L&E, it has rarely been addressed in a systematic fashion. The main contribution of this chapter is to show that an important but hitherto neglected aspect of the observable plurality within L&E is concerned with the interplay of theoretical and practical rationality in both parent disciplines and in L&E as well.

In the following, I shall first argue that Law and Economics is plural and that the dynamics of the meta-theoretical debates in its two parent disciplines do not fully determine how corresponding debates are carried out within Law and Economics. I shall also suggest that the distinction between the theoretical and practical is an important ingredient of this plurality (1). Then I briefly characterize the age-old divide between theory and practice, referring to Aristotle and Kant, and show that both parent disciplines, economics and legal scholarship, combine knowledge claims that are theoretical and practical (2). While for philosophers this is unsurprising, both economists and legal scholars tend to ignore this question. Yet, it has important implications for the various ways of interaction between the two disciplines. As an illustration, in section 3, I refer to a recent controversy in the United States over the use of quantitative data in supporting claims about case law in an authoritative Restatement of the Law (3). In the last substantive section, 4, I shall suggest a typology of the interactions between the theoretical and practical branches of legal scholarship and economics; these represent the main variants of Law and Economics. Section 5 concludes.

1. The plurality of interdisciplinary exchanges in Law and Economics

Philosophers of science have recently turned their attention to interdisciplinarity, distinguishing forms and modes of interdisciplinary exchange. Following the general trend in philosophy of science of moving from an *a priori* prescription to a humbler observation of scientific practices, researchers of interdisciplinarity have come to analyze and better understand exchanges of methods, models, tools and routines across disciplinary boundaries – before assessing them critically (Mäki and Grüne-Yanoff 2014, 54). In the course of this mapping, philosophers have provided illuminating typologies that help us better understand the variety of exchanges between disciplines, including law and economics. For instance, Mäki and Grüne-Yanoff (2014, 55) distinguish thirteen types of possible interdisciplinary exchanges in a two-discipline environment, according to "who uses" "what object" "to address what problem". The abstractness of such typologies is helpful: from a certain distance, it is easier to observe and also to conceptually grasp issues that would otherwise be easily missed by those who are working "in the field": more precisely on the borderline of economics and legal scholarship.

An important insight of this philosophical research is that interdisciplinarity itself is plural: "[t]here are many more varieties of interdisciplinarity than suggested by popular conceptions, which tend to require that they be integrative or collaborative to count". (Mäki and MacLeod 2016, 323–324) At closer inspection, Law and Economics seems to confirm this result: it turns out to be not a single interdisciplinary enterprise but a combination of several types of interdisciplinary interactions. This chapter will discuss some of these strands of L&E in more detail.

While the plurality of approaches within L&E has been noted previously, it is usually taken as a reflection of the plurality of economic schools, methods, assumptions or *explananda* which, in turn, reappear in L&E. To be sure, such typologies of various "schools and approaches" (Chicago, old institutional, new institutional, Austrian, public choice, New Haven etc.), as reconstructed in e.g. Mercuro and Medema's (1997) or Mackaay's (2000) overview and distinguished in the Elgar Encyclopedia (Bouckaert and De Geest 2000), make a lot of intuitive sense. For instance, mainstream or heterodox, institutional or Austrian economic approaches to law are indeed likely to result in significantly, even radically, different versions of L&E.[1]

One could argue, however, that L&E, such as it is, institutionally established through scholarly associations and specialized journals, does not in fact reflect the plurality characterizing economics – a certain version of mainstream microeconomics dominates L&E, perhaps even more than it dominates economics more generally.

One could also object that, in spite of its recognition of a certain kind of plurality, this perspective on pluralism simplifies the picture. It suggests, at least implicitly, that L&E is essentially the result of an imperialistic extension of the methods of economics (however plural) to legal problems. The umbilical cord of L&E links it to economics only.[2]

1 On schools or paradigms in L&E, see also Chapter 2, by Bystranowski, in this volume.

2 Incidentally, this simplified view is in line with Guido Calabresi's plea in his recent book (2016) for the role of law in enriching and reforming economic analysis. The pattern of disciplinary interaction

This is the point where some general insights of the philosophy of science prove helpful. For instance, Mäki and Grüne-Yanoff conjecture (2014, 55) that if agents in discipline A use methods of A to solve a problem in domain B and if agents in B borrow methods of A to solve a problem in B, these are two different types of disciplinary exchanges. Thus, economists' L&E – or economic analysis of law, in the terminology of Calabresi (2016) – is analytically distinct and possibly also empirically different from lawyers' L&E, i.e. legal scholars relying on economics. The typology I shall suggest in section 4 below takes some initial steps toward testing this idea. It would be a fruitful study to test this hypothesis systematically. Intuitively, such differences are plausibly expected to arise from different disciplinary cultures. One expression of this difference in disciplinary cultures is that different standards of adequacy apply to explanations in purely economic, purely legal and L&E contexts.

Further, again in line with insights from the philosophy of interdisciplinarity, it could be argued that after several decades of exchange and collaboration, there is an emerging disciplinary culture of L&E that reflects its "differences in epistemological or methodological conventions and practices" (Mäki and Grüne-Yanoff 2014, 57) from both of the parent disciplines. At the moment, this generalization is a hypothesis, mainly based on the intuitions of someone who has been reading L&E scholarship for over twenty years. A complete analysis would require an explanation of both the epistemic reasons and the institutional (historical, sociological) contingencies of this interdisciplinary dynamic of exchange and/or integration between legal scholarship and economics.

If this hypothesis is at least plausible, then this suggests a number of further related hypotheses about the interdisciplinary character of L&E. First, intradisciplinary controversies within economics and legal scholarship, respectively, carry over selectively to the new context. Second, L&E as an interdisciplinary field of research has not only inherited controversies from its parent disciplines but has also added a new layer of questions associated with the conflicting knowledge claims of the two disciplines. In sum, the dynamics of the meta-theoretical debates in the two parent disciplines do not fully determine how corresponding debates are carried out within L&E.

Let me briefly illustrate these two claims. First, the epistemic controversies of the parent disciplines are transposed to L&E selectively. On the one hand, questions that are at the forefront of discussions in, say, legal scholarship may hardly register within mainstream L&E. What counts as an important doctrinal distinction in legal scholarship may be irrelevant in L&E for when it comes to economic analysis, what matters is the ("extra-legal") impact of classifying a case

Calabresi envisions here is that of economics as an abstract theory being controlled and revised in confrontation with the richness of human experience, embodied in law. Yet, once we recognize that "law" is neither simply a passive subject matter of economic analysis (or even analyses in plural) or an undistorted atheoretical mirror of human experience, we are confronted with a(n even) more complex pattern of disciplinary interactions.

one way or another on the actual or potential behavior of legal subjects. For instance, in economic analyses, the intricate doctrinal categories of contractual duress are often reduced to a simple distinction between welfare-enhancing and welfare-reducing contracts.[3] On the other hand, what counts as a successful model in economics may be heavily discounted in L&E for its neglect of legal variables or disregard of institutional barriers to implementation in policy. And issues that seem settled in a particular way within economics at large may be openly questioned in legal context. This is illustrated in how economic analysis conceptualizes property rights.[4]

The second claim is that new perspectives may open in L&E that show methodological issues within the parent disciplines in a different light. In fact, compared to the parent disciplines, methodological pluralism may be reduced but new meta-theoretical questions emerge as well. For instance, new analytical techniques and substantive challenges may filter through to L&E in surprising ways. Thus, findings of the behavioral sciences often come into the view of legal scholars and practitioners through economics, rather than directly from psychology and cognitive science – an issue of double interdisciplinary exchange that surely deserves closer attention in science studies. Another example is a potential reverse effect of L&E on economics. The dominant self-perception of academic economic research seems to be linked to a strict divide between positive and normative analysis, with priority given to the former. The relevance and impact of L&E in practical policy contexts can give further support to the less prominent view, expressed e.g. by Varian (1989), namely that economics is ultimately a "policy science". To the extent that this view is accepted, it both highlights the age-old notion of economics being concerned with practical rationality, i.e. the good governance of a community, and makes economics a "natural ally" to at least certain kinds of legal scholarship which share this notion of being primarily a reflective endeavor concerned with practically relevant community matters.

As this last point about practice relatedness rarely registers on the radar of philosophers of science, it is important to pay closer attention to it. While the literature on interdisciplinarity occasionally refers to "extra-academic partners or stakeholders", who engage with academics to cocreate knowledge and solve practical problems at the same time as part of the "institutional framework within which ideas are transferred" (Mäki and Grüne-Yanoff 2014, 55), what is less frequently discussed in this literature is that academic disciplines themselves are more or less closely engaged with practice. It is therefore worth analyzing whether the variety of interactions between disciplines plays out differently in the case of those disciplines that stand with one foot in academia but one foot outside. Both law and economics are obvious cases in point. To be sure, there are also important second-level differences among disciplines in the degree they

3 On the distinction of legal and extra-legal consequences of laws, see Cserne (2011b).

4 See the chapters by Solari and Stojanović in this volume.

acknowledge and/or problematize the fact that they aim at or have their ultimate *raison d'etre* in some practical context.[5]

In sum, this section has made three meta-theoretical claims. First, L&E is in fact a collective term for interactions between the two parent disciplines. Second, the plurality of interactions classified as L&E cannot be reduced to the plurality of economic approaches to law. Compared to this simple view, disagreements in the parent disciplines only partly determine the dynamics of L&E as an interdisciplinary practice. In section 4 I shall introduce a typology that gives a different account of this plurality. Third, both parent disciplines of L&E have been historically closely linked to practice. L&E brings this connection between theory and practice to the fore in a number of ways. This is also one of the sources of the plurality of the interdisciplinary exchanges between economics and law. I shall return to this point in section 4. But first, in the next section, I shall clarify the sense in which I refer to theory and practice and to the practice relatedness of the two disciplines.

2. Theory and practice

The rhetoric of opposing "theory" against "practice" is well known to us from everyday experience. Since at least Kant's 1793 essay, referring in its title to the "Common Saying: That May Be True in Theory, but It Is of No Use in Practice" (Kant and Wood 1996 [1793])[6] and John Maynard Keynes's famous adage about "practical men" unknowingly driven by ideas of long-dead theorists,[7] there has been ample philosophical reaction to the philistine criticism of theory (and theorists) by practical (wo)men.

In Western philosophy, this dichotomy has a confusing(ly rich) history, starting from the opposition of philosophy (contemplation) and politics (political activity) as two forms of life in ancient Greece; Aristotle's distinction of forms of theoretical, practical and productive knowledge; "the dissociation of theory proper from contemplation in Neoplatonism; the opposition between 'contemplative' and 'active' life in medieval Christianity; the gradual transformation of a basically atheoretical 'practical philosophy' in the Greeks into the 'practical philosophy' of the post-Cartesian period, which actually is only an 'applied theory'; the emergence of a 'theory' involved in 'making' and 'production'; etc." (Lobkowicz 1967, xii). More recently, "anti-foundationalism" and "pragmatism" emerged in their various guises, either to downplay the distinction of theoretical and practical rationality or to recognize the distinction but criticize

5 There are, of course, further differences within individual disciplines as well, across time and space.

6 An extremely lucid and helpful interpretation of Kant's essay, with further references, is Murphy (1995).

7 "Practical men who believe themselves to be quite exempt from any intellectual influence are usually the slaves of some defunct economist. Madmen in authority, who hear voices in the air, are distilling their frenzy from some academic scribbler of a few years back" (Keynes 1936, 383).

"foundationalism" or "theory" more generally as sterile or irrelevant and argue for the primacy of "practice". These are intricate matters of philosophy and its history. The concern of this section is much more limited.

The distinction of theory and practice that is relevant for grasping the practice relatedness of economics and law is roughly the following. Theoretical philosophy is concerned with, among other things, what we can know about the world and how. Practical philosophy aims to answer the question "What is to be done?" or, as Finnis puts it, "What should I decide to do and equivalently, what kind of person should I resolve or allow myself to be?" (Finnis 2003, 115). Answering this question leads to a choice of conduct. But before we make this choice, we have to work out what to do. This working out is called practical reasoning, as opposed to theoretical reasoning, which guides belief and thinking (Ullmann-Margalit 2000).

Mariam Thalos (n.d.) argues that these two types of reasoning are categorically different. A good illustration of this is the following comparison of two examples. "We (correctly) judge Buridan's ass to be completely above reproach when he picks (randomly, if necessary) between two identical and equally convenient bales of hay". This is an instance of practical reasoning. But we also think that "a detective or judge faced with identical evidence for the guilt of two different suspects is decidedly at fault if she should simply 'pick' one as the guilty party". (Thamos, 1) This is an instance of theoretical reasoning, and what is at stake is the truth.[8] Even though categorically different, these modes of reasoning interplay both in economics and in legal scholarship.

2.1. *Economics between theory and practice*

To characterize economics as belonging to the domain of practical rationality meets quite general skepticism in mainstream academic economics, even though recently there is less self-confidence in styling economics as a science. In fact, classical thinkers from Aristotle to Adam Smith would easily subscribe to the view of economics as practical rationality (roughly, of managing the wealth of a private household or a political community). This view implies, and sometimes explicitly refers to, certain goals and values: most notably, a version of the idea of the common good (Mastromatteo and Solari 2014). It is relatively recently that economists have seriously claimed to be in the business of producing knowledge of a "scientific" pedigree about their subject matter and separated themselves from business and management studies.

8 To be sure, as Thamos would doubtless acknowledge, such exercises in truth seeking also take place in practical contexts, e.g. in procedures that publicly assess personal liability. The context can be such that evidence is not simply assessed for its contribution to the establishment of truth but responds to a host of institutional considerations. For instance, the timeliness of decisions and the goal of putting an end to disputes and rendering final decisions, considerations that are surely present in legal settings, may weigh against single-minded or even cost-justified truth seeking.

The status of economics as a scientific discipline and the nature of the knowledge economics claims to generate have been debated throughout the history of economic thought. Especially since the nineteenth century, this discussion has been prompted by, and focused on, the disciplinary identity, scope and method of economics and its relation to other scientific disciplines; versions of the positivism versus normativism opposition and the "unrealistic" character of economic theories and models.

Economics is not an exceptional case in this respect. More generally, the epistemic credentials of the social sciences have been debated throughout their history, with Mill's comments on Comte's sociology, Durkheim's introduction of the category of social facts and Weber's ideas of *Verstehen* (interpretative understanding of social behavior) and *Wertfreiheit* (value-free but value-related research in sociology) being classical examples which, in spite of specialization, had an impact on past methodological debates in economics as well.

With the classical trichotomy of positive science, normative science and art, John Neville Keynes (1891) suggested a plurality of approaches in economics, with corresponding theoretical and practical goals at least implicitly acknowledged. Then came logical positivists and others influenced by their ideas, such as Robbins, who questioned whether "normative science" is meaningful at all. Even among those who did not question this, much of the focus of methodological and epistemic debates has been on positive economics (see e.g. Friedman 1953, 1).

In modern economics the distance between theory and practice is perceived to be large, but ultimately, it is hard to deny that there is connection. Otherwise, it would be hard to justify employing economists in practical decision-making positions. Physicists and chemists may provide expertise but not directly practical decisions in their scientific qualities.

In a somewhat cryptic fashion, this duality has been expressed by Ross (2012), who characterized economics as "both objective science and normatively helpful engineering". Ross's interpretation of economics both distinguishes and links together "positive" or theoretical economics as an academic discipline aiming at "objectivity" and understanding and business studies or policy advice being directly relevant to economic practices or their regulation, thus aiming at practical rationality, in the sense referenced previously. While representatives of business and management studies would surely object to their exclusion from academia, one can acknowledge the valid core of this argument – as a matter of academic specialization (division of labor) it makes sense for certain segments of the discipline to focus on understanding, rather than advising. Yet the understanding is subservient to and dependent on a practice.

Economics thus seems to be a theoretically informed and sometimes highly general but practice-driven discourse on public policy. The rationale of pursuing it is its ultimate link to practice. To be sure, individual academics or their groups or even academic units can legitimately specialize in the more abstract sections of this pursuit (not every economist is or should be engaged with "helpful engineering"), but this is a contingent matter of division of labor within the discipline.

It is worth noting that sometimes the term "theoretical" is used in economics in opposition to "empirical", the former referring to formal (mathematical) models, the latter the use of quantitative and qualitative methods to analyze data.

The matter of theoretical and practical rationality in economics is further complicated, first, by the use of the concept of rationality, in itself a normative concept (Hahn and Hollis 1979, 13), as an assumption in positive (i.e. explanatory) models of human behavior, which are measured against standards of theoretical rationality. A second set of complications arises when such models are empirically tested: here the theoretical/practical divide can come into play in a different guise. In fact, some of the latest "turns" in economics – empirical, behavioral and neuro-economics – while seemingly concerned with the issue of the explanatory adequacy of abstract models also generate an important debate about theory and practice that concerns the evidential and/or rhetorical role of economics, behavioral or not, as "science" in public decision-making.[9] Deidre McCloskey quoted a brisk summary by psychologist Lola Lopes: "The idea that people-are-irrational-and-science-has-proved-it is useful propaganda for anyone who has rationality to sell" (McCloskey 1998, 244). This suggests a technocratic or managerial view of economics, which is surely on the practical side of the divide but nonetheless objectionable to McCloskey, who argues for economics as a humanistic discipline – its insights ultimately have to make sense and convince reasonable people in a public discourse, rather than being imposed on them in the name of science, be it economics or psychology.

2.2. *Legal scholarship between theory and practice*

How do practice and theory interact in law under usual accounts? To understand this, we should start with a number of distinctions among those dealing with law: lawyers, legal scholars and legal theorists. This is simply because the current division of labor and patterns of specialization need to be taken into account when mapping the heterogeneity of theory/practice interactions in law.

First, we have to distinguish law as an institutional practice and legal scholarship as a (conglomerate of) discipline(s). This is similar to but not quite the same as the distinction between economy (the domain or sphere of life) and economics (the discipline).

At the most general level, we can characterize (modern) law as a sophisticated regulatory technique: a normative practice of guiding behavior that is both conceptually and institutionally distinct from other practices. Law provides practical reasons and, as an institutional practice, surely pertains to practical rationality. Legal proceedings are, of course, also concerned with the establishment of facts and, in that respect, subject to the standards of theoretical rationality.[10]

9 As I argued elsewhere, the rise of behavioral economics acts as a litmus test or perhaps a catalyst of methodological disagreements within L&E (Cserne 2017).

10 See my discussion of Thamos's distinction and note 8 earlier.

The characterization of law as belonging to the domain of practical rationality is uncontroversial. Lawyers are then, in a way, the craftsmen or technicians of this institutionalized legal practice: they learn and follow methods but *qua* lawyers do not pursue academic work.

As a more or less systematic and institutionally specialized reflection on legal practice, legal scholarship has a tendency to take a certain distance from the practice. Legal scholarship is ambivalent about the nature of knowledge it generates and its relation to legal practice. In some respects, the functioning of this practice relies on academic insights of various levels of abstraction. There are, of course, other kinds of legal scholarship that draw their *raison d'etre* from law less directly. Overall, legal scholarship is secondary to or parasitic on and in some cases co-constitutive of legal practice.

In many legal cultures, further specialization has emerged. As law needs scholarship to be understood "internally", this intellectual work is performed by "jurists" who provide doctrinal legal scholarship. British legal theorist Roger Cotterrell defines jurists as "legal scholars with a particular concern for the general well-being of the idea of law as a value-oriented structure of regulation". (Cotterrell 2018, xi).

Law relies on everyday categories but operates with its specialized conceptual scheme, required by its systemicity. Thus, to the extent that law is formal, it embodies "artificial reason" (Fried 1981): legal reasons are not entirely reducible to everyday moral and instrumental reasons. Doctrinal legal scholarship as "system maintenance" provides commentaries on existing laws, pursues debates on controversial new cases, fits them into existing doctrinal categories or suggests new conceptual distinctions, adapts legal techniques to external changes as part of legal policy or legal reform etc.

As mentioned, this can happen at various levels of generality/abstraction. Some doctrinal work is concerned with, say, sales contracts in a particular jurisdiction; others with more general categories such as consent in law; still others with the most abstract ones such as rights or obligations. The latter is the domain of (general) legal theory or jurisprudence.

To be sure, the precise tasks of various players in "system maintenance" vary across jurisdictions because of different patterns in the division of labor among legal professions. Important differences include whether judges or law professors have more prestige, the canon of acceptable arguments by judges and whether public administrators are more trained in doctrinal knowledge or management. To the extent that legal practitioners rely on the conceptual schemes suggested in legal scholarship, the latter is co-constitutive of the law itself.

In short, doctrinal legal scholarship interprets the practice in light of its internal goals and values – although this point is a matter of controversy among methodologists. Many agree, however, that doctrinal legal scholarship is a hermeneutical exercise where conceptual, explanatory and normative questions are intermixed. For instance, when, in a key piece of mid–twentieth century analytical legal scholarship, Herbert Hart and Tony Honoré analyzed concepts of causation in law, their ambition was to provide a "rational and critical foundation" (Hart and

Honoré 1985, xxx) for legal doctrines and practice, combining both internal and external values in evaluating practice.[11]

Legal scholarship has faced debates about the nature of epistemic projects that evolved within it. In some languages the term referring to legal scholarship may be misleadingly translated as "legal science". It appears that the practical orientation of legal doctrine, as well as the normative character of law, pose a challenge for studying law in a "scientific" manner. Until very recently, in spite of the "scientific" ambitions or pretensions of some legal scholars, e.g. some American legal realists, mainstream legal scholarship has been reluctant to emulate social, let alone natural sciences.

Thus, we can speak of doctrinal theories in law or of law: these theories, developed by legal scholars, contribute to "system maintenance". Of course, law can also be analyzed "externally". This produces critical or scientific theories on or about law, such as historical or anthropological accounts or, closer to our topic, economic analysis.

3. Theory and practice in interdisciplinary interactions: an example from legal scholarship

The previous section illustrated one simple point about the parent disciplines of L&E. Within both economics and legal scholarship, the connections between theory and practice are both complex and controversial: there are various activities, and there is disagreement about their theoretical/practical character. One should not assume that all economists agree with the commonly shared view that economics is science, not art – nor that legal scholars agree on whether legal doctrine is a theoretical or scientific endeavor. This section is going to illustrate the importance of disagreements in the parent disciplines of L&E, in particular in legal scholarship, about the theoretical and practical character as well as the explanatory and normative dimension of the discipline.

In order to better appreciate the complexities and controversies involved, let us look at what has recently been called "positive legal methodology" in the United States, in the context of a debate about the use of empirical research in the drafting of the Restatement of Consumer Contract Law. As we shall see, the controversial use of quantitative research methods in drafting a Restatement of Law is an exemplary case to study the epistemic and hermeneutical tasks in a domain that sits somewhere between theory and practice, doctrinal and academic work, positive and normative analysis. The controversies around this restatement shall prove highly instructive for our purposes.

By this new-old term of "positive legal methodology", scholars mean the use of empirical methods (often but not necessarily by economists or L&E scholars) to determine what the law is (Baude, Chilton and Malain 2017). In a common law jurisdiction, when courts have to establish what the law is on a particular

11 I have analyzed Hart's method in Cserne (2012).

subject, they look at precedents: that is, previous cases on the same subject matter. Ordinarily, judges do not follow the methods of empirical research in either finding precedents or establishing what the law is. Judicial decisions depend on the selective memory of the parties and their representatives and ultimately of the court – from the vast number of precedents, those relevant and authoritative need to be found and cited. There are several reasons for this. The reporting of previous cases is incomplete and often unreliable. Judges have limited time and other resources under the constraints of actual court proceedings. Court cases also do not carry the same weight – it is often sufficient for the court to know a limited number of leading or landmark cases decided by higher courts. To be sure, as an empirical matter, the selection and interpretation of cases that a court considers and follows as binding precedent (or eventually distinguishes as different from the present case) are subject to all the usual motivational and cognitive biases judges ordinarily face. "Positive legal methodology", however, is not concerned with describing the behavior of judges – rather, with supporting them by providing a new method of establishing what the law is. As such, at least on the face of it, positive methodology promises a leap forward for legal practice. Thanks to developments in information technology, with the availability of large databases of cases and powerful search algorithms, it is possible to identify and quantify leading or influential cases (the ones that are cited approvingly in other courts), temporal trends (convergence toward a dominant solution or increasing deviation from an established majority, etc.) and many other features of the body of case law under scrutiny. (For an earlier overview, see Hall and Wright 2008.)

In order to help navigating areas of case law, various legal systems have developed a number of techniques and instruments to systematize the material. In the United States, in the last hundred years, many areas of the law have been systematized by restatements. These are not legally binding but highly persuasive authoritative sources – *de facto* codifications of the law in particular areas such as Contracts, Product Liability or Mortgages. These are usually drafted by leading experts in the particular area, appointed as "reporters", through long years of research and consultation, and approved by the American Law Institute, a prestigious private body of practicing and academic lawyers.[12]

When the drafting of a restatement is combined with positive methodology, this methodological innovation promises a high-quality output and also a highly influential scholarly achievement: an accurate and quantifiable description of

12 According to the Institute's website, its mission is "to promote the clarification and simplification of the law and its better adaptation to social needs, to secure the better administration of justice, and to encourage and carry on scholarly and scientific legal work. Restatements are primarily addressed to courts and aim at clear formulations of common law and its statutory elements, and reflect the law as it presently stands or might appropriately be stated by a court. Although restatements aspire toward the precision of statutory language, they are also intended to reflect the flexibility and capacity for development and growth of the common law. That is why they are phrased in the descriptive terms of a judge announcing the law to be applied in a given case rather than in the mandatory terms of a statute" (www.ali.org/about-ali/how-institute-works/).

what the law is, published as an authoritative source of the law. This is exactly what was promised, and later contested, when three established L&E and empirical scholars of consumer contract law, Oren Bar-Gill, Omri Ben-Shahar and Florencia Marotta-Wurgler were commissioned as reporters to draft the Restatement of Consumer Contract Law and decided to use mainly quantitative methods to establish what the law is on particular consumer contract issues in the US (Bar-Gill, Ben-Shahar and Marotta-Wurgler 2017).

Along with the improved opportunities provided by empirical methods, this restatement project has faced a number of difficulties. Ironically, one is the relative scarcity of data. Consumer law disputes are rarely litigated due to the high costs of legal proceedings and the high rate of settlements. The reporters aimed at a comprehensive list of all published cases – for the various issues, this resulted in samples of between 20 and 200 cases.

Second, as the reporters themselves say, this new data-driven quantitative method of establishing what the law is shifts the nature of abuse and of bias. Previously, it was the intuition, selective recall and difference in resources available for searching through largely printed material for relevant (or in a litigated case, favorable) precedents. With databases, "bias can creep in through the selection of search criteria or through filtering the 'most relevant' cases among those identified by the search engine. The advantage of a quantitative approach is in making the search selection criteria transparent and subject to replication scrutiny. The risk is that most lawyers are not trained in scrutinizing search algorithms and statistical calculations and thus may be handicapped in challenging biased analyses" (Bar-Gill, Ben-Shahar and Marotta-Wurgler 2017, 14). As we shall see, critics of the methodology, themselves lawyers, were not handicapped: they did not find it insurmountably difficult to produce replication studies with their own coding and analysis (Klass 2019; Levitin et al. 2019).

Third, there is an inherent ambivalence (or methodological difficulty) in the enterprise of "restating the law". Even if conducted in a fully transparent way, following uncontroversial criteria of coding, by its very nature this is not a value-free mapping exercise. When drafting a restatement, value-laden choices have to be made, not the least because the result has to be practically useful in providing a reasonably clear and consistent answer to all important questions in the area of law. A restatement should identify both the state of the law and eventual trends of development. In unclear cases drafters have to decide in favor of one solution or another. To be sure, the reporters in this case were not naïve positivists – they were aware of and, when pressed, open about the fact that the rules they proposed are based on normative choices. In particular, they identified and supported what they call the "grand bargain" in this area of the law: a trade-off between the relative lightness of ex-ante regulation at contract formation and the stronger judicial powers of ex-post regulation by striking down unfair or unreasonable clauses.[13] They also acknowledge that the prevalence of

13 "Thus, the 'grand bargain' that the common law of consumer contracts reflects allows for relatively permissive adoption of standard contract terms that businesses draft, balanced by a set of substantive

some established general principles of the law, such as rules on unconscionability and deception, were not subject to the empirical method: these principles are accepted as binding law irrespective of the quantitative results (Bar-Gill, Ben-Shahar and Marotta-Wurgler 2017, 9 n. 3).

Once the discussion draft of the restatement (American Law Institute 2017) was made available for comments and consultation, it also generated controversy that ended up in academic journals. The debate is clearly not academic, though: it has clear practical implications, given the prestige and influence of restatements, and urgency too, as the ALI was expected to vote on the final version of the restatement in May 2019. The *Yale Journal of Regulation* has opened an online symposium with short blog entries around the topic where several legal scholars have contributed, both criticizing and defending the reporters' methodology and the ALI's institutional rules of transparency (Symposium 2018–2019).

For our purposes, two aspects of this discussion stand out as particularly relevant. First, the coding of the cases and the epistemic as well as institutional aspects of transparency. Second, and more generally, the interplay of traditional legal methods of reading cases and quantitative and "positivist" social scientific methods.

As for the first, the reporters, being aware of the importance of transparency and the risk of abuse and bias, promised to "make [their] databases, search criteria, coding decisions publicly available once the Restatement is published". (Bar-Gill, Ben-Shahar and Marotta-Wurgler 2017, 9 n. 2) This, however, is likely to come too late for an informed and transparent discussion of these coding decisions. Luckily, however, the list of cases has been made available even in the discussion phase. When critics Gregory Klass (2019) and later a group of scholars (Levitin et al. 2019) in fact engaged in recoding the cases and replicated some of the analysis,[14] their results were very different from what the reporters found. In short, according to the critics, the quantitative analysis does not support the qualitative claims. In analyzing the case datasets on two particular issues, the critics claim to have found "substantial, uncontroverted evidence of serious flaws in the Reporters' reading of case law" (Levitin et al. 2019, 465).

The second criticism was that even if the positive methodology had been followed accurately, cases coded precisely etc., this quantitative approach resulted from overreliance on an inadequate methodology. There is something inherently qualitative and value laden in such an exercise of restating the law. Thus, even the best positivist methodology is inadequate to accomplish this task on its own (Klass 2019).

---

boundary restrictions that prohibit businesses from going too far. One the restatement's methodological cornerstones is the commitment, throughout, to reflect this fundamental tradeoff" (American Law Institute 2017, 29).

14 The results were first handed in to the ALI during the consultation process in 2017, then in amended versions published as academic articles – another example of the interplay between theory and practice.

Levitin et al. (2019, 453) report three brief points the reporters made in a memorandum to the ALI in response to these criticisms. The most important point for our purposes is their claim that quantitative data were merely supporting their traditional legal analysis as a basis for their positive and normative claims. Thus, the reporters have responded to the criticisms indirectly insofar as they changed the emphasis in their discussion of methodology, stressing that they have read all relevant cases. The latest draft of the restatement from December 2018 (Council Draft No. 5) "no longer makes such methodological claims and generally downplays the role of the quantitative empirical studies, even though it arrives at precisely the same positions as the earlier drafts of the Restatement . . . We read the Reporters' substantial downplaying of their empirical claims and their shift to averring reliance on traditional doctrinal analysis in Council Draft No. 5 as their response to the coding issues we and Professor Klass have identified" (Levitin et al. 2019, 465). In a brief answer to the criticisms, the reporters called their quantitative analysis "a secondary methodology to bolster the traditional legal analysis" and argued that as their conclusions were not debated, they are entitled to consider "the disagreement over which of the many cases are informative as a tempest in a teacup" (Bar-Gill, Ben-Shahar and Marotta-Wurgler 2019).

As this example shows, well-respected legal scholars applied an innovative empirical methodology in a quasi-legislative drafting project and thereby generated controversy about such elementary issues as what it means to know the law. Through this example this section has showed how legal scholarship is caught in the complexities of epistemic and nonepistemic norms of transparency and the intricate interplay of theory and practice. Similar issues arise in economics, as later chapters in this volume suggest.

4. Gaps and bridges in Law and Economics: a typology

In this section, I shall contribute to a better understanding of L&E as an interdisciplinary project by providing a typology of the most relevant interactions of theoretical and practical claims in L&E. Some of these interactions are merely mentioned, others briefly analyzed below.

First, however, let me summarize two simpler typologies which have been suggested by two pioneering and self-reflective L&E academics. The first one was put forward by Robert Cooter in an unpublished working paper (2015).[15] Through a historical overview of the main achievements of L&E, Cooter identified two distinctive enterprises that emerged as dominant modes of the economic analysis of law. "The first explains the causes and effects of law (the

15 In 2017, Cooter wrote, but did not publish, a later version of this working paper, in which he amended his classification, distinguishing positive and normative analysis within the "legal causes" enterprise and elaborated on the "legal content" enterprise. This, along with other typologies suggested by Posner, Trebilcock, Parisi and others, shall be analyzed and commented on in due course, but that discussion goes beyond the scope of this chapter.

'cause enterprise'), especially its effects on efficiency and distribution . . . The second explains the law's content (the 'content enterprise'). The content enterprise interprets what the law requires people to do. It presents itself as a theory of law, not merely a theory of its effects. Lawyers mostly reject economic interpretation as alien to law and offensive to morality, whereas economists mostly confuse legal interpretation with normative economics. Both need a philosophical account of Law and Economics that encompasses its two enterprises" (p. i).

Second, in the 2017 version of his masterful overview of L&E for the *Stanford Encyclopedia of Philosophy*, Lewis Kornhauser suggested a threefold distinction of the strands of "policy analysis", "political economy" and "doctrinal analysis" in the economic analysis of law (2017, ch. 1.3). "Both policy analysis and political economy examine behavior. The policy analyst focuses on the behavior induced by legal rules and institutions", i.e. "the effects of legal rules and institutions on *outcomes* . . . Political economy concentrates on behavior that causes legal rules and institutions", i.e. "investigates the operation of political institutions such as electoral systems, courts, legislatures, the executive and administrative agencies. These institutions make policy or determine which people make policy. Political economy thus seeks to explain how the content of the law is determined. . . . Doctrinal analysis, by contrast, focuses on the content of the legal doctrine developed by courts in adjudication. It asserts that efficiency rationalizes the content of the law" (Kornhauser 2017, 1.3).

Kornhauser also noted that, apart from the difference in explananda, "each strand makes different motivational assumptions about public officials. Policy analysis generally assumes that public officials in general and judges in particular, are conscientious. Judges thus enforce the legal rules as they are announced, regardless of the judge's own view of the desirability of the legal rule or its impact on her personally . . . Political economy assumes that public officials have the same motivation as private individuals; they are self-interested . . . Doctrinal analysis does not analyze the behavior of public officials; it rationalizes the decisions of judges without necessarily imputing motivations to them" (Kornhauser 2017, 1.3).

Arguably, Kornhauser's typology is more comprehensive than Cooter's.[16] It is easy to notice that Cooter's "content enterprise" roughly coincides with "doctrinal analysis" in Kornhauser's terminology. It is concerned with questions generally asked in legal scholarship, such as what the law requires of people and how to interpret laws, or it helps determine the law's correct categories. The "cause enterprise" encompasses both "policy analysis" (behavioral effects of law) and "political economy" (behavioral causes of law). While both require social scientific analysis (and as Cooter emphasized elsewhere, economics has a justified ambition to be a privileged one among the social sciences),[17] it is useful to

16 Cooter, of course, has many important new insights; they are especially illuminating on the proper role of economics in the "legal content" enterprise, i.e. as legal interpretation and doctrinal analysis.

17 See also Chapter 2 by Bystranowski on Cooter's meta-theoretical views.

distinguish between these two strands, i.e. whether one wants to find out the empirical consequences of laws or what caused officials to make or repeal a law.

These analytical distinctions, focusing on three dominant types of interdisciplinary exchanges, are helpful both in themselves and as representatives of the self-understanding of academic L&E. In the following I shall suggest a richer typology of possible connections between economics and law, starting by those dominant types featuring in the exemplary typologies by Cooter and Kornhauser.

First, in L&E *economic theory informs legal practice*. As mentioned earlier, the designers of legal policy and reform routinely rely on economic insights in interpreting empirical facts or making predictions about human behavior, in order to know how legal subjects will respond to changes in the law. This includes so-called "forensic economics", when economic expertise is used in legal proceedings, e.g. when calculating damages (Zitzewitz 2012). Economics can elucidate questions of legal design, e.g. as to the preferability of prior licensing versus supervision versus liability of certain risky but socially beneficial activities or, more generally, the structure of the legal system or the reliance on simple rules versus standards or principles. This is the domain of "policy analysis" (Kornhauser). It is not "doctrinal analysis" (Kornhauser) or "legal content" (Cooter) as it remains an external input to legal decisions, rather than acting on the concepts and categories in which those decisions are expressed.

Second, we can also talk about L&E when *economic theory aims at explaining legal practice*. This is what the "political economy" strand (Kornhauser) or the "legal causes" enterprise (Cooter) of L&E is concerned with. A large part of L&E research falls into this category.

On the face of it, the difference between "informing" and "explaining" legal practice is clear; the first is contributing to it, the second merely observing it. There are, however, some interesting intermediate cases, as the second approach may also feed back into legal practice itself, e.g. when a report, primarily aimed at the explanation of (maybe foreign) practice is used, secondarily, in legal reform or in a court as a (comparative) legal argument.

It is worth returning to a related point here. As mentioned earlier, the motivational assumptions of the first and second approach are different. The first approach assumes that legal decision-makers are conscientious. Somewhat generalizing, one could say that in that mode, L&E assumes a (notional) benevolent regulator waiting for advice and willing and able to enforce the policy recommendations through the judiciary or a loyal bureaucracy. As noted earlier, political economy (public choice/constitutional economics) relaxes the assumption of conscientiousness concerning public (legal) officials. This can be seen as a more consistent way of theorizing, as it does not acknowledge motivational and cognitive differences between private and public decision-makers. It is, however not always a theoretical choice based on epistemic considerations in favor of generality (Mäki and Grüne-Yanoff 2014, 53). It is indeed rare that economists explicitly reflect on the pros and cons of uniform motivational assumptions or the possible differences in motivations of, say, consumers and citizens (Brennan and Lomasky 1983).

When L&E scholars nonetheless reflect on this dichotomy of motivational and cognitive assumptions about private and public decision-makers, some come to an even more radical suggestion than political economy, called "eliminativism" (Kornhauser 2015). Kornhauser is right to point out that there is some oddity in the usual motivational assumptions of modern mainstream economics. Based on his earlier arguments (2004), in a 2015 paper he suggested that a consequent social scientific analysis of governance structures should not rely on doctrinal categories of law; in fact, a thorough-going social-scientific analysis has to eliminate the concept of law from its conceptual and explanatory vocabulary altogether. Governance structures can be explained on the basis of incentives, i.e. without the motivational assumptions of conscientiousness. "Law" or "rule of law" is justifiably used as a term of praise, characterizing certain governance structures if they conform to the value of "legality" – yet this is not a conceptual but a normative matter.[18]

More generally, the neglect of the motivational and cognitive differences between private and public decision-makers indicates a lack of reflection within economics. Once we realize that economics is both theoretical and practice related, "objective social science" but also a "policy science" or "helpful engineering" (see section 2.2), it becomes clear that these latter modes of economic analysis only make proper sense under the assumption of a reasonable audience that can be persuaded, rather than merely incentivized. In other words, when informing legal policy, economics has to rely on a richer set of assumptions – at the least, to acknowledge motivational and cognitive differences between private and public decision-makers.

A third mode of L&E is entirely practice related – it concerns interdisciplinary exchanges where *economic policy informs legal practice.* This is the case, for instance, when legal decisions and enactments adopt economic arguments as legal criteria, as in the "more economic approach" in EU competition law where substantive economic considerations are being decisive on the legality of certain business practices. More generally, the two disciplines are interacting in this mode in much of "economic law"; e.g. when economic policy ideas of ordo-liberalism guide substantive and procedural rules and the institutional setup of EU law, especially as far as the internal market is concerned.

The fourth mode, when *economic policy encompasses legal practice*, goes a step further than the previous one in integrating economic and legal thought. This is the case when established legal doctrine is reinterpreted in line with substantive (economic) policy arguments – thus, legal rules and decisions are perceived, not just from the outside but by participants as well, as techniques to achieve certain goals, justified in terms of economics.

Fifth, as a theoretical parallel of the previous case, we also talk about L&E when *economic theory* is conquering doctrinal *legal scholarship*, in the sense that particular areas of law are understood, taught and conceptually grasped in terms

18 For a legal philosopher's response see Murphy (2014, 89–102).

of incentive effects, transaction costs etc., i.e. the terms of (usually, mainstream micro)economic theory. This is the "legal content" enterprise in Cooter's terms and "doctrinal analysis" in Kornhauser's. As far as US legal academia is concerned, much of this is due to the genius and tirelessness of Richard Posner in reconceptualizing core areas of the common law in light of economic theory. To be sure, this endeavor has been more successful in some areas than in others. Arguably, its success in tort and contract law can be measured on the energy and intensity of efforts by intellectually powerful philosophically minded legal scholars who, in reaction to the growing influence of an economic understanding among doctrinal tort scholars, have generated nonconsequentialist accounts of increasing sophistication. To some degree, intellectual property law is in a similar situation. To be sure, as with every typology, this is a pure case – actual legal scholarship is never univocal and homogeneous.

In a sixth mode, *economic theory* can be seen as *informing legal theory*, i.e. the most abstract version of legal scholarship, concerned with the law's basic concepts and principles. For instance, this is the case when rational choice models, often although not always developed by economic theorists, appear in arguments of legal philosophy. Thus, game theory, including the coordination problem, the prisoner's dilemma and sometimes evolutionary game theory as well, have enriched and helped sharpen arguments about the nature of legal obligations and the normativity of law (e.g. Postema 1982; Lagerspetz 1995). Perhaps this mode of L&E comes closest to purely academic, i.e. theoretical interdisciplinary integration, especially in the form of constitutional political economy as political philosophy.

The aforementioned six modes of L&E are all driven, in one way or another, by economics, either through its disciplinary tools or normative arguments. There are, however, two important types of L&E scholarship which are driven the other way. Thus, a seventh mode is when *legal doctrine and scholarship inform economic policy*. Arguably, this was part of the rationale behind Coase's involvement with the legal doctrine of nuisance (Coase 1960), as far as his concerns were practice related. Note that this mode of L&E shows some affinity with the fourth one mentioned earlier (economic policy encompasses legal practice); the difference is that here economic policy is seen as gaining epistemic benefits by the use of the conceptual categories, analytical and normative arguments, employed in legal thought.

This mode of L&E is also somewhat similar to the last one, in which *legal doctrine and scholarship inform economic theory*. This mode of interdisciplinary exchange is going further and focusing on the theoretical benefits provided by law to economic theory. As Stefano Solari and Aleksandar Stojanović demonstrate in their respective chapters, there is a strong case to be made for the complex categories of property law to be integrated into (new institutional) economics, in order to enrich their accounts of the governance of resources. Another example is suggested in the introductory chapter of Cooter and Ulen's L&E textbook where, at least in the earlier editions, they suggested that economists should learn from law in the sense of integrating doctrinal legal insights into their rather simplistic accounts of what it means for a contract to be agreed voluntarily.[19]

While this typology is surely incomplete in the sense that it does not exhaust all logically possible or even historically observable cases of interdisciplinary interaction between economics and legal scholarship, it may prove helpful in systematizing the various modes of interdisciplinary exchange which are currently practiced under the label of L&E or in related academic endeavors. As some of the later chapters in this volume show, there are several more ambitious proposals for further types of interdisciplinary exchange in L&E, e.g. as far as legal reasoning is concerned.[20] Even more complex exchanges among disciplines are not mentioned here either, such as those that involve a third discipline: say, philosophy.[21]

5. Conclusion

The focus of this chapter has been on contrasting epistemic ambitions of the various interdisciplinary interactions brought together under the label of Law and Economics. What kind of knowledge is produced in L&E scholarship and how? In what sense is (this or that of the eight versions of) L&E a theoretical or a practical enterprise? Does it belong to the domain of and should it adhere to the norms of theoretical or practical rationality? As we have seen, the eight types of interdisciplinary exchanges differ substantially in these respects.

The main conclusion of the chapter, then, is the following. Epistemologically speaking, L&E is heterogeneous/plural. The diversity and controversies within it are inherited from both parent disciplines. It is thus important not to lose sight of the heterogeneity of the parent disciplines, especially as far as their academic and/or policy focus is concerned. Yet the disagreements in the parent disciplines only partly determine the dynamics of L&E as an interdisciplinary practice. This basic claim is hardly surprising from the point of view of the philosophy of science. After all, any interdisciplinary work that is worth the effort should generate such a new dynamic. Yet it shows the relevance of looking at L&E through philosophical lenses and also provides reasons to appreciate diversity where homogeneity is conventionally presumed. More specifically, the typology of interdisciplinary exchanges and the dichotomy of theory and practice provide a richer tool kit for observers of L&E to analyze it in action. This plurality of the forms of

19 "[E]conomists frequently extol the virtues of voluntary exchange, but economics does not have a detailed account of what it means for exchange to be voluntary. . . [C]ontract law has a complex, well-articulated theory of volition. If economists will listen to what the law has to teach them, they will find their models being drawn closer to reality". (Cooter and Ulen 2008, 12) For a brief critical discussion of this argument see Cserne (2011a, 57–58). Note that this suggestion is very similar to, and predates, Calabresi's (2016) argument for economics learning from law in L&E.

20 See the chapter by Esposito and Tuzet in this volume.

21 See the chapters by Marino and Solari in this volume. With regard to psychology as a third discipline, see Cserne (2017).

interdisciplinary exchanges in L&E provides ample evidence for the key insight of the philosophy of science literature, viz. that valuable interdisciplinary exchanges can take place without the disciplines changing their character.

References

American Law Institute. 2017. "Restatement of the Law: Consumer Contracts." *Discussion Draft*, April 17.

Bar-Gill, Oren, Omri Ben-Shahar, and Florencia Marotta-Wurgler. 2017. "Searching for the Common Law: The Quantitative Approach of the Restatement of Consumer Contracts." *University of Chicago Law Review* 84: 7–35.

Bar-Gill, Oren, Omri Ben-Shahar, and Florencia Marotta-Wurgler. 2019. "Reporters' Statement Concerning Research Methods" *Yale Journal on Regulation: Notice & Comment* 36 (28 March 2019), http://yalejreg.com/nc/reporters-statement-concerning-research-methods-by-oren-bar-gill-omri-ben-shahar-and-florencia-marotta-wurgler/

Baude, William, Adam Chilton, and Anup Malani. 2017. "A Call for Developing a Field of Positive Legal Methodology." *University of Chicago Law Review* 84: 1–5.

Bouckaert, Boudewijn, and Gerrit De Geest, eds. 2000. *Encyclopedia of Law and Economics, Volume I: The History and Methodology of Law and Economics*. Cheltenham: Edward Elgar.

Brennan, Geoffrey, and Loren Lomasky. 1983. "Institutional Aspects of 'Merit Goods' Analysis." *Finanzarchiv* 41: 183–206.

Calabresi, Guido. 2016. *The Future of Law and Economics: Essays in Reform and Recollection*. New Haven: Yale University Press.

Coase, Ronald H. 1960. "The Problem of Social Cost." *Journal of Law and Economics* 3: 1–44.

Cooter, Robert. 2015. "The Two Enterprises of Law and Economics: An Introduction to Its History and Philosophy." University of Berkeley Law School Working Paper, www.law.berkeley.edu/wp-content/uploads/2015/04/The-Two-Enterprises-of-Law-and-Economics.pdf

Cooter, Robert, and Thomas Ulen. 2008. *Law and Economics*, 5th ed. Boston: Pearson Education.

Cotterrell, Roger. 2018. *Sociological Jurisprudence: Juristic Thought and Social Inquiry*. London: Routledge.

Cserne, Péter. 2011a. "Duress." In Gerrit De Geest (ed.), *Encyclopedia of Law and Economics, Second Edition: Volume 6: Contract Law and Economics*. Cheltenham: Edward Elgar, pp. 57–79.

Cserne, Péter. 2011b. "Consequence-based Arguments in Legal Reasoning: A Jurisprudential Preface to Law and Economics." In Klaus Mathis (ed.), *Efficiency, Sustainability, and Justice to Future Generations*. Berlin, NY: Springer, pp. 31–54.

Cserne, Péter. 2012. "Between 'Metaphysics of the Stone Age' and the 'Brave New World': H.L.A. Hart on the Law's Assumptions About Human Nature." In Miodrag Jovanović and Bojan Spaić (eds.), *Jurisprudence and Political Philosophy in the 21st Century: Reassessing Legacies*. Frankfurt: Peter Lang, pp. 71–87.

Cserne, Péter. 2017. "Behavioural Law and Economics as Litmus Test" *Œconomia. History/Methodology/Philosophy* 7: 305–329.

Finnis, John M. 2003. "Law and What I Truly Should Decide." *American Journal of Jurisprudence* 48: 107–129.

Fried, Charles. 1981. "The Artificial Reason of the Law or: What Lawyers Know" *Texas Law Review* 60: 35–58.

Friedman, Milton. 1953. *Essays in Positive Economics*. Chicago: University of Chicago Press.

Hahn, Frank, and Martin Hollis. 1979. "Introduction." In Frank Hahn and Martin Hollis (eds.), *Philosophy and Economic Theory*. Oxford: Oxford University Press, pp. 1–17.

Hall, Mark A., and Ronald F. Wright. 2008. "Systematic Content Analysis of Judicial Opinions." *California Law Review* 96: 63–122.

Hart, H. L. A., and Tony Honoré. 1985. *Causation in the Law*, 2nd ed. Oxford: Clarendon Press.

Kant, I., and A. Wood. 1996. "On the Common Saying: That May Be Correct in Theory, But It Is of No Use in Practice." In M. Gregor (ed.), *Practical Philosophy* (The Cambridge Edition of the Works of Immanuel Kant). Cambridge: Cambridge University Press, pp. 273–310, 1793.

Keynes, John M. 1936. *The General Theory of Employment, Interest, and Money*. London: Macmillan, www.hetwebsite.net/het/texts/keynes/gt/gtcont.htm

Keynes, John N. 1891. *The Scope and Method of Political Economy*. London: Macmillan.

Klass, Gregory. 2019. "Empiricism and Privacy Policies in the Restatement of Consumer Contract Law." *Yale Journal on Regulation* 36: 45–116.

Kornhauser, Lewis A. 2004. "Governance Structures, Legal Systems, and the Concept of Law." *Chicago-Kent Law Review* 79: 355–381.

Kornhauser, Lewis A. 2015. "Doing Without the Concept of Law." *New York University Public Law and Legal Theory Working Papers* 527, http://lsr.nellco.org/nyu_plltwp/527

Kornhauser, Lewis A. 2017. "The Economic Analysis of Law." In Edward N. Zalta (ed.), *The Stanford Encyclopedia of Philosophy* (Fall Edition), https://plato.stanford.edu/archives/fall2017/entries/legal-econanalysis/

Lagerspetz, Eerik. 1995. *The Opposite Mirrors: An Essay on the Conventionalist Theory of Institutions*. Boston, Dordrecht, London: Kluwer.

Levitin, Adam J. et al. 2019. "The Faulty Foundation of the Draft Restatement of Consumer Contracts." *Yale Journal on Regulation* 36: 447–470.

Lobkowicz, Nicholas. 1967. *Theory and Practice: History of a Concept from Aristotle to Marx*. Notre Dame, London: University of Notre Dame Press.

Mackaay, Ejan. 2000. "Schools: General." In Boudewijn Bouckaert and Gerrit De Geest (eds.), *Encyclopedia of Law and Economics, Volume I. The History and Methodology of Law and Economics*. Cheltenham: Edward Elgar, pp. 402–415.

Mäki, Uskali, and Till Grüne-Yanoff. 2014. "Introduction: Interdisciplinary Model Exchanges" *Studies in History and Philosophy of Science* 48: 52–59.

Mäki, Uskali, and Neil MacLeod. 2016. "Interdisciplinarity in Action: Philosophy of Science Perspectives." *European Journal of Philosophy of Science* 6: 323–326.

Mastromatteo, Giuseppe, and Stefano Solari. 2014. "The Idea of "Common Good" and the Role of the State in Present Day Social Economics." *Rivista Internazionale di Scienze Sociali* 1: 85–102.

McCloskey, Deirdre N. 1998. "The Good Old Coase Theorem and the Good Old Chicago School: A Comment on Zerbe and Medema." In Steven G. Medema (ed.), *Coasean Economics: Law and Economics and the New Institutional Economics*. Boston, Dordrecht, London: Kluwer, pp. 239–248.

Mercuro, Nicholas, and Steven G. Medema. 1997. *Economics and the Law. From Posner to Post-Modernism*. Princeton, NJ: Princeton University Press.

Murphy, Jeffrie G. 1995. "Kant on Theory and Practice." In Ian Shapiro and Judith Wagner DeCew (eds.), *Nomos XXXVII: Theory and Practice*. New York: New York University Press, pp. 47–78.

Murphy, Liam B. 2014. *What Makes Law. An Introduction to the Philosophy of Law*. Cambridge: Cambridge University Press.

Postema, Gerald J. 1982. "Coordination and Convention at the Foundations of Law." *Journal of Legal Studies* 11: 165–203.

Ross, Don. 2012. "The Economic Agent: Not Human but Important." In Uskali Mäki (ed.), *Handbook of the Philosophy of Science: Volume 13: Philosophy of Economics*. Amsterdam: Elsevier, pp. 691–735.

Symposium. 2018–9. "Symposium on the Draft Restatement of the Law of Consumer Contracts." *Yale Journal on Regulation: Notice & Comment*, http://yalejreg.com/nc/category/symposia/symposium-on-the-draft-restatement-of-the-law-of-consumer-contracts/

Thalos, Mariam. n.d. "The Gulf Between Practical and Theoretical Reason" (Unpublished manuscript), www.academia.edu/7387603/The_Gulf_between_Practical_and_Theoretical_Reason

Ullmann-Margalit, Edna. 2000. "Introduction." In Edna Ullmann-Margalit (ed.), *Reasoning Practically*. New York, Oxford: Oxford University Press, pp. 3–14.

Varian, Hal R. 1989. "What Use Is Economic Theory?" (unpublished working paper), people.ischool.berkeley.edu/~hal/Papers/theory.pdf

Zitzewitz, Eric. 2012. "Forensic Economics." *Journal of Economic Literature* 50: 731–769.

2 References to Kuhnian philosophy of science in the Law and Economics literature

Piotr Bystranowski

1. Introduction

When the first edition of Thomas Kuhn's *The Structure of Scientific Revolutions* (hereafter, *Structure*) was published in 1962, just a couple of months had passed since the publication of two texts that were foundational to the economic analysis of law: *The Problem of Social Cost* by Ronald Coase and *Some Thoughts on Risk Distribution and the Law of Torts* by Guido Calabresi. Thus, one of the most important books in the twentieth-century philosophy of science was released in temporal proximity to the emergence of the most influential approach in contemporary American legal scholarship.[1] This proximity has turned out to be enduring: as soon as Law and Economics scholars started any reflection on their own approach, *Structure* would be amongst their most cited philosophical texts. Even today, one remains surprised by the willingness with which these scholars make use of Kuhnian terminology (most notably with notions of *paradigm* and *paradigm shift*). However, it is by no means certain whether Kuhn's popularity in the Law and Economics literature means that his philosophy is particularly illuminating in these contexts or whether it is merely a consequence of its omnipresence in contemporary culture.

It is oftentimes noted that Kuhn's *Structure* entered wider academic circles almost immediately after it was published. The result was that referring (generally in a rather superficial way) to Kuhnian thought and using the notion of *paradigm*,[2] both in common parlance and in academic scholarship, was not

1 However, this temporal proximity should not be confused with the existence of any direct mutual influence: there is no evidence suggesting that the founding fathers of Law and Economics took any inspiration from any philosopher of science (Kuhn included), and any stimulus going the other way would be even less likely. One notable exception is the fact that Kuhn and Ronald Coase got to know each other as fellows at the Center for Advanced Studies in Behavioral Sciences at Stanford (1958–1959), an encounter that, as Coase later recollected, had a fundamental impact on forming his views on the methodology of economics (Coase 1995, 26–28). The stay at Stanford was quite formative for Kuhn as well, although for different reasons; see note 13.

2 Of course, it should not be assumed that Kuhn was the only person responsible for the dissemination of the word *paradigm* in academic writings in recent decades. Neither was he the one to coin the term (it had been used for centuries in connection with grammar), nor was he the first person to use it in

always accompanied by much reflection and knowledge about Kuhn's philosophy (Hacking 2012). This chapter argues that references to *Structure* in the Law and Economics literature are both numerous and typically superficial. Such references most often take place in one of two contexts: (i) while discussing the scientific status of the economic analysis of law or (ii) while seeking the best interpretation of the historical development of this field.

The first of these two contexts, i.e. the discussion of the scientific status of Law and Economics, is clearly related to the claim that the emergence of the Law and Economics movement made it possible to conduct legal analysis in a scientific way. Proponents of Law and Economics expected that the transplantation of the economic methodology into law would enable legal academia to finally carry out systematic research that would generate testable predictions. However, the scientific status of Law and Economics has always been contested. Critics have mainly argued that the economic analysis of law can hardly meet the criteria of demarcation postulated by the most influential position in the twentieth-century philosophy of science – Popperian falsificationism. Consequently, turning to Kuhn appeared to be a promising option for the defenders of the scientific status of Law and Economics because Kuhn's criteria of scientificity, like the ability of a discipline to solve puzzles, seemed to be less demanding, at least at first glance.

Turning to the second context, a historical interpretation of the developments within the field shows that both the emergence of the economic analysis of law and the subsequent shifts in its assumptions and methodology (e.g. the development of the property rights approach, the theory of social norms and behavioral Law and Economics) occurred in a sharp and fierce manner. At the same time, those shifts were separated by periods in which previous methodology, commonly accepted at a given moment, was rather fruitfully applied to analyze various legal problems. It appears that such a picture of the development of Law and Economics can easily be accommodated into the Kuhnian scheme: *adoption of a paradigm – normal science – anomalies – crisis – revolution*. Moreover, as per the argument in this chapter, historical transformations in the economic analysis

---

the context of the philosophy of science; as Cedarbaum (1983) notes, it was Georg Christoph Lichtenberg, an eighteenth-century German philosopher of science, who was possibly the first author to use the notion in a meaning similar to Kuhn's usage. Lichtenberg's writings, as Cedarbaum further speculates, might have inspired the occasional employment of the term in Wittgenstein's *Philosophical Investigations*, which, in turn, could have inspired Kuhn to give the word a central place in his work. What is more, there were other authors applying the term to reflections on science before *Structure* was published, some of them even working in academic circles close to Kuhn's. For example, Wray (2011) devoted much attention to Robert K. Merton, a sociologist of science, who used the term in some texts published in the 1940s. Nevertheless, even though there were authors using the term before Kuhn in contexts related to science, both anecdotal evidence (Hacking 2012) and more systematic bibliometric research (Marx and Bornmann 2009) seem to show that the explosion in the usage of the term directly succeeded the publication of *Structure* and, indeed, was inspired by Kuhn's understanding of *paradigm*.

of law are often depicted as paradigm shifts, with many luminaries of Law and Economics taking pride in stylizing themselves as Kuhnian revolutionaries.

The aim of this chapter is to critically analyze references to Kuhnian philosophy in the Law and Economics literature on the two aforementioned issues. The chapter argues that despite the frequency with which Kuhn's name is referenced in these discussions, the Law and Economics scholars usually do nothing more than use the term *paradigm* in a rather superficial way and not in a manner that is faithful to the broader picture emerging from *Structure* and completely ignoring Kuhn's later philosophy. All this suggests that Law and Economics scholars mostly employ Kuhn purely for rhetorical purposes and, therefore, do not contribute much to the still largely scarce debate on the philosophical foundations of Law and Economics.

The chapter is organized as follows. Section 2 briefly recaptures the main points of the Kuhnian philosophy of science – the notion of *paradigm* – the central role it plays in organizing scientific research and in the Kuhnian scheme of the development of science, as well as the subsequent corrections and clarifications of Kuhn's original ideas in his later philosophy. Section 3 starts by signaling some of the problems with attributing scientific status to Law and Economics and shows why the Kuhnian philosophy turned out to be an attractive option for at least some of those wanting to defend the scientificity of the field. It will be shown why the Kuhnian framework is probably too weak a tool to achieve this goal. Section 4 discusses the way in which some Law and Economics scholars used the Kuhnian framework to describe the historical development of the field. It will show that events such as the emergence of new schools, for instance the theory of social norms and the behavioral analysis of law, have been interpreted as paradigm shifts in the field. It will be argued that interpretations of this kind are misguided and are based on a flawed understanding of the Kuhnian notion of paradigm. The conclusion will point to the fact that virtually all references to the Kuhnian philosophy of science in the Law and Economics literature have been made for rhetorical purposes and have failed to deliver scholarly, interesting or illuminative results.

2. Kuhnian philosophy of science

The importance of Kuhn's ideas, as presented in *Structure*, lay in his departure from many assumptions that were crucial to earlier philosophical pictures of science, in particular those associated with logical positivism, which dominated the philosophy of science for much of the twentieth century. Amongst assumptions questioned by Kuhn were the centrality of evidence and logic in the scientific endeavor; the conviction that scientists, in their research, follow some explicit rules of the scientific method; that only the context of justification (and not the context of discovery) should be the object of the philosophy of science and that sciences develop in a strictly cumulative way. Another novelty of Kuhn's work was setting the history of science as the primary source of data for the philosophy of science as well as postulating that the philosophical reflection on science should inspire and be inspired by the results of a descriptive sociology of scientific communities (Bird 2014; Wray 2011).

The central thesis of *Structure* is that scientific development is (most of the time) driven by scientists' adherence to what Kuhn called a *paradigm*: something that allows scientists to identify scientific problems (puzzles), to reach solutions to these problems and to provide a benchmark against which the quality of solutions is assessed. The term *paradigm* is used in *Structure* in a notoriously nebulous and somewhat inconsistent way, with one critical reader famously listing its twenty-one different meanings (Masterman 1970, 61–65; Hoyningen-Huene 1993). Consequently, in his later writings, Kuhn claimed that, in *Structure*, he used the term in two senses (Kuhn 1996, 176–191). The first sense – paradigm as exemplar – refers to one solution to a particular scientific problem (such as Ptolemy's computation of planetary positions or Maxwell's mathematization of the electromagnetic field) that, according to the consensus of a given scientific community, constitutes a model piece of science. Such exemplars are then used in training new adepts to a given discipline on how to solve problems. The other meaning of *paradigm* is broader[3] and encompasses many factors that unify a given discipline: basic theories or laws; metaphysical assumptions, instruments, techniques and heuristics used by scientists; epistemic values followed by the community and the paradigm as exemplar.

It is important, though often forgotten, that according to Kuhn, paradigms are hardly ever explicitly verbalized. They are transferred to new generations of scholars by exposing these scholars to model solutions to old problems and by encouraging them to solve "problems at the end of the chapters in science texts" (Kuhn 1977, 301) in a way modeled after the old solutions. This means that for Kuhn, the paradigm unifying a given scientific community lies in the *practice* they share, not so much in terms of the explicit theories they adhere to.

According to Kuhn, the lack of a dominant, commonly accepted paradigm is what characterizes a discipline at its prescientific stage (Kuhn 1996, 10–22). At this stage, there are a number of competing schools in a given discipline that adhere to incompatible theories and are unable to reach even the most basic agreement on the terminology used, the methodology or acknowledged facts. A discipline becomes scientific only after some of its practitioners come up with a problem solution so inspiring and convincing that it can be acclaimed and followed by other schools. After the community reaches a consensus on following this one paradigm, the period of what Kuhn called *normal science* starts.

During the normal stage, a science progresses through the strict adherence to its one paradigm. The paradigm enables a given scientific community to enter the "efficient mode of scientific practice" (Kuhn 1996, 178), as the scientific community may focus its attention on a small class of problems (that might appear esoteric outside this community) and ignore those problems that fall

3 To avoid confusion, Kuhn later tended to use term *disciplinary matrix* to refer to the second meaning.

outside its scope. This way, scientists engage in *puzzle solving*,[4] i.e. their identification of scientific problems and search for solutions are almost exclusively determined by the paradigm. As time passes, it turns out that some problems (which Kuhn calls *anomalies*) are not easily solvable in accordance with the paradigm. However, due to the conservatism of normal science, the emergence of anomalies does not necessarily lead to the rejection of the paradigm. For as long as is possible, anomalies are ignored (as mere lacunae) or somehow explained away. Only after a number of particularly troubling anomalies accumulate does the discipline enter into the stage of *crisis*, where the paradigm is openly questioned. Sometimes, a minor revision of the paradigm will suffice to return to the stage of normal science, but if the inadequacy of the paradigm is becoming more apparent, the discipline enters the stage of *revolution* or *paradigm shift*: the old paradigm is discarded. During a revolution, science looks much like during the preparadigmatic stage: practitioners start analyzing the most basic assumptions and foundations of their discipline; methodological and philosophical disputes, ignored in normal science, now attract the attention of scientists, and a number of candidates for a new paradigm start competing. If one of them prevails over others and gradually gains general acceptance among the community, the discipline enters another stage of normal science.

A characteristic vein in Kuhn's views, as presented in *Structure* (much moderated in his later writings), is the postulated radicalism of the change brought about by a revolution. First, after a discipline enters the revolutionary stage, there are no objective rules regarding choosing the new paradigm. Kuhn compared the acceptance of a new paradigm to religious conversion, based on trust rather than logic, often affected by sociopolitical factors specific to a given scientist.[5] He also believed that a scientist embracing a new paradigm goes through something like a *Gestalt* switch or change of worldview: he quite literally starts seeing the world in a different way than he used to under the old paradigm. Finally, theories developed under the new paradigm are *incommensurable* with their old counterparts. This means that two theories developed under different paradigms lack common measures that would facilitate their direct comparison: for example, because their terminologies, even when they use the same words, refer to different objects.[6]

4 By calling the problems that were dealt with in normal science "puzzles", Kuhn meant that they are assumed to have a relatively easily reachable solution. As with regular puzzles, if a scientist cannot find a solution to a given problem, she assumes it is due to her own inability, not to the fact that the problem does not have a solution at all.

5 This inclusion of sociopolitical factors inspired constructivist interpretations of Kuhn's philosophy. Kuhn himself always rejected such interpretations. Despite occasional references to extra-scientific factors in *Structure*, he believed that in the end, the development of science was determined by factors internal to science, hence the difficulty in labeling him an externalist in this regard (Wray 2011).

6 An example used in *Structure* points to the fact that it does not make sense to claim that Einstein changed the Newtonian understanding of mass, since *mass* refers to completely different objects in Newtonian and Einsteinian physics. Incommensurability is an idea that Kuhn expanded on in his

Much of Kuhn's later work in the aftermath of *Structure* was an attempt to correct misunderstandings caused by overly radical interpretations of the ideas presented in his most famous book. These attempts proved to be largely unsuccessful as most casual readers (including virtually all Law and Economics scholars cited in the next sections of this chapter) still identify Kuhnian philosophy with the ideas presented in the first edition of *Structure* (Hacking 2012). As mentioned earlier, in his later work, Kuhn gave up on using the notoriously confusing term *paradigm*, substituting it with terms such as *disciplinary matrix* and *exemplar*. Just as importantly, he stopped defining scientific revolutions in terms of paradigm shifts, focusing instead on *taxonomic* or *lexical change*. Finally, Kuhn started emphasizing the phenomenon of specialization as a fundament of epistemic development in science (Wray 2011).

3. Kuhn in the debate on the scientific status of Law and Economics

The postulate to make legal studies more scientific is by no means new. Over the last two centuries or so, many schools of jurisprudence have aimed to transform legal analysis into a rigorous scientific discipline. However, according to the proponents of Law and Economics, it was only with the advent of their approach that a proper way was established to conduct legal research that met the criteria of scientificity. Borrowing the methodology from a relatively mature social science (as economics appears to be) and using neoclassical price theory to describe how the law affects human behavior were expected to enable legal scholarship to generate consistent theories and empirically testable models.

Nevertheless, it should first be noted that the scientific status of the mother discipline of Law and Economics, neoclassical economics, is not as obvious as many proponents of the economic analysis of law would like it to be. Quite the opposite, its scientificity remains notoriously controversial (Blaug 1992; Boland 2005). What is even worse, objections to the scientific status of Law and Economics not only mimic those used against neoclassical economics, but also include some additional and more specific arguments).[7] According to De Geest, those objections to the scientificity of Law and Economics can usually be put into one of four categories: (1) Law and Economics does not meet the criterion of falsifiability: Law and Economics scholars do not abandon falsified hypotheses, nor do they try to falsify their hypotheses at all;[8] they use vague

later writings, and it remains one of the most controversial and influential of his philosophical ideas (Bird 2018).

7 De Geest argues that the intensity of these particular attacks on Law and Economics (even when compared with controversies surrounding economics in general) may be explained by its interdisciplinarity (the clash between economists and legal scholars) and by its close ties to politics.

8 An example given by De Geest is the efficiency of common-law hypothesis: virtually all its advocates were able to cite some examples of inefficient common-law doctrines, but none of them thought that this observation falsified the hypothesis. More generally, it is possible to argue that many theories

concepts such as *transaction costs*, thus making falsification impossible; (2) Law and Economics is based on unrealistic assumptions such as rational behavior; (3) Law and Economics scholars do not confront their theories with empirical data and are guilty of pursuing *armchair analysis*[9] and (4) almost all Law and Economics theories are based on the concept of Kaldor-Hicks efficiency, which requires interpersonal comparisons of utility (unscientific, according to critics) (De Geest 1996, 1000). As De Geest claims, all arguments that can be put into one of these categories are actually reducible to Karl Popper's philosophy of science and its criterion of demarcation: falsifiability.

Such a situation is not surprising. Since the 1960s, when logical positivism and the deductive-nomological model of explanation started losing ground in the philosophy of economics, it was Popperian falsificationism that became the dominant approach within this domain (Drakopoulos and Karayiannis 2005, 14). Thus, the charge of unfalsifiability could be seen as quite damaging for Law and Economics. However, proponents of Law and Economics attempted to deal with this challenge in one of two ways. First, some of them decided to ignore the charge of unfalsifiability and to justify the scientificity of the economic analysis of law by turning to the criterion proposed by Milton Friedman in his well-known essay "The Methodology of Positive Economics". Friedman (1966) claims that "[v]iewed as a body of substantive hypotheses, theory is to be judged by its predictive power for the class of phenomena which it is intended to 'explain'. . . the only relevant test of the validity of a hypothesis is comparison of its predictions with experience" (Friedman 1966, 8–9). Moreover, "[t]ruly important and significant hypotheses will be found to have 'assumptions' that are wildly inaccurate descriptive representations of reality, and, in general, the more significant the theory, the more unrealistic the assumptions (in this sense)" (Friedman 1966, 14). Friedman's criterion, which equated scientificity with the potential to generate useful, interesting predictions, could to some degree overcome the difficulties raised by points 1 through 3 of De Geest's aforementioned list.[10] In this sense, the criterion would be more "liberal" with regard to the scientific status of Law and Economics than Popperian falsificationism. However, despite its popularity among economists, Friedman's criterion of scientificity as the ability to generate testable predictions, irrespective of its general empirical

used in Law and Economics (starting with the paradigmatic analysis of tort law by Landes and Posner) are not essentially empirical theories (Johnston 1990). Even if Law and Economics generates unempirical theories, its scientific status might still be upheld because it studies social phenomena using assumptions and theories borrowed from microeconomics, where scholars have been able to generate testable predictions with regard to social phenomena (though this line of argumentation is obviously non-Popperian).

9 De Geest published his article in 1996, before the advent of behavioral law and economics and the blooming of empirical legal studies. Consequently, it might be argued that objections 3 and 4 were a bit less applicable to Law and Economics back then as they are today.

10 However, it would not necessarily invalidate the charges belonging to class 4 (see De Geest 1996, 1002).

plausibility of the given discipline's assumptions, has always been attacked by philosophers of science (Hausman 1992, 162–169; Mäki 2009). Thus, some defenders of the scientific status of Law and Economics chose another strategy: they openly rejected the Popperian criterion as overly strict and sought to employ some other approach developed in the philosophy of science. Kuhnian philosophy of science could be one of these alternative approaches.[11]

Before we turn to analyzing whether Kuhn's ideas can be applied to the foundations of Law and Economics, it is worth asking whether they can be applied to social sciences in general. As is commonly argued, Kuhn himself (at least in the earlier stage of his career) found this unlikely. In an often-cited passage from the preface to *Structure*,[12] Kuhn suggested that the main difference between social and natural sciences is the fact that the former remain in the preparadigmatic stage, since they usually lack one dominant paradigm and are usually strongly divided between competing schools and methodologies. This would imply that social sciences are not capable of solving puzzles, do not deserve the scientific status and, ultimately, should not be analyzed using the Kuhnian framework.[13] It may be argued that Kuhn was not excessively radical in criticizing the scientific status of social sciences, but it remains undebatable that *Structure* was based on the history of natural sciences: physics, astronomy and chemistry. It is then quite paradoxical that, while Kuhn's ideas were initially met with hostility by natural scientists, social scientists welcomed them with great enthusiasm.[14]

11 One feature of Kuhnian philosophy that makes it look particularly liberal when compared to Popperianism is that while the latter postulates that scientists actively look for falsification of their hypotheses, the former claims something almost antithetical: at the stage of normal science, scientists virtually never discard the paradigm on the basis of a single anomaly.

12 In the preface, Kuhn recalled a year he had spent at the Center for Advanced Studies in the Behavioral Sciences at Stanford, where he entered a community dominated by social scientists. He was struck by "the number and extent of the overt disagreements between social scientists about the nature of legitimate scientific problems and methods", something that would be unusual among natural scientists. According to Kuhn, it was this observation that inspired him to coin the notion of paradigm (Kuhn 1996, ix–x).

13 It should be stressed, though, that the unscientific status of social sciences has always been a matter of interpretation regarding *Structure* rather than part of any explicit statement by Kuhn in this regard. What is more, later in his philosophy, Kuhn conceded to charitable agnosticism in this matter: "I'm aware of no principle that bars the possibility that one or another part of some human science might find a paradigm capable of supporting normal, puzzle-solving research . . . Much of what is ordinarily said to argue the impossibility of puzzle-solving research in the human sciences was said two centuries ago to bar the possibility of a science of chemistry and was repeated a century later to show the impossibility of a science of living things. Very probably the transition I'm suggesting is already under way in some current specialties within the human science. My impression is that *in parts of economics and psychology, the case might already be made*" (Kuhn 2000, 222–223, emphasis added).

14 It is worth stressing that Kuhn's philosophy has never gained any widespread popularity in the philosophy of natural sciences, and no Kuhnian school in the philosophy of natural sciences has ever emerged (Bird 2014). For a philosopher who based his framework on the history of natural sciences, this obviously counts as a drawback.

There are at least two reasons for this enthusiasm (Bird 2018). First, Kuhn's framework suggests that external social factors may have played a greater role in the historical development of science than was acknowledged by earlier philosophers of science.[15] As such, Kuhn's philosophy appeared to allow the social sciences to become more involved in science studies. Second, and more importantly for this chapter, Kuhn's criterion of demarcation (the existence of a community following the same paradigm to solve puzzles) seemed to be less restrictive when compared to the older criteria of logical positivists or of Popper. Social scientific disciplines, starting with those that obviously could not meet the harsher criteria (such as psychoanalysis) to those that met them in a problematic way at best (such as economics), could have hoped that their scientific status would be somewhat easier to demonstrate under the Kuhnian framework.

Thus, it is hardly surprising that Kuhn's ideas once gained some popularity in the philosophy of economics. We will not go into too much detail here, but it should be mentioned that the popularity of Kuhn's ideas reached its peak in the philosophy of economics at the beginning of the 1970s, seemingly in reaction to the (largely unwelcome) popularity of falsificationism in the philosophy of economics (Drakopoulos and Karayiannis 2005).[16] However, even then, Kuhn's philosophy remained quite controversial in this context, with many philosophers of economics criticizing it as overly vague, even deceptive (Hausman 1992). From the perspective of the debate on the scientific status of economics, it is important to note that, while the structure of economic scientific practice does not seem to conform to the Kuhnian model of disciplinary matrix, Kuhn himself never offered normative clues on how the scientific quality of a discipline should be assessed against this benchmark (Hausman 1992, 85). In other words, it appears that economics does not possess a *par excellence* Kuhnian paradigm; however, it is unclear whether, from a Kuhnian perspective, this justifies the assertion that economics is not a science. The heyday of Kuhn in economics was quite short lived, although his vision of science is still frequently cited by economists, especially those describing more specific fields of economic research (Drakopoulos and Karayiannis 2005).

Taking into account the huge influence that Kuhn has had on the contemporary philosophy of science and the noticeable, even if by no means overwhelming, reception of his ideas in the philosophy of economics, it is natural to expect that his work would be frequently cited in philosophical discussions about the foundations of Law and Economics, especially as a shield against charges questioning the scientific status of the approach. Indeed, Kuhn is often mentioned

15 As referenced in note 5, this fact triggered more constructivist interpretations of Kuhnian thought, of which Kuhn himself was not particularly fond.

16 It should be noted, however, that even at its peak in the 1970s, the popularity of Kuhn's ideas in the philosophy of economics was largely overshadowed by Lacatos's philosophy, to the effect that Kuhn has never really entered the mainstream of this discipline.

in texts devoted to the foundations of Law and Economics (e.g. De Geest 1996; Mackaay 2000b; Ulen 2002), in particular, those written by authors who, despite having accepted that the scientific status of Law and Economics could not possibly be defended on Popperian grounds (and finding the Friedman alternative unappealing), still wanted to defend it. Thus, the Kuhnian philosophy of science is often presented as being able to deliver an alternative justification for the scientific status of Law and Economics. What is striking, though, is the fact that these expositions of Kuhnian thought are almost always limited to a rather superficial sketch of his philosophy (occasionally accompanied by a list of the most common objections to it). What is lacking in the Law and Economics literature is a wholehearted attempt at using the Kuhnian concept of scientificity (as puzzle solving guided by a paradigm) to defend the scientific status of the economic analysis of law.[17]

Most of the authors referred to here, while abandoning the Popperian or Friedman concepts of scientificity, only briefly consider Kuhnian thought as a viable alternative, going on to find the best philosophical basis in probabilistic (De Geest 1996) or Bayesian (Ulen 2002) concepts of science. De Geest's argument against referring to Kuhn is that his framework provides no tools that enable one to choose between competing theories. Consequently, it does not allow us to discriminate among different incompatible schools within Law and Economics in terms of their scientificity, nor does it allow us to justify the claim that Law and Economics as a whole is 'scientifically superior' to other theories of law.[18] Nevertheless, Ulen (2002) appeared more sympathetic to a Kuhnian apologia of Law and Economics. According to Ulen, just like the adoption of a common paradigm enables the establishment of a scientific community that is capable of communicating in an efficient way, so does adopting the Law and Economics framework enable legal scholarship to overcome its parochialism.[19] He admitted that there are genuine reasons for legal scholarship's parochialism (cultural context and path dependence of every legal system and close links to legal practice), arguing that the "scientification" of legal studies requires ignoring these details in favor of what he calls "a shared, core theoretical perspective" (p. 914), allowing the legal research community to enter the efficient mode of scientific practice. The Kuhnian inspiration is quite explicit here. For Kuhn, the crucial features of a discipline exiting the prescientific stage were overcoming locality and finding a way in which previously separated groups could conduct common research. For Ulen, these are precisely the features that Law and

17 One impresses that most of the authors cited here consider Kuhnian philosophy to be a bit outdated. This is not surprising if we remember that the texts under discussion were written in the eighties or later – when the peak of the interest in Kuhn among economists had long disappeared.

18 While the first argument makes sense, it could always be said that other approaches to legal analysis do not possess a paradigm, which is not the case for Law and Economics.

19 Ulen means mostly the lack of communication between legal scholars from different countries. However, one might argue that Law and Economics might also help overcome another kind of parochialism: lack of communication between scholars of different branches of law.

Economics brought to legal studies, allowing it to achieve its scientific status. However, having spent much time defending the scientificity of Law and Economics from a Kuhnian perspective, Ulen eventually conceded that theories based on Bayesian inference provide a better (than the traditionally understood Kuhnian philosophy) basis for describing the scientific development of Law and Economics.

While Ulen's account, as presented earlier, employed Kuhn's philosophy to show how the advent of Law and Economics brought scientificity to legal scholarship, Rubin's (1985) paper exemplified a more apologetic enterprise. Rubin responded to a number of critics (e.g. Markovits 1979; Dworkin 1980; Horwitz 1980; Kennedy 1981) who generally claimed that Law and Economics failed to meet the criteria of scientificity and should instead be taken for a controversial ideological enterprise. Rubin saw the philosophical views of Kuhn and Lakatos[20] as the best shield against such charges. He claimed, like other authors referenced in this section, that Law and Economics was the first approach to bringing a well-developed paradigm to legal studies, and what is more, this paradigm remains "the only game in town" (p. 33), meaning that no other existing approach could guide research in such a productive way. At the same time, Rubin reminded us that Kuhn (and Lakatos) rejected the idea of a crucial experiment: hardly ever is a theory rejected because one observation was inconsistent with it; a theory can guide productive research even in the presence of many anomalies. "The only way to kill a theory is with a better theory", noted the author (p. 34), implying that Kuhnian philosophy of science allows for a theory change only when a better alternative is available. Since there is no better alternative on the table when it comes to legal scholarship, philosophical criticisms of Law and Economics should not affect its status as a productive mode of scientific practice.

Rubin's analysis is obviously flawed for at least two reasons. First, Kuhn would never agree (neither would Lakatos) that one should question the adopted paradigm (or theory) only when a better alternative is at hand. Quite the opposite: a situation in which the existing paradigm is already put into question, while no viable alternative is visible on the horizon, is almost a definition of a Kuhnian crisis, which is an indispensable stage in the Kuhnian vision of the development of science. Second, according to Mercuro (1986), the two assumptions made by Rubin (that Law and Economics is a productive approach to legal analysis and that no alternative could offer another paradigm) beg the question and are not justified in any convincing way. All in all, Rubin's short piece is a striking example of a very superficial and failed application of the Kuhnian philosophy of science in the context of Law and Economics.

20 In fact, he does not pay much attention to the differences between these two philosophers, claiming that their theories have "similar implications" from the viewpoint of law and economics and using their terminologies almost interchangeably.

A more wholehearted, even if sketchy, attempt at characterizing Law and Economics in terms of Kuhnian "normal science" can be found in a recent short paper by Cooter (2011), who presents his vision of the development of Law and Economics within the Kuhnian framework. He claims that the birth of Law and Economics half a century ago was a new paradigm being adopted in legal scholarship. At the same time, he denies that any subsequent turn in the history of this approach might count as a scientific revolution.[21] His most original point, though, is that Law and Economics has not yet reached the status of normal science in its history, claiming that it is only now approaching this point. According to Cooter, the economic analysis of law is reaching its maturity in our times, thanks to the dissemination of empirical legal research,[22] which finally allows legal scholars to engage in Kuhnian puzzle solving: formulating hypotheses about the consequences of legal rules *and* empirically testing them.

Cooter (2011) observed that until quite recently, even in the United States, original research in Law and Economics had been carried out only at top law schools. The reason was that only those upper-tier law schools could afford to invest in highly abstract theoretical research whose practical importance remained uncertain. According to Cooter, with the advent of Law and Economics as normal science, however, research in this field will require less brilliance while being more likely to produce interesting results. Therefore, Law and Economics research should now spread beyond the top universities and should start exercising greater influence on the everyday practice of law.

Cooter's analysis, sketchy as it is, seems to be both insightful and more faithful to the Kuhnian spirit than is usually the case in the field. Cooter stresses the social dimension of Kuhn's epistemology of normal science and points out that, in order to be called a normal science, Law and Economics needs to reach more of a consensus than it possessed in the initial decades of its development.[23] Notwithstanding, Cooter's account fails to explicitly identify the paradigm (or disciplinary matrix) that would unify Law and Economics as a scientific discipline to guide normal research. Without an attempt at describing what the disciplinary matrix consists of, it is difficult to defend the scientific status of Law and Economics in Kuhnian terms. Moreover, such an attempt to spell out the paradigm guiding the Law and Economics research could prove to be an interesting enterprise for a number of reasons. Most obviously, Law and Economics is

21 This is in sharp contrast to other Kuhnian accounts of the development of law and economics, which will be analyzed in the next section.

22 Cooter observes that the main reasons for a rapid dissemination of empirical research in Law and Economics are increased availability of statistical software and access to new datasets. Of course, this list can now be expanded. For example, we can see that the costs of conducting vignette experiments have gone down drastically in recent years.

23 By saying that Law and Economics is only now reaching its maturity, Cooter suggests that the great theoretical arguments of the previous half century will no longer play such an important role. Law and Economics scholars will no longer be bothered by philosophical questions about the foundations of their approach and will turn to normal puzzle solving.

an example of transplanting a methodology that has been relatively successfully employed in one field of study to the analysis of problems in another field.[24] The issue of interdisciplinary enterprises fascinated Kuhn even at the stage of writing *Structure* and gained even more prominence both in the later period of his thought and in contemporary reinterpretations of it, but Law and Economics scholars referring to Kuhn's thought seem to remain unaware of this part of his work.

However, there is reason to remain skeptical about the possibility of a fully Kuhnian apologia of Law and Economics. It is not by accident that the Kuhnian vision of science has never been the mainstream of philosophical reflections on economics: as argued earlier, the practice of economic research is not easy to incorporate into Kuhn's disciplinary matrix. In all likelihood, the practice of research in Law and Economics is not different in this respect. Further, since Kuhn did not leave much normative guidance on the problem of demarcation, it is not clear what a proper Kuhnian argument in favor of the scientificity of Law and Economics would look like. Thus, Kuhn's framework seems to be too weak a tool in the discussion of the scientific status of Law and Economics. Future apologies of Law and Economics should not stop at referring to a handful of generally known philosophers of science but, rather, should make more extensive use of existing discussions in the philosophy of social sciences, something that is still largely missing from the discussion.

4. Kuhn and the reflection on the history of Law and Economics

As argued earlier, although Kuhn is often cited in disputes on the methodological foundations of Law and Economics and its scientific status, his ideas have yet to play a major role in these disputes. The situation is quite different when we turn to discussions on the historical development of Law and Economics: in particular, on the emergence of new schools and approaches within it. The history of Law and Economics, as presented by its main protagonists, is full of sharp turns, many of which are described (often by the authors themselves) as Kuhnian paradigm shifts. In the remainder of this section, we will focus on three events that are often interpreted in the following way: the formulation of the so-called Coase theorem and the emergence of two influential schools within Law and Economics, i.e. the theory of social norms and the behavioral analysis of law.

24 There is a temptation (that Law and Economics scholars cited here often succumb to) to describe the emergence of Law and Economics as a transfer of the "paradigm" of economics to legal studies. In this context, this paradigm is often understood as assumptions of rational choice theory. As per the next section, such an understanding of the notion of paradigm is rather incompatible with Kuhnian philosophy.

The interpretation of the introduction of the so-called Coase theorem as a paradigm shift was offered by Ronald Coase himself in his well-known article on the early history of the Chicago School in Law and Economics (Coase 1993). Coase found it interesting that his ideas presented in the publications *The Federal Communication Commission* and *The Problem of Social Cost* initially triggered much more reaction in legal academia than in economics. This happened despite the fact that Coase had intended for them to be purely economic texts, in which legal norms served only as an example of external factors influencing the distribution of goods in a world of positive transaction costs (Coase 1993, 251).[25] It is in this context that Coase referred to the Kuhnian vision of a paradigm shift to explain the initial reluctance, or even lack of understanding, of economists who refused to accept his analysis of the problem of externalities.

As most of the Law and Economics scholars referenced in this section would agree, the original paradigm of Law and Economics was coined in the 1960s (Mackaay 2000a; Ulen 2002). There seems to be something like a consensus among these authors that the original paradigm of Law and Economics should be identified as some assumptions taken from neoclassical economics, most notably those associated with rational choice theory.[26] The interpretation of the history of Law and Economics favored by these authors is that the adoption of those assumptions would lead to two to three decades of normal science during which new puzzles would be successfully identified and solved.[27] However, normal science would gradually lead to the discovery of new classes of phenomena, which would be hardly explainable using the existing paradigm. As those anomalies were becoming more and more prevalent, some scholars decided to abandon the old paradigm, and new schools in Law and Economics emerged, such as the theory of social norms and the behavioral analysis of law.

25 Coase's predilection to stress his total lack of interest in law is well known.

26 Richard Posner: "Although economics, including economics of law, is technically more sophisticated and, above all, much broader in scope today than it was 25 or 30 years ago, it employs the same basic paradigm, namely the theory of rational choice, of which both game theory and public choice can be viewed as extensions" (Posner 1998, 565); Robert Ellickson: "Kuhn's framework can be applied to the situation of classical law and economics – the paradigm developed by Ronald Coase, Guido Calabresi, Posner and others in the 1960s and 1970s. The core of this paradigm was borrowed from economics. It consists of methodological individualism . . . and the assumption that individuals are self-regarding and rational" (Ellickson 1998, 539); Thomas Ulen: "My strong sense is that behavioral economics and [rational choice theory] are engaged in a struggle like that of the geocentric and heliocentric theories of our planetary system. There have been attempts by [rational choice theory] to accommodate the anomalies found by Kahneman, Tversky, and others. But my impression is that those accommodations are ad hoc rather than general, as I shall indicate in the following section. I further sense that the weight of the anomalies within [rational choice theory] is increasing and that a new paradigm is coming" (Ulen 2002, 112).

27 Ejan Mackaay: "It will be helpful, in dealing with the current law and economics movement, to distinguish several periods: the beginnings, paradigm proposed (1958–1973), paradigm accepted (1973–1980), paradigm questioned (1976–1983) and the movement shaken (from 1983 onwards)" (Mackaay 2000a, 71).

It is easily perceptible how well such a vision of the history of Law and Economics fits the Kuhnian framework. First, unlike in the case of some natural sciences (such as biology), in Law and Economics, it can be argued that the development of this approach resulted from the discovery of anomalies under the existing paradigm (Ellickson 1998). However (again according to Kuhn), there will be arguments between different generations of scholars on whether the irregularities discovered are anomalies that will eventually lead to the demise of the old paradigm or just lacunae to be filled later – still under the old paradigm (Kuhn 1996, 90).

Moreover, when the old paradigm has been discarded, the manner in which it restricted the perception of the scholars who followed it becomes visible. In the context under discussion, it is interesting that traditional Law and Economics scholars did not deny that human decision-making was largely determined by socialization (and not only by narrowly understood cost-benefit analysis) and cognitive shortcomings. However, they did claim that incorporating these factors into their analysis was not necessary under the existing paradigm and, consequently, not useful for solving puzzles. This way, the existing paradigm turned their attention away from the observation that many legal problems cannot be satisfactorily explained without taking into account social and psychological variables (Ellickson 1998). The unavoidable (according to Kuhn) conservatism of normal science could be easily seen in the days in which the traditional economic analysis of law remained unchallenged.

To exemplify, let us look at a paper by Langevoort (1992) on the anomalies that accompany the application of economic methods to the analysis of the regulation of capital markets. Langevoort complained that despite the existence of mature results in cognitive psychology that could be useful for legal analysis, they were not at all used by Law and Economics scholars. Contrast this with the state of affairs twenty years later when the behavioral approach was already widely accepted, and Korobkin (2011) could announce that this approach was already dominant in the economic analysis of law.

Yet another thread of Kuhnian thought in the Law and Economics literature is the picture of science during a crisis and the subsequent revolution caused by the emergence of anomalies: during this period, science looks as if it has returned to the preparadigmatic stage. Passionate philosophical and methodological debates take place, and there is fierce competition between candidates for a new paradigm. As noted by Ellickson (1998), something like that happened at the outset of the theory of social norms: there was a rivalry between a number of approaches in this new area. What is quite disappointing, despite the fact that some years have passed since the publication of Ellickson's paper, is that none of these competing approaches seems to have transformed into the new paradigm in the field.

As we see, a Kuhnian interpretation of the history of Law and Economics favored by many scholars (with rational choice theory being the original paradigm, subsequently leading to some anomalies and the emergence of new paradigms) can offer some interesting ways of conceptualizing the development of the approach. However, despite this, there are reasons to claim that such an interpretation is not fully consistent with Kuhn's philosophy.

First, it defines the "classical" paradigm of Law and Economics with reference to explicit assumptions of rational choice theory, i.e. the rationality of individuals and methodological individualism, among others. However, as discussed here, Kuhn understood paradigms as broad *practical* structures, of which explicit assumptions were only one element and possibly not the most important. To define the paradigm of Law and Economics correctly, much more attention should be turned to the question of other elements of the disciplinary matrix, such as paradigm as exemplar (would it be Coase's analysis of external costs, Posner and Landes's theory of tort law or something else?) and the epistemic values shared by the Law and Economics community.

Second, and more importantly, none of the subsequent changes in Law and Economics seemed to have been radical enough to constitute a Kuhnian revolution. This is particularly clear when we observe that Kuhn would later stop defining revolutions using the obscure term *paradigm shift*, which is still being used by all Law and Economics scholars cited here. According to Wray (2011), Kuhn later seemed to give three necessary conditions for a scientific revolution to take place: "(1) a research community must make a taxonomic or lexical change that violates the no-overlap principle; (2) the change must undermine the shared standards of the research community; and (3) there must be widespread disappointment with existing practices" (p. 26). As discussed here, even the advent of behavioral Law and Economics, arguably the most plausible candidate for a scientific revolution within Law and Economics (Cooter 2011, 1478), still falls short of it. First, the behavioral approach was accepted relatively quickly and painlessly into the mainstream scholarship.[28] Now, behavioral tools are presented in textbooks *alongside* those of the traditional approach. Law and Economics journals usually accept papers written from either perspective, and they are often employed *within* the same research paper. Second, it does not appear that the behavioral approach propelled Law and Economics scholars to revise their worldview, as would be necessary in the case of a paradigm shift. It seems that despite the change in some behavioral assumptions, the operations of the legal system look more or less the same from a behavioral Law and Economics perspective. This is a picture of legal actors reacting to incentives, among which are legal norms. Finally, it is difficult to talk about behavioral Law and Economics as introducing some new lexicon, which would lead to incommensurability between the theories developed under traditional and new

28 As Robert Cooter notes, "[w]hile I think that law and behavioral economics comes closest to a paradigm shift inside [law and economics], my view is that it still falls short. Instead of a revolution, I would describe law and behavioral economics as a successful insurrection that ended by granting the insurgents a prominent seat in the government" (Cooter 2011, 1478).

approaches.[29] It seems apparent that, despite occasionally different results, their terminologies refer to the same classes of objects. It seems rather clear that there have been no Kuhnian revolutions in Law and Economics.

5. Conclusion

Much of what has been said in this chapter has aimed to demonstrate that, despite their numerosity, references to the Kuhnian philosophy of science in the Law and Economics literature are usually superficial, often inconsistent and, virtually without exception, based on the stereotypical reading[30] of *Structure*, not affected by substantial clarifications that were later offered by Kuhn. The chapter occasionally suggested that a more faithful employment of the Kuhnian framework could lead to some interesting (not only for philosophers of science but also for the general Law and Economics public) results in philosophical reflections on Law and Economics, such as the identification of research communities existing with Law and Economics or of epistemic values shared by these communities. However, so far, Kuhnian references in this literature have introduced more obscurity than insight.

Law and Economics scholars most eagerly employ two notions from the Kuhnian lexicon: *paradigm* and *paradigm shift*. Ironically, these two terms were accused most harshly of introducing unclarity into *Structure*, and their role was subsequently marginalized in Kuhn's later thought. However, the imprecise meaning of these terms does not seem to pose a problem for Law and Economics scholars, who use them mostly for rhetorical purposes. The former term is usually employed to defend the scientific status of Law and Economics, to find a simple way to describe the methodological transfer from economics that gave birth to the economic analysis of law or to succinctly label the core theories and assumptions of the field. The notion of *paradigm shift*, in turn, is typically used to stress the putative radicalism of methodological transformations within Law and Economics, which, in turn, can be thought of as a way of self-congratulation and self-stylization as pioneers by the main protagonists of these turns. As the chapter argues, in none of these contexts is the usage of the Kuhnian terminology faithful to his philosophy.

There are many reasons to think that the Law and Economics community would benefit from greater reflection on its foundations, especially from reflection that is better informed by a contemporary philosophy of the social sciences. It is possible that Kuhnian philosophy would play an inspiring role in such an

29 Although an analysis assessing the differences between traditional and behavioral lexicons would be much welcomed.

30 Oftentimes, it is not even that: as shown in this chapter, some Law and Economics scholars used the term *paradigm* as synonymous with explicit assumptions and basic theories of a given discipline, which is obviously at odds with the Kuhnian understanding of this term, even as vaguely described in *Structure*.

enterprise. However, until then, Law and Economics scholars should be more cautious about their use of Kuhnian vocabulary. As suggested by Blaug (1975) in one subfield of economics, they should put the term *paradigm* in inverted commas.

References

Bird, Alexander. 2014. *Thomas Kuhn.* London: Routledge.

Bird, Alexander. 2018. "Thomas Kuhn." In Edward N. Zalta (ed.), *Stanford Encyclopedia of Philosophy*, https://plato.stanford.edu/entries/thomas-kuhn/

Blaug, Mark. 1975. "Kuhn Versus Lakatos, or Paradigms Versus Research Programmes in the History of Economics." *History of Political Economy* 7(4): 399–433.

Blaug, Mark. 1992. *The Methodology of Economics: Or, How Economists Explain.* Cambridge: Cambridge University Press.

Boland, Lawrence. 2005. *The Principles of Economics: Some Lies My Teacher Told Me.* London: Routledge.

Cedarbaum, Daniel Goldman. 1983. "Paradigms." *Studies in History and Philosophy of Science Part A* 14(3): 173–213.

Coase, Ronald H. 1993. "Law and Economics at Chicago." *The Journal of Law and Economics* 36(1): 239–254.

Coase, Ronald H. 1995. "How Should Economists Choose?" In Ronald H. Coase (ed.), *Essays on Economics and Economists.* Chicago: University of Chicago Press, pp. 15–33.

Cooter, Robert. 2011. "Maturing into Normal Science: The Effect of Empirical Legal Studies on Law and Economics." *University of Illinois Law Review* (5): 1475–1483.

De Geest, Gerrit. 1996. "The Debate on the Scientific Status of Law & Economics." *European Economic Review* 40(3–5): 999–1006.

Drakopoulos, Stavros A., and Anastassios D. Karayiannis. 2005. "A Review of Kuhnian and Lakatosian 'Explanations' in Economics." *History of Economic Ideas* 13(2): 51–73.

Dworkin, Ronald M. 1980. "Is Wealth a Value?" *The Journal of Legal Studies* 9(2): 191–226.

Ellickson, Robert C. 1998. "Law and Economics Discovers Social Norms." *The Journal of Legal Studies* 27(S2): 537–552.

Friedman, Milton. 1966. "The Methodology of Positive Economics." In Milton Friedman (ed.), *The Essays in Positive Economics.* Chicago: University of Chicago Press, pp. 5–48.

Hacking, Ian. 2012. "Introductory Essay." In Thomas S. Kuhn (ed.), *The Structure of Scientific Revolutions*, 4th ed. Chicago: University of Chicago Press, pp. vii–xxxviii.

Hausman, Daniel M. 1992. *The Inexact and Separate Science of Economics.* Cambridge: Cambridge University Press.

Horwitz, Morton J. 1980. "Law and Economics: Science or Politics?" *Hofstra Law Review* 8(4): 905–912.

Hoyningen-Huene, Paul. 1993. *Reconstructing Scientific Revolutions: Thomas S. Kuhn's Philosophy of Science.* Translated by Alexander T. Levine. Chicago: University of Chicago Press.

Johnston, Jason Scott. 1990. "Law, Economics, and Post-Realist Explanation (Book Review)." *Law and Society Review* 24(5): 1217–1254.

Kennedy, Duncan. 1981. "Cost-Benefit Analysis of Entitlement Problems: A Critique." *Stanford Law Review* 33: 387–445.

Korobkin, Russell. 2011. "What Comes After Victory for Behavioral Law and Economics." *University of Illinois Law Review* (5): 1653–1674.

Kuhn, Thomas S. 1977. "Second Thoughts on Paradigms." In Thomas S. Kuhn (ed.), *The Essential Tension*. Chicago: University of Chicago Press, pp. 293–319.

Kuhn, Thomas S. 1996. *The Structure of Scientific Revolutions*, 3rd ed. Chicago: University of Chicago Press.

Kuhn, Thomas S. 2000. "The Natural and the Human Sciences." In Thomas S. Kuhn (ed.), *The Road Since Structure: Philosophical Essays 1970–1993, with an Autobiographical Interview*, edited by James Conant and John Haugelant. Chicago: University of Chicago Press, pp. 216–223.

Langevoort, Donald C. 1992. "Theories, Assumptions, and Securities Regulation: Market Efficiency Revisited." *University of Pennsylvania Law Review* 140(3): 851–920.

Mackaay, Ejan. 2000a. "History of Law and Economics." In Boudewijn Bouckaert and Gerrit De Geest (eds.), *Encyclopedia of Law and Economics*, vol. 1. Cheltenham: Edward Elgar, pp. 65–117.

Mackaay, Ejan. 2000b. "Schools: General." In Boudewijn Bouckaert and Gerrit De Geest (eds.), *Encyclopedia of Law and Economics*, vol. 1. Cheltenham: Edward Elgar, pp. 402–415.

Mäki, Uskali. 2009. *The Methodology of Positive Economics: Reflections on the Milton Friedman Legacy*. Cambridge: Cambridge University Press.

Markovits, Richard S. 1979. "Legal Analysis and the Economic Analysis of Allocative Efficiency." *Hofstra Law Review* 8(4): 811–903.

Marx, Werner, and Lutz Bornmann. 2009. "How Accurately Does Thomas Kuhn's Model of Paradigm Change Describe the Transition from the Static View of the Universe to the Big Bang Theory in Cosmology? A Historical Reconstruction and Citation Analysis." *Scientometrics* 84(2): 441–464.

Masterman, Margaret. 1970. "The Nature of a Paradigm." In Imre Lakatos and Alan Musgrave (eds.), *Criticism and the Growth of Knowledge*. Cambridge: Cambridge University Press, pp. 59–90.

Mercuro, Nicholas. 1986. "Research in Law and Economics: Normative Law and Economics (Book Review)." *Journal of Economic Issues* 20(4): 1146–1151.

Posner, Richard A. 1998. "Social Norms, Social Meaning, and Economic Analysis of Law: A Comment." *The Journal of Legal Studies* 27(S2): 553–556.

Rubin, Paul H. 1985. "Some Notes on Methodology in Law and Economics." *Research in Law and Economics* 7: 29–39.

Ulen, Thomas S. 2002. "A Nobel Prize in Legal Science: Theory, Empirical Work, and the Scientific Method in the Study of Law." *University of Illinois Law Review* (4): 875–920.

Wray, K. Brad. 2011. *Kuhn's Evolutionary Social Epistemology*. Cambridge: Cambridge University Press.

Part II

Symmetric and asymmetric transfers of methods and concepts

3 Disciplinary collisions

Blum, Kalven and the economic analysis of accident law at Chicago in the 1960s[1]

Alain Marciano and Steven G. Medema

1. Introduction

The history of Law and Economics is tightly linked to the University of Chicago and its law school. What is less well understood is how the Law and Economics tradition has evolved at Chicago since its inception in the 1930s.[2] As Medema (1998, 2011) has noted, there are really *two* Law and Economics traditions at Chicago. The first, which we shall label "law and economy", examines the impact of legal rules on the economic system.[3] This is the Law and Economics of Henry Simons, Aaron Director and Ronald Coase, the economists who established and solidified the Law and Economics program at Chicago, and its goal is to inform economic analysis and economic policy making. The second, which we shall label the "economic analysis of law", applies the tools of economic analysis to the legal system. This is the Law and Economics of Gary Becker, Richard Posner and William Landes – and, indeed, makes up most of what is identified as "Law and Economics" today – and its goal is to inform legal analysis and decision-making. (Fleury 2015).

The study of "law and economy" has a long tradition in economics, antedating Adam Smith, but is represented in twentieth-century America by the institutionalist tradition of John R. Commons, Robert Lee Hale, Walton Hamilton and others (many of whom were also associated with the legal realist movement); by Chicagoans such as Simons, Director and Coase and by the New

1 Earlier versions of this chapter were presented at the ANR workshop (Ecole Normale Supérieure de Cachan, France 2010), at the History of Recent Economics conference (Duke University, 2011), at the University of Lausanne (seminar of the Walras-Pareto center, 2012), at the University of Paris 1 (CES seminar, 2013), at the Law and Society annual meetings (Boston, 2013 and at the Center for International Research in the Humanities and Social Sciences (New York, 2014). We thank all the participants for their comments. We are grateful for the assistance of the staff of the Special Collections Research Center at the University of Chicago's Regenstein Library, which houses the papers of Walter Blum and Harry Kalven. Usual disclaimers apply.

2 Internalist discussions of this history can be found in Kitch (1983) and Coase (1993).

3 Harnay and Marciano (2009) refer to this as the "law and economics" tradition, but we have elected to use the expression "law and economy" to avoid confusion with the more general "Law and Economics" label, which is often applied to both the older and newer Chicago traditions.

Institutional Economics. The "economic analysis of law", in contrast, is a much more recent creature. Its roots trace to the 1960s and early 1970s, when Yale's Guido Calabresi (1961, 1965a, 1965b, 1970) was working out an economic analysis of accident law (Marciano 2012; Marciano and Ramello 2014); Becker (1968) developed an economic theory of crime and punishment and Posner published his sweeping treatise, *Economic Analysis of Law* (1972). But the standard history suggesting that the economic analysis of law arrived on the scene in Chicago in the late 1960s and early 1970s and immediately took root there overlooks an important early episode in the history of Law and Economics at Chicago – one that involved a collision between the "law and economy" tradition and the emerging economic analysis of law and in which the economic analysis of law – at Chicago, at least – came out the loser.[4] The underlying story here is one of interdisciplinarity and its limits; of disciplinary definitions, boundaries and scope and of differing perceptions as to the legitimacy of certain types of boundary crossing.

The "law and economy" tradition at Chicago dates to the appointment of Henry Simons to the law school faculty in 1939, but its profile increased significantly with the appointment of Aaron Director following Simons's death in 1946. Under Director's influence, the late 1940s and early 1950s witnessed the development of the "Free Market Study" and "Antitrust Project", both funded by William Volker,[5] which turned the lens of economic analysis on the legal institutions of the American capitalist system. But "Law and Economics" was anything but central to the law school ethos at this time. Indifference and even outright hostility were much more the order of the day (Kitch 1983; Medema 2009, ch. 7), with a few exceptions. Among these exceptions were Walter J. Blum (1918–1994) and Harry Kalven, Jr. (1914–1974).

Blum and Kalven, though largely absent from traditional histories of Law and Economics, were, as Dean Geoffrey Stone put it in 2007, two of the "towering figures who redefined and reconstituted the University of Chicago Law School after World War II" – standouts for their scholarship and their roles in institution building (Stone 2007, 439). But they were also important transitional figures in the history of Law and Economics, evidencing elements of both its "law and economy" and "economic analysis of law" threads. As such, their story provides insight into how legal scholars at Chicago attempted to grapple with the tension between traditional legal thinking and what economics might offer to the analysis of legal issues, as well as into the history of the interactions between actors from these different disciplines. Blum and Kalven were at once open to considering what economics might have to offer to the analysis of legal issues, interested in engaging with Chicago colleagues on this score and ultimately

4 See, e.g. Kitch (1983) or Stigler (1992). This view is also reflected in many of the essays found in Cohen and Wright (2009), Butler and Klick (2018) and, in particular, Priest 2005.

5 On William Volker and the Volker Fund, see the analyses by Van Horn and Mirowski (2009) and Van Horn (2009).

critical of the normative conclusions for law drawn by others based on the use of economic logic. While they did not hesitate to invoke the economist's position as they understood it and to analyze economic arguments, Blum and Kalven consistently found themselves rejecting the economic approach that was soon to become so closely associated with Chicago on the grounds that it was unconvincing on logical, empirical and ethical grounds.

The objective of this chapter is to explore the trajectory that led Blum and Kalven to a discussion and criticism of the use of economic arguments in the law. We begin with an examination of the early years that both these scholars spent as members of the law school at the University of Chicago, demonstrating their lengthy immersion in economics and interactions with their colleagues in the economics department. We also discuss and analyze their arguments against expanding the use of economics in law and how they presented and refined them during a controversy that found them doing battle with Calabresi over the adaptation of the American legal system to the problem of motor-vehicle accidents.

2. Blum and Kalven, engaged with economics

Walter Blum earned his undergraduate and law degrees (AB, 1939; JD, 1941) at Chicago, graduating first in his law school class. His matriculation to the law school in 1939 coincided with the appointment of economist Simons to the law school faculty. Simons had been associated with the Chicago economics department for some years, teaching and writing (for professional and public audiences) on matters related to the US monetary system, taxation and the competitive/free-enterprise system. A 1930s controversy over the granting of tenure to Simons ended with his appointment in the law school, where the dean, Wilbur Katz, was attempting to build an interdisciplinary legal studies curriculum that included courses in economics and accounting. Simons's appointment and his offering of a law school course on "Economic Analysis of Public Policy" marked the inauguration of the economics tradition at the University of Chicago Law School (Shaviro 2013, 7; van Horn and Mirowski 2009, 169).

Blum's exposure to Simons was early and extensive. He was a student in the economics course that Simons offered in the law school and quickly became his "protégé" (Shaviro 2013, 3).[6] Blum also took the law school course in accounting taught by Katz, whose interdisciplinary perspective on law – one very much in keeping with the legal realist mood of the period – made him one of the forerunners of the "Law and Economics" field (Blum, in Kitch 1983, 168). The obvious proximity between Blum and the precursors of the Law and Economics movement, along with his "immersion" in economics, fed into the areas of research that Blum pursued upon joining the law school faculty in 1946. His research agenda was tilted heavily toward topics – bankruptcy law,

6 Blum recounted that he "got to know [Simons] as a result of drinking beer with him in Hanley's tavern about once a week over a period of about six or eight months" (in Kitch 1983, 179).

corporate law and tax law – which, even at that time, were considered to have an "economic" aspect and, as it happened, tacked closely to Simons's own research interests. But it was not simply a matter of Blum publishing in areas with overt links to economics. Blum's interest in economic issues also carried through to his teaching. When Henry Manne, one of the founders of the modern Law and Economics movement and a 1952 law school graduate, reflected back on his student days, he recalled "It was clear to me very early that economics was important in most of the courses I was taking in law school", and Blum's tax course was one of the three examples he cited to illustrate his statement (Kitch 1983, 184).[7] One of the other two examples cited by Manne, as it happens, was the course on torts that he took with Harry Kalven (Kitch 1983, 184).

Yet Kalven's connection to economics was not as overt as Blum's. Kalven was, at least in the beginning, interested in more strictly legal issues. Like Blum, he had earned both his undergraduate and law degrees from the University of Chicago, and he joined the law school faculty in 1945 – one year prior to Blum. Kalven's research focused on the functioning of the legal system and the role of juries, as well as the law of torts (more specifically, accident law), and he quickly became a leading authority on tort law, coauthoring, with Charles O. Gregory, one of the most widely used textbooks in the field, *Cases and Materials in Torts* (1959). Kalven's interest in economics built up progressively through formal and informal interactions with his professorial colleagues – both economists and lawyers – at Chicago. As Manne later related, no small amount of this came through informal interaction that took place over the daily afternoon tea in the law school's student lounge, where Blum, Kalven, Bernard Meltzer, Ed Levi, Aaron Director and Allison Dunham could be found discussing legal questions from an economic perspective (Kitch 1983, 187).

This period also featured a "kind of roving seminar" each month, in which Blum, Katz, Kalven, Malcolm Sharp and Director regularly participated. Even Milton Friedman attended on a number of occasions. The seminars typically focused on an assigned reading, which would then form the basis for the seminar discussion. Blum later noted that when Friedman presented his educational voucher plan to this group, "it had a great deal of influence" on him and on Kalven in particular. All of this affected Kalven's way of thinking about the law. "As Harry began to develop his materials in torts", Blum said, "more and more he began looking for economic dimensions in the subject". Blum acknowledged that, viewed through the lens of modern Law and Economics, these were "minor steps", but "compared to where we are today", he said, "they were important steps" (Kitch 1983, 186).

7 Blum used for his courses on taxation a "textbook" entitled *Law and Economic Organization: Materials on Federal Taxation*, published by the University of Chicago Law School (1947). He also coauthored with Katz a volume entitled *Materials on Reorganization for the Course in Law and Economic Organization in the University of Chicago Law School*, a revision of Katz's *Materials on Bankruptcy and Reorganization for the Course in Law and Economic Organization in the University of Chicago Law School* from 1942.

Blum and Kalven's intersection with "Law and Economics" had a number of facets, both direct and indirect. Their interest in the light that economics could shed on social and political issues was sufficiently strong that they agreed to participate in the organization of a three-day conference, held in early April 1951, on "The Economics of Mobilization", spearheaded by Aaron Director and sponsored by the University of Chicago Law School with financial support from the Volker Fund. The objective of this conference, the proceedings of which were published as *Defense, Controls, and Inflation* (Director 1952), was, as Director spelled out in his foreword to this volume, to discuss "issues concern[ing] the effectiveness of alternative measures to achieve economic mobilization [for war] as well as the influence of these measures on the more permanent objectives of public policy" (1952, v). The "markets versus controls" theme that overarched the discussion of how best to manage wartime resource allocation was one that was "of obvious importance to law and economics" (Director 1952, v) and reflected the broad nature of the "law and economy" approach that characterized the first several decades of Law and Economics at Chicago.

Blum and Kalven's most extensive early engagement with the interaction of economics and law came in their analysis of the case for progressive taxation (1952, 1953). This work carried forward Simons's interest in the subject, as seen particularly in his 1938 book, *Personal Income Taxation*. In contrast with the approach that later was to dominate the economic analysis of law, and its Chicago variant in particular, Simons had argued that the discussion of the appropriateness of a progressive tax system should be grounded *beyond* economics proper. "The case for drastic progression in taxation", he said, "must be rested on the case against inequality – on the ethical or aesthetic judgment that the prevailing distribution of wealth and income reveals a degree (and/or kind) of inequality which is distinctly evil or unlovely" (1938, 18–19). Moving the discussion in this direction, beyond a narrower economics of the issue, for Simons, would reveal that "the case for equality (for less inequality) is enormously stronger than any utility foundation on which it can be rested" (1938, 14). Blum and Kalven quoted Simons approvingly on this score (e.g. 1953, 72) and praised him for "insisting that in any discussion of progression the problem of inequality 'be dragged out into the open'" (1952, 487; see also 1953, 73).

But Blum and Kalven did not rest their position on moral arguments alone. Taxation, for them, also had important legal and economic dimensions. They brought numerous references from the economics literature into their discussion, though; as David McCord Wright pointed out in a review of their book, Blum and Kalven ignored the important recent writings on progressive taxation by economists including Paul Samuelson, Tibor Scitovsky and D.H. Robertson (McCord Wright 1954, 583). One particularly noteworthy feature of this discussion, in light of their later debate with Calabresi on accident law, is their treatment of the relatively technical issue of incentives and deterrence – the potential effect of progressive taxation on economic incentives. Here, we find Blum and Kalven taking issue with the incentive effects central to economists' analysis of taxation. Progressive taxation, they asserted, "does not impair the incentive" to find the most attractive jobs – which "are also the best paid" – because individuals who try to get better jobs tend to do so at least as much for the "prestige" that accompanies the high salary as for its income-augmenting aspect (1953, 438). In fact, they argued, "there is some plausibility to the notion that being subject to higher tax rates may even be an inducement to persons to work harder in order to maintain their net position after taxes" (p. 439). In fact, they considered the "technical" – that is, the economic – arguments to be among "the weakest" of those offered in support of a progressive tax structure, finding it "hard to gain much comfort from the special arguments, however intricate their formulations, constructed on notions of benefit, sacrifice, ability to pay or economic stability" (1952, 519). Economic arguments, then, could not be accepted in straightforward fashion but instead needed to be evaluated alongside those from other intellectual arenas.

Although Blum and Kalven developed their analysis of progressive taxation when Law and Economics already had a foothold at Chicago, this work bore no apparent marks of connection to the people then involved in what are now generally considered the early manifestations of the Law and Economics movement at Chicago. Though the links to the work of Simons are obvious, both the subject matter and perspective brought to bear were distinct from the Director-led "Antitrust Project" around which Chicago Law and Economics had come to revolve during the 1950s.[8] As we shall see, however, their hesitance about the conclusions that one could draw based on the insights of economic theory did not deter Blum and Kalven from taking up economic analysis when they were of the mind that it might be useful for their work.

3. Car accidents, tort law and compensation plans

Blum and Kalven took largely independent research paths in the years following the publication of their book on progressive taxation, with Blum continuing along the tax path and Kalven focusing on civil liberties and torts – in particular, accidents, insurance and compensation. This last was anything but a purely academic exercise for the 1950s saw a growing concern in the US with automobile accidents and highway safety.

In the late 1950s, the number of car accidents and associated fatalities in the US rose dramatically. The annual number of fatalities increased by 52 percent – from 36,981 to 56,278 – between 1958 and 1972 (National Council for Highway Safety),[9] leading one commentator to remark that "automobility was no longer

8 The areas covered by the Antitrust Project were vertical integration, predatory pricing, tying arrangements, the Sherman act, fair trade and trade regulation. Coase (1993, 242) later emphasized the disconnect between Simons's work – of which Blum and Kalven's was an offshoot – and the later Chicago approach to Law and Economics. Blum and Kalven's approach also likely would not have appealed to the Antitrust Project's funder, the Volker Fund. See Rothbard (2010).

9 See www.cdc.gov/nchs/data/dvs/lead1900_98.pdf. The death rate from automobile accidents had increased by 500 percent between 1912 and 1932, with more than 30,000 deaths occurring in 1930,

an historically progressive force for change in American civilization" (Flink 1972, 452). The toll associated with automobile accidents was both striking and troublesome for obvious human reasons, but also for what it cost American society. Franklin, Chanin and Mark put forward some particularly impressive figures in documenting the economic toll of accidents generally, finding that "lost wages and medical expenses alone amount to almost $5,000,000,000 annually . . . and the total economic cost of accidents may well exceed $15,000,000,000" (1961, 1–2). Automobile accident costs loomed large within these totals.[10] The *legal* costs associated with these accidents only added to that total as the number of lawsuits related to car accidents increased steadily – by 50 percent between 1955 and 1970 (Anderson, Heaton and Carroll 2010, 28). In Cook County, which was home to the University of Chicago, lawsuits arising from automobile accidents represented 66 percent of the civil cases between 1960 and 1975 (Peterson and Priest 1982, 6). Not surprisingly, the dramatic increase in accident numbers brought with it an increase in automobile insurance liability premiums, from $2.4 billion in 1955 to $8.9 billion in 1970 (Anderson, Heaton and Carroll 2010, 28),[11] even though insurance was not compulsory in any of the states in the union. The lack of compulsory automobile accident insurance meant that compensation was often granted only if fault or negligence was proved at trial, a fact that played a significant role in the increased number of lawsuits. As such, what people could obtain in the way of compensation for accident losses depended, at least partly, on the legal system.

The heavy reliance on the courts for dealing with accident-related claims led to a number of problems, including significant delays in the resolution of injury claims and mismatches between injuries and compensation awards. A study conducted by James and Law in 1951 showed that very little progress had been made since 1932, when the first compensation plan for automobile accidents was proposed, for "the same facts and the same problems are still with us today" (1952, 81).[12] Writing seven years later, James found that the central problems remained unresolved. There was "good reason to believe that the

while the death rate from other types of accidents *fell* by 20 percent during that same period. See Anderson, Heaton and Carroll (2010, 23): Abraham (2008, 70–71) and Smith, Lilly and Dowling (1932, 786).

10 Automobile accidents represented roughly a third of all accident-related fatalities at this time.

11 It was not only the number of car-accident-related lawsuits or the costs of liability that were problematic but also the strategic behaviors that this implied. As Anderson, Heaton and Carroll stressed, medical – overall and per-capita – expenses increased over the same period of time. This led "injury victims" to search for more "amounts from defendants to cover that care". (2010, 29). And attorneys started to devise methods that would allow victims to obtain "much higher verdicts for pain and suffering than had been common" (Abraham 2008, 83–84; cited in Anderson, Heaton and Carrol 2010, 28).

12 The proposal was made in the report of the Committee to Study Compensation for Automobile Accidents, also known as the "Columbia Report" or "Columbia Study". Car accidents and the compensation of victims were viewed as a problem already in the 1930s. The Columbia Report suggested that compensation should be paid from a general fund and that accident losses should be

bulk of automobile victims fare no better today than they did at the time of the Columbia Study", he argued, and the same "underlying inequities" continued to plague the payments system (1959, 424).

Many scholars actually suggested that these compensation issues could only be effectively resolved through a turn away from the legal system toward a centralized administrative solution. Under such a system, victims would not be fully compensated – particularly for noneconomic losses, such as pain and suffering – and liability would no longer be based on fault or negligence.[13] Kalven (1955, 1959) reacted strongly against such proposals. Though he found much to agree with in the basic diagnosis of problems with the tort-based system of accident law, the idea of removing fault from the equation, he felt, would throw out the baby with the bathwater. While some considered fault an outdated notion, Kalven insisted that it is a "deeply held category of thought in our culture" (1959, 686). More importantly, however, it was one of "the possible big ideas for *allocating liability*" – one that, for Kalven, made "enough sense to always deserve serious attention" (1959, 686, emphasis added). Though a significant segment of the literature was moving toward the position that loss spreading or the compensation of victims should be the chief function of tort law, Kalven was adamant that *liability allocation* should remain tort's primary objective. As we shall see, these conflicting visions of tort law's ultimate purpose were at the heart of Blum and Kalven's debate with Calabresi.

4. Applying economic analysis to the law of accidents

A. Calabresi and the case for economics

Though their most influential work on accident law was still ahead of them, Blum and Kalven were anything but ignorant of the debate around torts, liability and accidents when Guido Calabresi arrived at the University of Chicago Law School in 1960 to present a paper on the subject. He had been invited by the dean, Edward Levi, as part of an effort to lure Calabresi to Chicago. At that time, Calabresi had only recently assumed a professorship at Yale[14] and had just one paper written: "Some Thoughts on Risk Distribution and the Law of Torts" (1961).[15] This paper was to form the basis for Calabresi's seminar.

---

spread over a large population with a view to providing appropriate compensation to the maximum number of victims.

13 See, e.g., Ehrenzweig (1951, 1955) and Green (1958).

14 Calabresi graduated from the Yale Law School in 1958 and then spent a year clerking for US Supreme Court Justice Hugo Black.

15 This paper had been several years in the making. In 1955, while still a law school student, Calabresi wrote an essay entitled "Some Thoughts on the Distribution of Risks and Insurance" as part of his application for a position on the staff of the *Yale Law Journal*. The paper received the prize for the best student essay, which included the promise of publication in the *Journal*, but its appearance was delayed until 1961 because of, as Calabresi noted some thirty years later, the "cold reaction [of the]

Calabresi's analysis in the paper posed a stark challenge to the received legal approach to accident law. For Calabresi, the only question lawyers should concern themselves with was "when and how . . . to distribute" the risk, or losses, associated with accidents (1961, 500). His argument, in essence, was that tort law was an optimal-allocation problem – a problem in *economics* rather than one to be addressed by reference to traditional legal norms and concepts. This, as Calabresi noted, put him squarely at odds with the position taken by Gregory and Kalven (1959) in their casebook on torts. For Gregory and Kalven, the central question of tort law was whether liability for accident-related harms should be grounded in the legal conception of individual fault or instead should be distributed more broadly, on a no-fault basis. Calabresi argued that this ignored what he considered the central problem in tort law – how to compensate victims of accidents, spread losses and distribute risks.[16] For Blum, and even more so for Kalven, who had defended fault-based liability not only in the casebook on torts, but also in his aforementioned criticisms of auto compensation plans, ignoring fault as a criterion for liability and focusing on compensation made little sense, at once running afoul of an important social norm and robbing law of an important vehicle for determining the assignment of liability.

Calabresi's interest in applying economics to the analysis of accident law had its roots in his extensive economics training at Yale and Oxford. As he moved through his legal studies at Yale, following his return from Oxford, Calabresi began to sense that economics could provide insight into certain problems of tort law, and the paper that eventually became his celebrated 1961 article on accident law represented his initial attempt to bring economic thinking to bear on a torts-related issue. Though space limitations preclude a full exposition of Calabresi's use of economic reasoning here, two findings must be noted.

First, and like Ronald Coase, who was working along similar lines during this same period,[17] Calabresi found that there are some situations – those in which the pricing system is able to account for all relevant costs – where economics *cannot* provide guidance for the assignment of accident liability because the allocation of resources will be identical regardless of which party is made liable (1961, 506).[18] But in many more cases, he said, the pricing system does *not* lead

outgoing board" (Calabresi 1991a, 1482). This paper was eventually published as "Some Thoughts on Risk Distribution and the Law of Torts", and it appeared in print at almost the same time as another of the pioneering works in the modern field of Law and Economics, Ronald Coase's article, "The Problem of Social Cost" (1960). Coase's article, though bearing a 1960 publication date, actually appeared in the late winter or early spring of 1961. These articles represented two of the earliest attempts to apply modern price-theoretic economic reasoning to analyze common law problems and, specifically, to apply market principles to questions of legal liability for harm.

16 In this, Calabresi had been influenced by his Yale Law professor Fleming James (Marciano and Romaniuc 2015).

17 Coase was on the University of Virginia faculty at this time and moved to the University of Chicago Law School in 1964.

18 As in the case, for example, of workers compensation, where holding employers or workers liable for accidents would have identical effects, channeled through the labor market into wages, etc., a result

to the internalization of all accident-related costs, as a result of which it actually *does* matter which party is made to bear the loss. The determination of liability in these situations, Calabresi argued, should be based on *economic* criteria rather than ethical ones, with efficiency considerations – specifically, the minimization of accident-related costs – governing the determination of liability for damage.

Calabresi's rationale for bringing efficiency into the mix posed a stark challenge to traditional legal thinking. Criteria such as justice and fairness, he said, are too "vague", too general and not practical enough to serve as guideposts for judicial decision-making (1961, 501). The appropriate justification for liability assignment was what he termed "the 'allocation of resources' justification" (1961, 502), the theory underlying which suggested to him that "the most desirable system of loss distribution . . . is one in which the prices of goods accurately reflect their full cost to society" (1961, 505). Accomplishing this required not simply that the cost of accidents be placed on *someone*, but on the agents who could avoid them most cheaply. That was Calabresi's second finding.

B. The answer from Blum and Kalven

The circulation of Calabresi's paper at Chicago prior to his seminar had provided both Blum and Kalven with the opportunity to read it in advance. They found the paper brilliant, Kalven greeting Calabresi by exclaiming, "I wish I had written an article like that when I was your age!" (Calabresi 1975, 69). Nonetheless, they disagreed completely with its contents, with Kalven even insisting that the paper was "all wrong" (Calabresi 1975, 69).

Though Calabresi's article was published in 1961, not long after his visit to Chicago, it was not until 1964 that Blum and Kalven offered a published response to his economics-infused argument – stimulated in part, as it happened, by Calabresi's invitation to have them deliver the 1964 Schuman Lectures at Yale Law School. These lectures, subsequently published in the *University of Chicago Law Review* as "Public Law Perspectives on a Private Law Problem: Auto Compensation Plans" (1964), attempted both to clarify the nature of their disagreement with Calabresi and, more broadly, to express their opposition to proposed automobile accident compensation plans that would move the system away from its basis in fault. It is only the former aspect of their analysis, though, that concerns us here. It should be noted, however, that Blum and Kalven also objected to the methodology employed by Calabresi in his analysis of accident law, that of economic analysis and, specifically, the minimization of accident costs.

Blum and Kalven's assessment of the accident law literature suggested to them that economics appeared to be increasingly in play as a tool that might shed light

---

that had been well established in the economics literature for several decades. See Marciano (2012) and Medema (2014b) for discussions of the commonalities and differences between the arguments of Calabresi and Coase.

on the determination of liability. Indeed, they said, the suggestion that lawyers look to economic analysis had recently become "the *fashionable* response" (1964, 692, emphasis added).[19] They found this economic turn objectionable, though, and for two reasons.

First, Blum and Kalven did not believe that economic analysis was capable of informing the theory of legal liability for accidents, in that it could not pinpoint a legal rule to govern liability assignment (1964, 692–703). Both Calabresi and Coase, they noted, had demonstrated that, under certain conditions, the determination of liability would not affect the allocation of resources. Calabresi had argued that there was no allocative distinction between alternative liability rules when markets worked smoothly, and Coase had shown that if transacting was costless, agents would bargain to the outcome that maximized the value of output, regardless of where liability was initially placed.[20] Because allocations did not vary with legal rules under such conditions, Blum and Kalven pointed out, economics was of no assistance in determining the appropriate rule for assigning liability. And when these restrictions were loosened – when markets did not function smoothly and the exchange process was costly – the liability assignment *did* affect resource allocation, but economic analysis did not have the capacity to predict, and so to tell us, which rule among the alternatives could be relied upon to best promote efficiency (1964, 701). The implications, for Blum and Kalven, were not friendly to the economist: "To exaggerate only a little", they said, "when the economist is helpful he says that the legal problem is not worth arguing about; when he finds the legal problem consequential, he cannot be helpful in fashioning a solution" (1964, 703).

More concerning to Blum and Kalven was the fact that economics and law do not have the same objectives at their respective hearts. At issue was what they considered the "sharp collision" between the lawyer's criterion of "justice" and the economist's concern with resource allocation and efficiency.[21] Foreshadowing the debates over the economic analysis of law that was to take place during the 1970s and 1980s, Blum and Kalven argued that questions of justice and equity, which are "the *ultimate* concern of the law" and which "the law cannot escape its *obligation* to answer, appeared to lie beyond the scope of economic analysis (1964, 703, 702, emphases added). Given that the question of justice "is one on which our hypothetical economic advisor takes no position" (1964,

19 See the references given by Blum and Kalven (1964, 692). Among them, of course, one finds Calabresi. Later, they also noted that "economic analysis seems to be in command of a firm blueprint for inquiry" (Walter J. Blum Papers, Box 31, Folder 2, Document 20, "Economic Analysis", n.d., p. 1). All references to "Document _" in the subsequent discussion refer to this box and folder. Of course, it is possible that Blum and Kalven's proximity to economics-infused discussions of legal issues at Chicago also informed (and perhaps biased somewhat) this opinion.

20 Though Blum and Kalven found Coase's negotiation analysis interesting and were the first to reference it within the legal literature, they considered it rather unhelpful because they found the idea of prior negotiation among the parties to an accident a bit far-fetched.

21 Document 2, p. 10.

703), they were left to conclude that the economist was not the one to whom the law should turn to resolve the question of how best to deal with accident-related harms. This was exemplified in Calabresi's use of economic thinking to remove fault from the equation, thereby moving the goals of law in nontraditional directions.[22] "The law", they said, "ought not to break sharply with the moral traditions of the society, as it would if it no longer recognized fault and personal responsibility in human conduct".[23] To them, the economic analysis advocated by Calabresi, grounded in optimization analysis – but, one could also argue, interdisciplinarity in general – thus posed a threat not just to traditional legal methods but to legal and social norms.

5. Struggling with economics, 1966–1967

A. Car accidents and the law: the ongoing debate

Blum and Kalven's 1964 article did anything but mark the end of the discussion. In 1965, they attempted to take their case to a broader audience by publishing a book that bore the same title as their 1964 article and utilized the same arguments. Calabresi, meanwhile, undertook to elaborate and defend his own position. In 1965, he published "The Decision for Accidents: An Approach to Nonfault Allocation of Costs" (1965a), an extension of the central themes of his 1961 article, and "Fault, Accidents and the Wonderful World of Blum and Kalven" (1965b), which responded directly to Blum and Kalven's critique of his position and of the economic approach generally. Each of these pieces, the first published in the *Harvard Law Review* and the second in the *Yale Law Journal*, further developed Calabresi's arguments for allocation of liability based on the economic principle of cost minimization, but his basic line of reasoning did not change.[24]

Calabresi insisted that questions about liability and the goal of accident law "are not meant to herald a metaphysical search for ultimate causes" (1965a, 725). Such "[g]reat moral issues", he argued, are a matter of "collective choice" and have to be "decided in whatever political way our society chooses to decide moral questions" (1965a, 717). When it comes to everyday life situations, by contrast – dealing with "rotary mowers versus reel mowers" or "one method of making steel as against another" – we are dealing with "questions difficult of collective decision" (1965a, 717). The frequency with which these (often idiosyncratic) situations occur and the often widely differing circumstances that attend them, said Calabresi, do not lend themselves to thoughtful resolution through the political process or via larger overarching principles. Instead, he argued, they should be resolved on a case-by-case basis and grounded in practical considerations rather than ethical concerns. Economics is ideal for resolving these more practical issues,

22 On the outward turn of law during this period, see, e.g., Posner (1987).

23 Document 1, p. 14.

24 See, for example, the discussion in Medema (2014b).

he argued, since "the marketplace serves as the rough testing ground" for assessing the efficacy of the alternatives before us (1965a, 717).[25]

The significance of automobile accident costs, meanwhile, was increasingly on the public radar. Alfred Conard's 1964 article on "The Economic Treatment of Automobile Injuries" and his related book, *Automobile Accidents Costs and Payments: Studies in the Economics of Insuring Reparations* (Conard et al. 1964), published that same year, provided empirical evidence for the broad scope of accident-related costs borne by victims and by society as a whole. The increasing toll of automobile accidents motivated the passage of the National Traffic and Motor Vehicle Safety Act and the Highway Safety Act in 1966 – by which time, as President Lyndon Johnson noted when signing the bill into law, automobile fatalities had reached a number nearly triple that of the lives lost in all America's wars.[26]

Between the currency of the accident problem and Calabresi's critique of their arguments, Blum and Kalven had ample justification to press forward with their case for the redesign of accident law. This time, though, their salvo was aimed directly at Calabresi. "The Empty Cabinet of Dr. Calabresi: Auto Accidents and General Deterrence" was published in the *University of Chicago Law Review* in 1967, and the archival record reveals the processes through which they developed their argument. Beginning in January 1966, Blum and Kalven exchanged a lengthy stream of memoranda, notes and drafts of ideas which demonstrate the extent of their concern not just with the details of Calabresi's proposal, but with the appropriateness of using economic analysis to inform legal reasoning – an approach that they seem to have considered a true threat to traditional legal methods.

Befitting a discussion that was taking place on boundaries between disciplines, the archival record demonstrates that Blum and Kalven went to some lengths to improve their understanding of economic analysis as they prepared a response to Calabresi's attack. Evidence for this can be found throughout the notes and memoranda they exchanged in the process of drafting their response, in their notes from a conversation with Chicago economist Harold Demsetz, in several mimeographed pages from the famous Henry Simons Syllabus for Economics 201 ("The Divisional Course in Economics" for University of Chicago undergraduates), and in repeated references to Chicago economist George Stigler's approach to dealing with problems of deterrence.[27] Why would Blum

25 Calabresi (1965a, 717) cites as examples here the determination of whether manufacturers should be allowed to produce rotary lawn mowers in addition to reel lawn mowers and alternative processes for manufacturing steel. A ban on the sale of fireworks, on the other hand, fits more neatly into the ethical-concerns category where collective decision-making is perhaps the sensible way forward.

26 See www.presidency.ucsb.edu/ws/index.php?pid=27847.

27 It is unclear by what means Blum and Kalven arrived at a sense for Stigler's views on the subject of deterrence; there is no record of correspondence between them and Stigler in the Blum papers or the Stigler papers, and there is nothing in the articles that Stigler had written to that point which is suggestive. Apart from personal conversations, of which there is no record, one possible source

and Kalven go to this effort rather than simply rejecting economics out of hand as a lens through which to analyze legal problems? It is reasonable to surmise that their attitude was at least in part a result of the economic tradition in which they had been steeped at Chicago, going back to their student days. Having seen how economics *could* inform the discussion of *some* legal issues, they clearly did not want to reject the possibility that economics could inform the discussion of accident law without first having examined the details of the proposal that economists and economic reasoning would favor to minimize the costs of accidents – general deterrence.[28] But their attitude seems to have gone beyond one of mere respect: their hope seems to have been to discover an argument, grounded in economic analysis, that might point the way to their own favored system for dealing with accident-related losses, one involving a government-administered "social security" plan.[29]

B. General arguments against economics

As with their 1964 article, the notes they took and memoranda they wrote when preparing "Empty Cabinet" found Blum and Kalven emphasizing the divergent normative visions of economics and law – that while the economist is concerned with efficiency, "the primary concern of the law has been the corrective justice aspect of the matter".[30] The question of which party should bear the burden of losses was, in their reading of the common-law tradition, "a question of fairness".[31] This distinction, and their desire to "bring justice back into the discussion" (1967, 264), were at the heart of Blum and Kalven's 1967 assault on Calabresi's reasoning. From where they stood, the use of economics and economic criteria was not sufficient for law. The domain of law, for Blum and Kalven, was one on which the economist, at least so far as prescription went, could not trespass, for within law "there very likely are hidden values that cannot be translated into economic costs, such as the value of having individuals understand why they are being subjected to a special tax and the value of

of this view is Stigler's discussion of divergences between private and social costs in the 1952 and 1966 editions of his book *The Theory of Price* – the 1966 edition of which took up Coase's argument explicitly. Stigler mentions the possibility of using a tax to achieve deterrence (e.g. 1952, 105), and this is the context in which Blum and Kalven reference Stigler in their discussion. Stigler was also quick to draw the conclusion, from Coase's analysis, that law is often without effect on the allocation of resources. There is no mention of Stigler in either of Blum and Kalven's articles on accident law – a fact that is less surprising when one understands that Stigler was an ardent *proponent* of the application of economic reasoning in the legal realm.

28 Blum and Kalven noted in their exchanges that "General deterrence is a familiar objective to the economist", and that when one looks at the arguments in support of general deterrence, "[m]ost of the talk comes from the world of economics" (Document 1, pp. 18, 16).

29 This would entail creating a compensation for accident victims – a "welfare remedy" (1964, 721) – that paralleled the social security system. See Blum and Kalven (1964, 680–681, 711–712, 721–723).

30 Document 10, p. 2.

31 Document 1, p. 2.

not departing too lightly from traditional and accepted ways of doing things" (1967, 266). The values of law, then, made a truly interdisciplinary collaboration between economists and lawyers difficult to envisage.

But Blum and Kalven found other, more practical reasons to be skeptical of the benefits of an economic analysis of (accident) law. First, they questioned the empirical foundation underlying the claims an economist would make regarding human behavior within the legal realm – a concern that seemed to be rooted in their sense that the economist here was operating outside of his area of primary expertise. "What", they asked, "do we know that shows that general deterrence ever works? What is the economists' expertise and experience here? With what kind of accident? Or is the point simply that as price goes up, demand goes down; and that people with variable costs will try to reduce these costs?"[32] This, of course, led them to question the deterrence thesis that was at the heart of Calabresi's economic analysis of accident law, but their concerns were much larger than this, going to the issue of whether the economist's contention that the basic behavioral assumptions and the conclusions drawn from them translated outside the traditional economic realm had any substance. At a minimum, Blum and Kalven questioned the economist's willingness to make such a leap without having done the sort of empirical work necessary to ground these conclusions.[33]

These concerns led directly to Blum and Kalven's second argument against economics: absent such empirical evidence, they were not willing to walk down the behavioral road with the economist, at least when it came to matters related to automobile accidents. In particular, Blum and Kalven questioned the assumed propensity of motorists to adapt their driving habits in response to a legal framework, such as that advocated by Calabresi, which imposes the entire cost of accidents on motorists. The disconnect between their view of human behavior within the legal realm and the economist's perspective is reflected in the seeming disbelief with which they reacted to a conversation on this subject with Demsetz. "[E]verything the economist says here", they noted, "rests on the notion that humans can be made to change their conduct and that different configurations of conduct result in different degrees of efficiency in the utilization of resources".[34] And, at a minimum, Blum and Kalven were suspicious of the idea that legal rules inevitably functioned as price incentives, and thus, in the case of driving, that increases in these "prices" would induce individuals to exercise additional precaution. Echoing their earlier assessment of the questionable links between income tax rates and labor-market incentives, noted earlier, Blum and Kalven argued that "since the personal safety of the individual driver will almost certainly be involved in any accident, what reason is there to believe that the sanction of price will operate in instances where the sanction of personal safety

32 Document 5, p. 3.

33 See also Document 11, p. 2; Document 16, p. 1 and Document 18, February 4, 1966, p. 1.

34 Document 4, p. 2.

has failed to operate?"[35] Beyond this, they insisted that the incentive to avoid a charge of negligence under the extant fault-based system likely already induced motorists to exercise the *maximum* feasible amount of precaution, meaning that the move to a no-fault system such as that advocated by Calabresi would *not* result in *additional* deterrence (e.g. 1967, 252, 254).[36] In short, Blum and Kalven believed that existing incentives induced maximum precaution on the part of motorists and that additional price incentives would have no further deterrent effect.[37]

But even if the law actually does provide the price incentives suggested by economists, Blum and Kalven were not convinced that agents could or would make the "meaningful calculation" necessary to assess the benefit-cost trade-off between additional precaution and, say, a $100 savings on insurance premiums. The typical driver, they contended, "is likely to find the economic calculus somewhat remote and difficult".[38]

Blum and Kalven's final concern with the economic approach – the economist's neglect of distributional considerations in favor of those related to efficiency – brought them back around to their emphasis on traditional notions of justice. In the case of automobile accidents, they stressed that a deterrence system, by making a motorist liable for injuries to others that are not attributable to that motorist's negligence, involves an "injustice".[39] Even if the economic argument is correct up and down the line and strict liability does, in fact, have the efficiency properties asserted by Calabresi, this system provides no rationale grounded in justice for making motorists bear *all* the costs, including for accidents in which they were not negligent. Though the economist acknowledges that injuries from accidents affect the distribution of income and wealth, these effects "would not bear upon his proposal for optimizing accident conditions". Instead, he would respond by "disclaim[ing] any interest or competence, as economist, in such questions of distribution" or by asserting that "auto accident injuries are no different from other misfortunes; and that if welfare payments are thought desirable, they should be based on income and wealth status and not on the nature or cause of the particular misfortune".[40]

Though Blum and Kalven were not finding the economist of much use on the justice front, they did find one opening that seemed, to them, to provide some scope for harmony between the economist's views and their own. If the economist *was* concerned about policies to deal with the distributional effects

35 Document 5, memo from Blum to Kalven, "Questions and Reactions on Re-reading Calabresi", October 6, 1966, p. 2.

36 The economist would object to this argument, pointing out that since the probability of being found negligent under a fault-based system is less than 1, additional precaution will reduce expected costs.

37 For more details on Blum, Kalven and Calabresi and rationality, see Marciano and Romaniuc (2015).

38 Document 18, memorandum from Kalven to Blum, "Further Thoughts on Super-Carefulness", February 4, 1966, p. 4.

39 Document 10, p. 3.

40 Document 10, p. 1.

of auto accidents, they suggested, he would insist that the measures employed not impact incentives in such a way as to affect the attainment of the optimal level of accidents. This led them to conclude that such an economist would be likely to favor a system of government transfer payments to victims – a possibility that they had first raised in their 1964 article.[41] Levying a general tax on motorists to create a fund out of which victims would be compensated would not, in their estimation, impact incentives, leaving them convinced that no less an economist than Stigler would find this system "desirable".[42] In essence, the economist could potentially be useful to the law by suggesting efficient mechanisms for satisfying goals that were central to the law – though only to the extent that the economist's descriptions of individual responses to legal rules could be empirically validated.[43]

C. An economic argument against the economics of liability

Despite their concerns about whether economics could usefully inform legal decision-making, Blum and Kalven were convinced that they could turn economic logic to their advantage in rebutting Calabresi's claim that strict liability for auto accidents – putting the costs of accidents on motorists – was preferable to a common law negligence system. They initially sketched this argument in a 1966 exchange of memoranda and repeated the claim in their 1967 article, noting in the process that they had "benefitted greatly from discussions with Harold Demsetz" in the formulation of their arguments and pointing to "two especially relevant pieces by economists" – Demsetz's "The Exchange and Enforcement of Property Rights" (1964) and Simon Rottenberg's "Liability in Law and Economics" (1965) – that had informed their thinking (Blum and Kalven 1967, 239, n. 1).[44]

Certainly, Blum and Kalven agreed, one could accept the economist's claim in favor of the imposition of liability on manufacturers of potentially dangerous products, as this would indeed accomplish the desired level of deterrence at least cost. Strict liability puts the costs on the manufacturers, but a portion of these costs are passed on to consumers of these products in the form of higher prices. If the

41 See note 30.

42 Document 6, "Notes", p. 3. Blum and Kalven seem to have been of the mind that Stigler's desire to achieve an appropriate level of deterrence but yet separate deterrence from compensation for victims would be satisfied via a general tax on motorists (an idea to which they did not seem to be completely opposed, since it would fall on all motorists and not just those involved in accidents), *a la* Calabresi, combined with a transfer scheme such as the one they proposed in their 1964 article. What Blum and Kalven seem not to have realized is that the economist would argue that their transfer scheme *did* impact incentives, and thus efficiency, by reducing the level of precaution on the part of *potential victims*.

43 For a similar view of the appropriate role for the economist here, see the chapter by Esposito and Tuzet in the present volume.

44 Rottenberg was at that time a professor of economics at SUNY-Buffalo, having previously served on the faculty at Chicago.

costs and thus prices are properly set, the products' users are exposed to the potential costs associated with using the product, meaning that the relevant costs will be internalized to both parties at the lowest cost to society (1967, 248–249). However, they asserted, the same result *would not* obtain in *automobile* accident law if all costs were placed on motorists – the accident-law equivalent of the manufacturer – and for two reasons. First, unlike the manufacturer, the motorist cannot easily estimate accident risk and associated losses. Second, one cannot justify strict liability on the grounds that market forces will see to the proper allocation of costs. While consumers bear a share of the costs in product liability cases (either through harm incurred or higher prices), the absence of a pricing system to reallocate potential costs associated with auto accidents means that these costs fall on motorists if they are liable and on the victims if they are liable (pp. 250–251). One cannot then presume that motorists will bear the appropriate share of accident costs regardless of where liability is assigned, and thus the structure of law here, unlike in the product liability case, would affect the ultimate allocation of costs.

Their conversations with Demsetz and immersion in the literature of economics, though, did nothing to deter Blum and Kalven from their dim view of the price-related deterrent effects of legal rules, at least as applied to accidents. Blum and Kalven's article saw them continue to emphasize that the deterrent effect of strict liability was unlikely to be significant because drivers already faced the potential harm to themselves associated with accidents. This risk alone induced drivers to exercise maximum feasible care, or something approaching it, and adding to this the potential costs associated with harm to others, they argued, was not likely to increase the safety with which people drove. Here, then, we find Blum and Kalven taking an economic position that would be unrecognizable to their economist colleagues at Chicago. The claim, in short, is that there are limits to the link between costs and behavior. In the present instance, the costs associated with the risk to personal safety do indeed have a deterrent effect, but this effect is so substantial that the benefits associated with further cost internalization would be zero (1967, 254). And even if one allows that some people will respond to additional cost-internalization incentives, Blum and Kalven suggested that the difficulties of structuring insurance premiums to accomplish this would be practically insurmountable. This, along with other factors, such as the costs associated with drivers using slower speeds, the need to alter/build roads to account for these slower average speeds etc. raise the specter of further costs which, contrary to Calabresi's claim, may make the strict liability scheme *inefficient*. Moreover, they alleged, the strict liability approach does not offer the prospect of deterring those motorists most likely to be involved in accidents (in contrast to a fault-based system) and, because of the absence of a market process for reallocating costs, does not induce potential non-motorist victims to take sufficient precaution (1967, 255–259). When all of these effects were taken into account, it was not clear to Blum and Kalven that a move to strict liability would, in fact, "yield . . . a net reduction in costs to society" (1967, 259). Differently put, strict liability may well fail to satisfy the economic efficiency standard that Calabresi was using to justify it.

Perhaps the most serious difficulty with the application of the economic approach, Blum and Kalven repeatedly stressed, is the fact that *we do not know what the optimum is* and thus could not say whether putting any particular share of costs on motorists would move us any closer to it.[45] The standards for making such a determination were unrealistically stringent, in their view – so much so that they came away from a conversation with Demsetz feeling that, "[i]n essence, [the economic] approach is based upon the notion that we might be semi-omniscient, but not wholly so".[46] The idea that the analyst could determine or even get a sense for the optimal number of auto accidents, they said, gives accident law "a science-fiction flavor" (1967, 262). Thus, while a system based on economics might be "perfect", it would also be "Utopian" (1967, 263).

What is interesting about Blum and Kalven's criticism of the optimality standard is that it seems to part company with Demsetz's view of the appropriate "economic" approach to such problems in two important ways. First, Blum and Kalven – consistent with their emphasis on "justice" – were assuming that all victims must be fully compensated, whereas the wealth maximization approach advocated by Demsetz (and by Coase) did not necessitate this. Second, Blum and Kalven appeared to ignore the costs associated with administering the social insurance scheme that was their preferred method for accident-loss compensation. The determination of the optimal number of auto accidents requires building into the system *all* costs that vary with the number of accidents, and these include the costs of administering the compensation system. That Blum and Kalven did not put such costs on a par with the more direct costs associated with auto accidents is reflected in the introduction to the 1965 book version of their original article, where they note that "On our scale these matters are entitled to weight, but only as by-products and side effects of adopting a plan" (1965, vi). Here, too, then, Blum and Kalven were not prepared to go all the way with the economist's wealth-maximization approach. What makes this all the more curious is their insistence, in their private writings leading up to the publication of their article, that Calabresi was remiss in not considering the indirect costs associated with *his own* proposed revision of accident law. Blum and Kalven, the evidence suggests, were guilty of another version of the same sin. In attempting to push the limits of the "economic approach" and adapt it to their purposes, it would seem that they were still not able to completely loose themselves from other concerns.

6. Conclusions

This marked the end of Blum and Kalven's debate with Calabresi, though not the end of either party's work on accident law. Calabresi's approach, of course, became highly influential in legal thinking, both helping to drive and riding the

45 See, e.g., Document 7, "A Note on the Calabresi Formulation", p. 2.

46 Document 4, p. 1. They also note here that this is the basic position taken by Stigler. Interestingly, "semi-omniscience" was replaced with "omniscience" in their 1967 article.

ascendancy of the economic analysis of law in the 1970s and 1980s, and Blum and Kalven's proposed mechanisms for dealing with accidents never received serious traction in theory or practice.

The story of the origins of the economic analysis of law is often portrayed as an exercise in economics imperialism (e.g. Duxbury 1995, 367–377; Fine and Milonakis 2009). But there is a growing body of evidence to suggest that this was anything but the case and thus that the traditional view is misguided at best, that legal scholars, rather than colonizing economists, were at the center of the application of economic thinking to new areas of law. As Medema (2014a) has demonstrated, it was lawyers, not economists, who brought the Coase theorem to bear on law in the 1960s, and the place of a "Chicago school" in that history is anything but central.[47] The present chapter adds weight to this alternative perspective on legal-economic history by focusing on the interactions between lawyers and economists at Chicago and the earliest steps toward interdisciplinarity. The lawyers at Chicago are central to the story here, and these legal scholars were reaching out to economists for insights that would further their efforts to determine whether, and the extent to which, economic thinking could properly inform legal analysis and how that thinking might shed light on a legal issue of major social and legal importance.

What our analysis reveals is that *all* the players examined here have in common a sense that economic thinking *can* be fruitfully applied to the analysis of legal issues. Where they differed was in the utility, appropriateness and extent to which one should do so and the conclusions that one could, and should, properly draw from the analysis so applied. Blum and Kalven were amenable to the application of economic analysis to legal questions so long as it did not challenge the traditional prerogatives of law; Calabresi, in contrast, was willing to shake up the apple cart and allow economic thinking to dictate to law in new and transformative ways.

In short, the interdisciplinary effort that became known as the economic analysis of law was alive and well at Chicago throughout the 1960s in areas beyond antitrust. Chicagoans such as Gary Becker and Richard Posner walked into a conversation already in progress, one in which the perspectives on how economic analysis should inform law and the lessons to be taken from it were anything but homogeneous.

47 See also Medema (2017) for a more broad-based historical discussion of the "imperialism" question as it pertains to the economic analysis of law. On how economists understood "The Problem of Social Cost" and used the Coase theorem during this period, see Marciano and Frischmann (2015) and Medema (2014c).

References

Anderson, J. M., P. Heaton, and S. J. Carroll. 2010. *The U.S. Experience with No-Fault Automobile Insurance: A Retrospective.* Santa Monica, CA: Rand Institute for Civil Justice, Rand Corporation.

Becker, G. S. 1968. "Crime and Punishment: An Economic Approach." *Journal of Political Economy* 76(2): 169–217.

Blum, W. J., and H. Kalven Jr. 1952. "The Uneasy Case for Progressive Taxation." *University of Chicago Law Review* 19(3): 417–520.

Blum, W. J., and H. Kalven Jr. 1953. *The Uneasy Case for Progressive Taxation.* Chicago, IL: University of Chicago Press.

Blum, W. J., and H. Kalven Jr. 1964. "Public Law Perspectives on a Private Law Problem: Auto Compensation Plans." *University of Chicago Law Review* 31(4): 641–723.

Blum, W. J., and H. Kalven Jr. 1965. *Public Law Perspectives on a Private Law Problem: Auto Compensation Plans.* Boston, MA: Little, Brown & Company.

Blum, W. J., and H. Kalven Jr. 1967. "The Empty Cabinet of Dr. Calabresi: Auto Accidents and General Deterrence." *University of Chicago Law Review* 34(2): 239–273.

Butler, H. N., and J. Klick, eds. 2018. *History of Law and Economics.* Aldershot: Edward Elgar.

Calabresi, G. 1961. "Some Thoughts on Risk Distribution and the Law of Torts." *Yale Law Journal* 70(4): 499–553.

Calabresi, G. 1965a. "The Decision for Accidents: An Approach to Nonfault Allocation of Costs." *Harvard Law Review* 78(4): 713–745.

Calabresi, G. 1965b. "Fault, Accidents and the Wonderful World of Blum and Kalven." *Yale Law Journal* 75(2): 216–238.

Calabresi, G. 1970. *The Costs of Accidents: A Legal and Economic Analysis.* New Haven, CT: Yale University Press.

Calabresi, G. 1975. "Concerning Cause and the Law of Torts: An Essay for Harry Kalven, Jr. *University of Chicago Law Review* 43(1): 69–108.

Coase, R. H. 1960. "The Problem of Social Cost." *Journal of Law and Economics* 3(1): 1–44.

Coase, R. H. 1993. "Law and Economics at Chicago." *Journal of Law and Economics* 36(1): 239–254.

Cohen, L. R., and J. D. Wright, eds. 2009. *Pioneers of Law and Economics.* Aldershot: Edward Elgar.

Conard, A. 1964. "The Economic Treatment of Automobile Injuries." *Michigan Law Review* 63(2): 279–326.

Conard, A., J. Morgan, R. Pratt Jr., C. Voltz, and R. Bombaugh. 1964. *Automobile Accidents Costs and Payments: Studies in the Economics of Insuring Reparations.* Ann Arbor: Michigan Legal Studies, University of Michigan Press.

Demsetz, H. 1964. "The Exchange and Enforcement of Property Rights." *Journal of Law and Economics* 7(1): 11–26.

Director, A. 1952. *Defense, Controls and Inflation.* Chicago, IL: Chicago University Press.

Duxbury, N. 1995. *Patterns of American Jurisprudence.* Oxford: Oxford University Press.

Ehrenzweig, A. 1951. *Negligence Without Fault.* Berkeley: University of California Press.

Ehrenzweig, A. 1955. "Full Aid Insurance for the Traffic Victim – A Voluntary Compensation Plan." *California Law Review* 43(1): 1–48.

Fine, B., and D. Milonakis. 2009. *From Economics Imperialism to Freakonomics: The Shifting Boundaries Between Economics and Other Social Sciences.* London: Routledge.

Fleury, J-B. 2015. "Massive Influence with Scarce Contributions: The Rationalizing Economist Gary S. Becker, 1930–2014." *European Journal of Law and Economics* 39(1): 3–9.

Flink, J. J. 1972. "Three Stages of American Automobile Consciousness." *American Quarterly* 24(4): 451–473.

Franklin, M. A., R. H. Chanin, and I. Mark. 1961. "Accidents, Money, and the Law: A Study of the Economics of Personal Injury Litigation." *Columbia Law Review* 61(1): 1–39.

Green, L. 1958. *Traffic Victims: Tort Law and Insurance.* Evanston, IL: Northwestern University Press.

Gregory, C. O., and H. Kalven Jr. 1959. *Cases and Materials on Torts.* Boston, MA: Little, Brown & Company.

Harnay, S. A., and Marciano. 2009. "Posner, Economics and the Law: From 'Law and Economics' to an Economic Analysis of Law." *Journal of the History of Economic Thought* 31(2): 215–232.

James, Jr. F. 1959. "The Columbia Study of Compensation for Automobile Accidents: An Unanswered Challenge." *Columbia Law Review* 59(3): 408–424.

James, Jr. F., and S. Law. 1952. "Compensation for Auto Accident Victims – A Story of Too Little and Too Late." *Connecticut Bar Journal* 26(1): 70–81.

Kalven, Jr. H. 1955. "Review of Albert Armin Ehrenzweig, *'Full Aid' Insurance for the Traffic Victim: A Voluntary Compensation Plan.*" *Texas Law Review* 33(5): 778–782.

Kalven, Jr. H. 1956. "The Jury in Auto Cases: Invitation to Research." *Virginia Law Weekly*, 22.

Kalven, Jr. H. 1957. "Compulsory Auto Insurance." *Chicago Sun-Times*, November 24, p. 3.

Kalven, Jr. H. 1959. "Review of Leon Green: *Traffic Victims: Tort Law and Insurance.*" *University of Chicago Law Review* 26(4): 679–686.

Kitch, E. W. 1983. "The Fire of Truth: A Remembrance of Law and Economics at Chicago, 1932–1970." *Journal of Law and Economics* 26(1): 163–234.

Marciano, A. 2012. "Guido Calabresi's Economic Analysis of Law, Coase and the Coase Theorem." *International Review of Law and Economics* 32(1): 110–118.

Marciano, A., and B. Frischmann. 2015. "Understanding the Problem of Social Cost." *Journal of Institutional Economics* 11(2): 329–352.

Marciano, A., and G. Ramello. 2014. "Consent, Choice and Guido Calabresi's Heterodox Economic Analysis of Law." *Law and Contemporary Problems* 77(2): 97–116.

Marciano, A., and R. Romaniuc. 2015. "Accident Costs, Resource Allocation and Individual Rationality: Blum, Kalven, and Calabresi." *European Journal of the History of Economic Thought* 22(6): 1084–1114.

McCord Wright, D. 1954. "Review of *the Uneasy Case for Progressive Taxation* by Walter J. Blum and Harry Kalven." *Stanford Law Review* 6(3): 583–584.

Medema, S. G. 1998. "Wandering the Road from Pluralism to Posner: The Transformation of Law and Economics, 1920s–1970s." In M. S. Morgan and M. Rutherford (eds.), *The Transformation of American Economics: From Interwar Pluralism to Postwar Neoclassicism: History of Political Economy Annual Supplement.* Durham, NC: Duke University Press, vol. 30, pp. 202–224.

Medema, S. G. 2009. *The Hesitant Hand: Taming Self-Interest in the History of Economic Ideas.* Princeton, NJ: Princeton University Press.

Medema, S. G. 2011. "Chicago Price Theory and Chicago Law and Economics." In R. Van Horn, P. Mirowski, and T. Stapleford (eds.), *Building Chicago Economics: New Perspectives on the History of America's Most Powerful Economics Program.* Cambridge: Cambridge University Press, pp. 151–179.

Medema, S. G. 2014a. "Debating Law's Irrelevance: Legal Scholarship and the Coase Theorem in the 1960s." *Texas A&M Law Review* 2(2): 159–213.

Medema, S. G. 2014b. "*Juris Prudence*: Calabresi's Uneasy Relationship with the Coase Theorem." *Law and Contemporary Problems* 77(2): 65–95.

Medema, S. G. 2014c. "1966 and All That: The Birth of the Coase Theorem Controversy." *Journal of the History of Economic Thought* 36(3): 271–303.

Medema, S. G. 2017. "Scientific Imperialism or Merely Boundary Crossing? Economists, Lawyers, and the Coase Theorem at the Dawn of the Economic Analysis of Law." In U. Mäki, A. Walsh, and M. Fernández Pinto (eds.), *Scientific Imperialism: Exploring the Boundaries of Interdisciplinarity*. London: Routledge, pp. 89–116.

Peterson, M. A., and G. L. Priest. 1982. *The Civil Jury: Trends in Trials and Verdicts, Cook County, Illinois, 1960–1979*. Santa Monica, CA: RAND Corporation.

Plant, M. L. 1955. "Review of '*Full Aid' Insurance for the Traffic Victim* by A. A. Ehrenzweig, and *the Law of Compulsory Motor Vehicle Insurance in South Africa: A Treatise on the Motor Vehicle Insurance Act* by A. Suzman and G. Gordon." *American Journal of Comparative Law* 4(1): 117–121.

Posner, R. A. 1972. *Economic Analysis of Law*. New York: Little, Brown & Company.

Posner, R. A. 1987. "The Decline of Law as an Autonomous Discipline." *Harvard Law Review* 100(4): 761–780.

Priest, G. L. 2005. "The Rise of Law and Economics: A Memoir of the Early Years." In F. Parisi and C. K. Rowley (eds.), *The Origins of Law and Economics: Essays by the Founding Fathers*. Cheltenham: Edward Elgar, pp. 350–382.

Rothbard, M. N. 2010. *Strictly Confidential: The Private Volker Fund Memos of Murray N. Rothbard*. Edited by D. Gordon. Auburn, AL: Ludwig von Mises Institute.

Rottenberg, S. 1956. "The Baseball Players' Labor Market." *Journal of Political Economy* 64(3): 242–258.

Rottenberg, S. 1965. "Liability in Law and Economics." *American Economic Review* 55(1): 107–144.

Shaviro, D. 2013. "The Forgotten Henry Simons." *Florida State University Law Review* 41(1): 2–38.

Simons, H. C. 1938. *Personal Income Taxation: The Definition of Income as a Problem of Fiscal Policy*. Chicago: University of Chicago Press.

Stigler, G. 1966. *The Theory of Price*. Chicago: University of Chicago Press.

Stigler, G. 1992. "Law or Economics?" *Journal of Law and Economics* 35(2): 455–468.

Stone, G. R. 2007. "In Memoriam: Bernard D. Meltzer (1914–2007)." *University of Chicago Law Review* 74: 439–441.

Van Horn, R. 2009. "Reinventing Monopoly and Corporations: The Roots of Chicago Law and Economics." In P. Mirowski and D. Plehwe (eds.), *The Road from Mont Pelerin*. Cambridge, MA: Harvard University Press, pp. 204–237.

Van Horn, R., and P. Mirowski. 2009. "The Rise of the Chicago School of Economics." In P. Mirowski and D. Plehwe (eds.), *The Road from Mont Pelerin*. Cambridge, MA: Harvard University Press, pp. 139–178.

Woodard, C. 1988. "Charles O. Gregory." *Virginia Law Review* 74(1): 3–10.

4 Rights, entitlements and the law

The ambiguous status of legal elements in economic discourse

Stefano Solari

1. Economics and the law: love will tear us apart. . .

Law and Economics is a broad field of investigation. The largest part of it deals with the benefits of regulations, seen from the perspective of the ruler. Here, we deal with a component of the field: the economic analysis of contracts and of the legal elements involved in private interactions. The perspective is alternatively that of the private actor analyzing efficient choices in a juridically framed space or that of the ruler in terms of good market design.

Economics and law have a reciprocal attraction.[1] The two disciplines are often complementary in business practice. Law is often a fundamental subject in business school, and some economics is taught in law schools to make students aware of both the context and some hard constraints to any legal discourse. In general, legal scholars would be happy to benefit from some solid economic input for their arguments. This actually happens for a variety of specific subjects. Unfortunately, delusions and misunderstandings are also frequent for a variety of reasons, primarily because economists sometimes supply judgments in fields usually reserved for legal disciplines and they do this by developing their own simplified legal categories functional to their method of analysis. However, adopting law categories in standard economics raises some serious methodological challenges. Rights and the law are ambiguous inputs for economic discourse and, therefore, are often best understood as simple constraints.

Indeed, the contact between economics and law may be differently conceived according to which subdiscipline is concerned. Here, microeconomics – enjoying a more compact theoretical *corpus* – will be considered, and political economy, business and accountancy, which have a more practical orientation, will not be discussed.[2]

1 We should not forget that the success of political economy came with British classical economists evaluating alternative institutional arrangements relative to the poor laws and to corn laws.

2 The interpretation of the practical dimension of legal study proposed here is based on the approach of the University of Padua's school, which has always kept a deep hermeneutical stance, basing its research on the logics of argumentation.

The fundamental idea of this chapter is that standard microeconomics has an epistemology that makes it fit to very specific and short-term evaluations. It is quite simplificatory of human and social cognition, and therefore it cannot supply normative assessments on very broad practical questions involving political and ethical issues. Law and Economics builds over an epistemological mismatch, and this problematic relationship suggests caution when incorporating economic knowledge into juridical discourses (Cserne 2011).

Consequently, this chapter will argue that these different epistemologies are responsible for some crucial problems in the interaction between economics and legal studies, particularly in the theorization of economic choice in a juridical context. This difficulty is mostly due to the ambiguous status assumed by legal concepts in the model of economic choice. Economics requires clearly defined variables, while juridical concepts, from this perspective, suffer from a certain indeterminacy and dependence on context. Some epistemological difficulties related to the static objectivization of options typical of economics and the difficulty of considering interdependencies related to the context will be highlighted in particular. In the next section, some epistemological difficulties in interaction between the two disciplines will be analyzed. In the third section, the problem of the status of legal elements in the model of choice is studied. The outdated or oversimplified notion of property rights adopted by economists is illustrated and criticized in section four. At that point, the chapter scrutinizes in more depth the specific problem of the notions of goods, rules and entitlements relative to agency and the poor economic framing of these concepts.

2. The epistemological mismatch between legal and economic studies

Standard microeconomics is a well-ordered set of consequential reasoning tools based on a few axioms. Its theoretical core tends to be perfectly nomological-deductive, while the belt is constituted by empirical studies based on econometrics.[3] In Law and Economics, the epistemological clash is particularly evident in legal systems based on the traditions of Roman law. The main problem is that economists do not use in their Law and Economics studies actual legal categories, instead inventing their own, simplified and functional to their model of individual choice.[4] These categories are based on a common-sense-of-the-economist kind of ontology, where distinctions are instrumentally shaped to hide the process of framing, exalt the act of choice, simplify the elements that enter evaluation and wipe off uncertainty. In this way, economics

3 In fact, the economic theory landscape is not so homogeneous, as heterodox economics represents a good share of the total population, but heterodoxies are fragmented and of uncertain classification (Cartwright and Davis 2016, 53).

4 I am not arguing that legal categories are rationally organized and perfectly functional to their scope. However, they are the categories used in legal work.

hopes to detect some laws of economic behavior or some principles of universal application which lay beyond the veil of corrupted reality, and indeed some of these principles actually have a general validity. Nevertheless, the result is either an oversimplification of the world or a tendency to exclude the context from theorization due to the sharp *isolating abstractions* necessary to keep the mathematical reasoning. This is particularly evident in the debates about *property rights*.

A further epistemological diversity concerns the different metrics used to evaluate facts adopted in the two disciplines (Sunstein 1994). The metrics of law is not specified: it refers to individual interest or general interest but, in any case, tends to keep reasons and action motives separate. Sunstein affirms that "the use of a single metric is often unhelpful for law" (Sunstein 1994, 797). Economics operates by imploding all variables into a single metric that is in the end comparable to monetary value (often leaving many residuals in the open category of *social costs*). It tends to be inconceivable for economists *reasoning without comparing* (Chan 2010), which is, instead, everyday practice for law scholars. All this has some relevant *performative* consequence, as individuals may be guided by economic theory to privilege monetary aspects over any other or to look at moral and cultural rules as hindering their action. The specification of context and categories through which we arrange perceptions is usually left by economists in a second plan or grouped instrumentally. This makes economic intervention in legal reasoning very specific and limited to definite knowledge inserted instrumentally to inform discourses based on different logics (Sunstein 1995, ch. 1).

There is also some conceptual difference in the definition of variables. Economic concepts such as "good", "utility", "preference", "property", "choice" and "value" are synthetic notions that assume a precise meaning in actual circumstances but are usually used in very broad and abstract ways (Taylor 1982). Economics, even in its more recent developments as game theory, privileges the "syntactical connections" between these pre-ordinate elements. The actualization, contextualization and fitting of real situations into theoretical categories is an aspect of the theorizing process that is usually left to applied economists, who are an extinction-endangered species.[5] In this way, the inquiry into theoretical categories is virtually absent in present-day economics. The language of the law scholar, when not intentionally ambiguous, is much more precise because it directly enters laws, contracts and treaties that are intended to frame or be an unambiguous reference to concrete action. Moreover, contracts are always preceded by long specifications, clarifications and elucidations on the actual meanings of terms used, so as to avoid any misunderstanding.

Another fracture between economic and legal language is due to the positivistic endeavor of the former versus the ethical or political setting of the latter.[6]

5 The present tendency is that of testing of theories through econometrics, based on variables taken as "proxies" of phenomena to be studied, avoiding any really applied approach.

6 Economics is usually divided between a positive and a normative perspective, according to its aim. The separation between a positive and a normative theory is rooted in rationalistic positivism. This

Backhaus (1979, 2) observed that Chicago-style Law and Economics was an attempt to blend a positive science into a normative body of knowledge and reasoning. Although specific, this criticism should be seriously considered when working in the interface of the two disciplines: optimization tends to boil down to a normative discourse when imported into another discipline. The *practical science* approach (broadly conceived as Aristotelian) or any ethical approach to economics can find a more consistent bridge with legal studies (Crespo 2017), but this is a radically heterodox approach.

Finally, a specific demand from law scholars (as well as from other disciplines) to economists is to supply reliable evaluations, or a reliable method of evaluation, in specific contractual situations. This could really be the role of economics in legal research. Unfortunately, evaluation techniques from economics are quite specific to very specific cases, and their reliability should be accurately questioned when translated into other domains. Economics tends to rely on a simple consequentialist approach, while in legal disciplines, it is necessary to integrate other value criteria (Cserne 2011; Mathis 2011). In economics, individual preference deals with *overall comparative evaluations* (Engelen 2017), but law scholars would be more interested that economists dissect preferences and analyze subjective value according to its composite elements. Related to this issue is the problem of comparability and incommensurability (Sunstein 1994), a problem that, despite the wide discussion in Law and Economics, has still not found an audience in the economic mainstream. The idea of incommensurability clashes with the idea that economists should not discuss preferences but should simply deal with ways to calculate best options. Moreover, economics is seldom about considering relationships or studying relational dimensions of value. In legal studies, despite the general attempt to reduce variables to individual rights, reciprocal interaction is fundamental for the same definitions of rights and obligations. This argument will be analyzed in the fourth section.

3. Choice and action in a legally framed context

Free will is the protagonist of the two disciplines. However, the individual reason supporting the will is conceived differently in the two disciplines. The difference resides not only in what is included (and how) in individual motivation for action, but also in which variables are considered and which are discarded, what is subject to choice and what is considered as given. Moreover, what is relevant here and the way the same variables are conceived differ substantially, particularly in the case of rules and rights.

Legal studies certainly assume a more comprehensive and less precise *model of man*. They do not require a strong hypothesis of rationality as the simple idea of individual interest is sufficient. Economics is more clear cut in its framing of choice

---

division has been defined as untenable (Davis 2014). Moreover, in ethical approaches, the *fact-value* dichotomy does not hold.

but tends to adopt a relatively poor conception of human motivation and a computational view of reason. The economic model of choice divides variables between what is the object of calculation (prices and quantities of a good), what contributes to define preferences and what does not enter the problem (often an overpopulated group). Rationality, therefore, can be resumed in the problem of having complete information and performing appropriate calculation: *constrained preference satisfaction* (White 2017). The standard model of economic choice presented in textbooks is particularly deceiving because costs are presented as objective and given, while benefits are subjective, depending on preferences. In this way, choice takes place in a given context that helps calculation and comparison. By contrast, to find a bridge with legal studies (and with actual situations), costs should also include subjective elements. More radically, the economic agent should be best interpreted as an opportunity builder: a framer of situations rather than a simple exploiter of given opportunities. In fact, legal rationality is much more focused on framing problems (partly because given concepts are often obsolete); in this sense, it can be considered practical. Consequently, problems are continuously reinterpreted according to the changing context (which is never discarded).

These are problems that can apparently find a conciliation. However, the most intricate issue is the inclusion of typical legal elements into the model of economic choice. Economists have attempted various ways to include rights and rules in economic decision-making. The mainstream of political economists tends to endogenize duties, norms and commitments in a broad definition of preferences (Sen 1997), nonetheless expressing them in a simplified and static way. In particular, moral norms are included in preferences, while formal rules are seen as limits to choice, more or less effective according to their enforcement and to the probability of being sanctioned. However, qualitative features of rules, such as the difference between regulative norms and constitutive rules (Searle 2017), are difficult to understand in the economic model of choice. The former are simply seen as a more or less stringent bound; the latter are hardly considered or simply conceived as belonging to the context. The fact is that economics does not and cannot inquire the cognitive role of norms because it implies a radically different notion of rationality.

We also find a paradoxical theoretical situation in which rights and duties are (by and large) symmetrical in the law perspective, while they are conceived in very different positions in economic reasoning: duty is, in principle, included in preferences, and rights are seen as individual endowments. Rights, however, have a very ambiguous status. They may be connected to resources, as in the case of real rights, being in this way part of a tradable good. But they may also be seen as structuring the space of choice, as a component of capabilities, defining what can and cannot be done. Certainly, economists tend to overlook that rights and duties include deontic powers that produce reasons for action which are independent of individual desires (Searle 2017). All this makes the application of the model of *constrained preference satisfaction* (White 2017) to rights and rules rather difficult as a consequence of the freezing implication it has on the status of legal variables.

Some economists (although not mainstream) have tried to explain (unspecified) rights. Sen (1970) has defined individual rights as the possibility of determining the social ordering of social states.[7] However, this interpretation has been criticized by Gärdenfors (1981), who argued, in support of Nozick's (1974) interpretation, that rights, if exercised, put constraints on the set of alternatives open to social choice. That allows a distinction between having a right and exercising it, which is an interesting issue in Law and Economics. Gärdenfors (1981) introduced the idea of expressing rights through *game forms*: that is, games where utilities are undefined. Greenberg (1990) further developed this kind of modeling into a whole compendium for the study of social situations. Yet Chapman (1982) questioned the ability of these models to grasp rights, arguing that the incorporation of individual rights into maximization frameworks is problematic with respect to deontological perspectives (as well as from *virtue ethics*). The "concern for *how* (i.e. the process by which) a state of affairs is chosen over another has serious implications both for the conventional models of economic rationality and for certain proposed models of individual rights" (Chapman 1982, 460). Rights should resist utilitarian calculation; otherwise, they have no separate existence and independence. More recently, Dowding and van Hees (2003, 284) have resumed the criticisms of Sen's idea that rights are defined as a form of power to determine the social preference relation, by arguing that people may have rights without power. Moreover, it is difficult to distinguish having rights from exercising them, and preferences in this view are seen as coinciding with choices (which is a bad shortcut). Actually, the true idea Sen had in mind was the *positive freedom* approach, which has nothing particularly legal in it.

There is a further aspect of rules, which has been discussed in the *expressive function of law* literature. There are many versions of this concept; however, it essentially states that "the social meanings of actions are very much a function of existing social norms" (Sunstein 1996, 2022). Sunstein lists two possible versions: that based on the social consequences of law and that based on individual interest in integrity. Rules are not always effective and well accepted, but Cooter admits that when "many people in a community internalise an obligation, it becomes a social norm" (Cooter 1998, 585), and this leads to commitment. Laws announce or signal an expected change in practices. Their effectiveness depends much on how a law influences social norms; this means that it is not a simple tie to human behavior, but it goes more deeply into how reason takes decisions (Raz 1990). Cooter concludes that law can induce a change in individual preferences (Cooter 1998). His view is that law can create a focal point by expressing values. Changing individual values is exactly what Cooter means by the expressive use of law (Cooter 1998, 586). The analysis of Anderson and Pildes (2000)

7 This definition, in fact, has expressed an attempt to model *positive freedom* that eventually led to the idea of *capabilities*. Sen tried to connect his theory to juridical variables in his book on justice (2009), but, again, at the end, that work is about *positive freedom*, confirming the ajuridical nature of Sen's thought.

is even more philosophically and sociologically elaborate, as it considers three dimensions: the ontological, the epistemic and the normative. According to these researchers, "expressive norms regulate actions by regulating the acceptable justifications for doing them" (Anderson and Pildes 2000, 1510). Therefore, relative to consequentialism, the expressive effect of law consists of telling us "*why* the consequences matter, and *which* consequences matter" (Anderson and Pildes 2000, 1514). This is a typical framework based on practical reason, where the individual decides by balancing reasons. This model is considered valid by such Aristotelian economists as Ricardo Crespo (2017), but it cannot be well (coherently) framed by the standard theory of choice.

Economics has difficulty in packing various motivations into preferences also because of the problem of noncomparability and incommensurability (Sunstein 1994; Crespo 2017). Engelen (2017) has proposed to unpack *other motivations* (cravings, duties, commitments) from overall preference ranking to allow a better study of final individual choice. This has the advantage of keeping preferences stable (following the manual of the good economist) and including such intractable elements as duties and commitments in economic reasoning. In this way, many specific legal variables enter the *other motivations*, enhancing the comparability with legal studies. The side effect is that *other motivations* would inevitably be traded off with monetary gains emerging from the standard part of the calculation. Nonetheless, some variables (such as duties and contractual promises) still retain ambiguous status.

Consequently, the microeconomic interpretation of rules, rights and duties misses some important qualitative aspect, as well as the interdependent nature of these elements. Individual rights are enforced by rules that impose some specific or universal obligation on other individuals.[8] This interdependency makes the context of individual choice rather changeable. Rules have an impact on the rights and, consequently, on the endowments of individuals. At the same time, rules cannot be interpreted as simple bounds to admissible actions because rules affect individual evaluation. They affect the value of resources, as well as the use that individuals can have for them. They even help defining if a thing is a resource or not (in the fifth section, this element will be further analyzed). The next step is to explore in more detail the notions of property rights, goods and the relationship between rules and entitlements.

4. The controversial definition of property rights

We have seen that the definition of legal elements in Law and Economics theory is quite problematic. An emblematic case is the very broad notions of property rights adopted by economists as they are not prepared for a proliferation

8 This idea is particularly supported by *legal realism*, but it makes sense in general. Sen (2000) is well aware of the difficulty of cost-benefit analysis. He argued that "[t]he neglect of the freedoms that people enjoy is no less serious a limitation than the neglect of rights" (Sen 2000, 944).

of specific concepts that would make their models unmanageable. Therefore, they adopt definitions of property rights that require no modification of their model of choice or that even reinforce it. What is more, Hodgson has accused this discipline of confusing categories, as in the case of possession and property (2015), forgetting the role of the state in assuring property. Exchange concerns property, but property is a right that has a social dimension, and it is produced by mutual recognition in a political community context (Ege and Walraevens 2011; Solari 2015). The discipline of Law and Economics has, according to Hodgson (2015), wiped off the state as a legal structure defining the various dimensions of rights and obligations connected to property. The progressive simplification of categories has led this discipline to just theorize about possession: that is, about the factual control over the asset. However, property, properly defined, is not the factual control of the good as control is often left to other individuals; sometimes, it is correctly defined as a *residual control right*. Such a right is weakly enforceable without the jurisdictional institutions of the modern state, which also needs social and political recognition. Hodgson's critique tends to bring the state and social control into the theory, but it tends also to hold on to the old notion of property that has been here defined as very problematic in section five.

We can distinguish different economic definitions of property rights. Alchian (1965) defined property rights as the *ability to choose the use of goods*. This ability has been specified as an *exclusive authority* granted by the law and/or by custom and convention. This definition is based on *de facto* powers of control rather than on legal or moral rights but suffers from both Hodgson's critique and from an industrialist bias.[9] This is a quite useful and effective definition for many individual entitlements, but it can surely be extended to a variety of rights that are not property. However, it would not help in understanding the position of managers in regard to the control of companies.

Barzel (1997, 3) distinguishes between abstract legal property rights (*de jure*) and economic rights (*de facto*), relating the latter to the ability to control or use assets. This definition, confining the law to the realm of abstract things, sanctions a separation between legal and economic concepts that is not quite useful in any sense. It appears an artifact to bypass the expressive role of law. It remains fully concentrated on actual possession and does not further an understanding of contemporary issues. Barzel adds that

> The term "property rights" carries two distinct meanings in the economic literature. One . . . is essentially the ability to enjoy a piece of property. The other, much more prevalent and much older, is essentially what the state assigns to a person. I designate the first "economic property rights" and the

9 Alchian (1977, 238) also defined property rights as *the probability that the decision about the uses of the resource will determine the use.* Nevertheless, the probabilistic setting does not help the interaction with legal studies.

> second "legal rights". Economic rights are the end (that is, what people ultimately seek), whereas legal rights are the means to achieve the end. Legal rights play a primarily supporting role.
>
> (Barzel 1997, 3)

This distinction goes in the direction of Coase (1960) but, again, is too wide. In fact, we can enjoy or manage many goods without holding any property on them. The term *a piece of property* is not defining a crucial issue we deserve to know: what can be included in it and what is not? Moreover, it is avulsed from rules and duties that evidently frame this right when we consider property not related to commodities.

Allen, on the other hand, has defined property as "the ability to freely exercise a choice" (Allen 2015, 2). This definition rightly invades the domain of "liberty" and is broad and not precise at all. It misses the endowment effect of property and omits the duties connected to it. It has the defect of not identifying the relational nature of legal positions as it is focused on individual choice alone. While property may in a sense assure liberty (the old Republican position), liberty does not necessarily need property.

All these conceptualisations of property rights are nonetheless quite interesting and indicative of the needs of developing some specific legal form to frame new exchanges. The old legal categories are seen as abstract and unfit, and economists rightly try to find a pragmatic and simple way to frame the entitlements that are modified in economic intercourses. It is nevertheless not clear why they indulge in focusing on property rights while the protagonists of exchanges are a wide array of entitlements. Additionally, these novel tendencies in the conception of property can be already distinguished in the justifications of property rights of modern theorists. The idea of *property right*, from Grotius to Pufendorf and Locke, has been defined as an extension of the notion of occupation functional to the *protective* definition of one's personality (Buckle 1991; Pennington 1998; Schlatter 1951). Therefore, the *suum* has been seen as a prelegal idea of a personality needing essential possession in order to assure his/her life. Possession of goods is not factually problematic. It becomes a legal concept when a political community allows a specific sphere of control to individuals – in which possession of a good is a specific case. Therefore, classical liberal scholars defined property as the right to a variety of personal entitlements needed to protect the *suum* (including limbs, honor etc.), thereby distancing themselves from Roman law. The right to self-preservation results in the right to exclude others from affecting this sphere of the *suum*, but it inevitably depends on others' acceptance. Hegel's theory simply asserts that ownership is a basic human interest, and it is included in the ethical development of individual persons. The consequence is that property is seen as a subjective right rather than a real right (Hegel 1820). Hegel's liberalism also tended to consider that everyone should have some property in order to obtain democracy based on property owners (distributionism). This subjective right, however, was seen as embedded in the ethical institutions of the state and in practice resided in reciprocal recognition (Solari 2019), which socially frames and limits these rights. Consequently, property was theorized as something related to personality and not as a simple *dominium* on things. This is why property is also a necessary condition to the effective participation in civil society for Hegel (1805–1806).

Legal scholars have, by now, resisted the evolution of property rights in this direction, holding on to the original category of *in rem* rights of Roman law. Modern theories apparently have assimilated the idea of a right functional to individual autonomy and perhaps the Hegelian transformation into a subjective right; forget, nonetheless, all social and ethical dimensions of rights that liberal thinkers conceived in their works, particularly the Hegelian ethical state that was able to coordinate individual rights. However, the factual development of the economy is going in a direction that makes the claims of Allen and Barzel (and Hegel) understandable.

5. On goods and rules in the era of access

Some difficulty of communication between economics and law studies arises regarding the notion of economic good in relation to property rights. In economic studies, *good* is a general notion, including all that can have a value: that is to say, inducing individuals to work out some reservation price (individual evaluation). The economic good is regarded as an original category and a phenomenologically defined entity, independent from the juridical framing of it. The law is generally considered a useful device, even if sometimes costly or cumbersome, to enforce the property of valuable resources by excluding others from their use. However, in the view of economists, it remains a superstructure with no foundational value. Moreover, rules are introduced ex-post, compared to reservation prices, to define the field of admissible choices. In this way, regulation is often understood as limiting profitable options. Therefore, evaluation, deriving from need or from scarcity, is phenomenologically seen as the foundational element, while the law is a social accessory.

This mainstream view has also diffused to contemporary Law and Economics, particularly in areas of common law.[10] A challenge deriving from this need-based evaluation fundamentalism is the difficulty in clearly understanding why contracts subscribed in a state of necessity are voidable (Cserne and Szalai 2010; Cserne 2011). This means that the legal framework assumes a wider variety of principles compared to economics to understand what a just price is. Limiting evaluation to a need/scarcity approach, however, might create merciless situations, as well as lead to paradoxical situations, such as measuring the value of human life (Hammer 2011).

The good in economics is typically framed by *real rights*, usually further reduced to *property rights*, functionally assuring exclusion, even if, as just argued,

10 Differently from institutionalism that considers need and rules as co-substantial. Consider the manifesto of "Legal Institutionalism" of Deakin et al. (2017).

the good can involve very different situations. This fact is a legacy of the *industrialist* derivation of microeconomics, where goods have usually been intended as *commodities*, and *property right* was the main legal category for both the good itself and, above all, the means of production. Standard economics teaching texts are shaped by the problem of defining prices of commodities by connecting their demand for consumption to their production. The theoretical device used to connect demand and supply consists of defining both production costs and consumers' subjective evaluation, variable in the short term relative to quantity. Therefore, the primary focus of microeconomics is to study prices relative to changing quantities. Moreover, the student is exposed to simplifying notions when the theme of quality is treated and the role of the context is considered. Nonetheless, all this works relatively well when discussing the working of commodity markets.

In actual society, real consumers tend to be price takers and seldom have much to do with *ceteris paribus* decisions about the quantity of goods.[11] What would be more interesting is evaluation and negotiation, two poorly studied issues. Consequently, legal studies are also only partially interested in how prices are formed in markets. More commonly, the problem that does interest legal scholars is *evaluation* of discrete options in the absence of well-defined markets. In this case, microeconomic theory, which is all shaped around markets, perfect or not, supplies no certain answer as everything depends on abstract variables we do not know (e.g. elasticities). Some insight is supplied by advanced business courses teaching how to evaluate a firm, but little is said about other goods, particularly services.

The industrialist-commodity interpretation of "goods" has been dominant and exported to any new domain in which the production and conservation of value became relevant. Intellectual property rights are the typical example of a commodity view translated to a field where goods are not material and fungible. Even in this case, the legal framework to define rights and their tradability has been seen as over-imposed to an original phenomenon seen as categorically evident (the intellectual good), while the legal element is, in this case, really foundational. Therefore, the conflict between economics and the law is for the ontological primacy of their respective concepts: the good and the right (entitlement).

Today, we mainly consume services. An increasing share of services is today produced at nearly zero marginal costs, their consumption cannot be framed by the notion of quantity and what is relevant is simply having access to these goods (imagine the access to web platforms where we interact or share various contents). Exclusion is here essential to determine the possibility to have access to the satisfaction of desires (Rifkin 2000). But there is much confusion between the technical exclusion and the legal exclusion. The latter is not simply a barrier to access, as theorized by economists. It is part of a whole set of rights and duties

11 When prices are lower than their reservation prices, they spare and spend elsewhere.

defining the *position* of individuals, at their time defined by rules that shape how interactions take place, as well as how prices are formed. Therefore, law shapes price systems by designing which interactions take place, how they are managed, what and when is to be paid and what is for free. The formation of prices in these mechanisms is increasingly similar to auctions and tenders, where specific entitlements are confronted. In these mechanisms, often designed to grant a dominant position to suppliers, the market price mechanism represents simply an old metaphor.

A further consequence of the industrialist framework is that the rationale for contributing to specific public goods is difficult to grasp, particularly public goods that are prerequisite to civil interaction, often confused with standard public services. No space of the *common good* is defined at a higher hierarchical level compared to the production of standard goods (Mastromatteo and Solari 2014). Constitutional economics has attempted to separate the choice of constitutional rules from ordinary economic choices, but it has avoided including the ethical-political dimension that is normally considered in legal studies.

All that notwithstanding, these categories of economics, derived in part from common sense and in part from the need to keep mathematics at a treatable level, have particular difficulty in dealing with the legal sense of rules and have an insufficient understanding of immaterial goods and situations deriving from the relational nature of the legal framework in which the economy is defined. The evolution of the economy is increasingly putting these categories under stress, as most contemporary transactions concern some commodity less and less. In particular, the use of the notion of property rights simply to designate the faculty of excluding someone from the benefits of acceding to a specific environment is tremendously poor and limiting the development of promising interactions between economic analysis and the law.

6. The idea of legal position and property rights

Coase, in his seminal 1960 contribution to the notion of social costs, introduced the idea of individual *legal position*, including a whole set of organizational and rule arrangements in which the allocation of resources takes place. This includes property rights in strict terms and general rules affecting the use of property, as well as the way governance of exchanges is organized. This is an explicit acknowledgement that property rights were intended by Coase as a far more complex notion than a simple, typical real right. The idea of transaction cost, which is a very synthetic notion, further highlighted the complexity of factors affecting the pursuit of economic interests. In particular, transaction costs are deeply determined by cognitive problems involving poor information, uncertainty, unreliability and time inconsistency of partners' interests, which have been frozen in the simplificatory idea of information asymmetry to avoid questioning the standard model of rational choice. In this way, any connection with the cognitive role of rules, with the expressive role of law, has been cut off.

The literature that followed Coase (1960) developed these ideas in a very useful set of instruments to analyze legal arrangements and actual economic problems. It also represents an excellent didactical framework. Unfortunately, even here, the connecting bridges with legal studies have not been precisely established. In fact, as Hutter (1978) points out, Alchian and Demsetz (1972) tended to focus on a subset of the *legal position* named property rights to get a (*ceteris paribus*) more tractable economic problem of optimization. Nonetheless, Demsetz (1966, 158) stated that bundles of property rights are the object of economic exchanges. In this way, *exchange* can be defined as the reciprocal modification of specific rights by two individuals, keeping a legal dimension well in sight. Nonetheless, here there is a first approximation of the various legal entitlements into property rights, unwisely limiting them to a specific real right.

In this second generation of studies, we can notice a certain endogenization of rights and rules, without a clear distinction, but this framework still allows for the study of the legal structure of economic processes. Nevertheless, Hodgson (2015) has accused Law and Economics of having forgotten the social-legal nature of property, confusing it with simple possession. This is due to the fact that property rights are not understood in their full architecture but are limited to the relationship between the thing and the owner, in a way that cannot be distinguished from possession (Stojanović 2019). Therefore, Coase's rich notion of legal position has been excessively simplified in recent years.

Some years earlier, Grey (1980) published a paper that further developed the idea of *bundle of rights*. As Epstein has argued, the key advantage of the idea of a *bundle of rights* image is that it allows individuals to sell off bits and pieces of a thing to various persons (Epstein 2009–2010, 463). In this sense, this notion exploded the core of property rights, questioning the usefulness of the synthetic idea of property. However, the definition of property rights from its constituent parts has been criticized by many (Arruñada 2012; Mossoff 2003; Smith 2012). Actually, in legal research, the idea of a property right, originally a *real right*, has been translated to frame a variety of issues involving immaterial, intellectual or financial rights. Therefore, the notion of a *real right* (*in rem*), meaning typical, direct and absolute power over a thing (even belonging to others), has been stretched to lose its original meaning. In particular, it has been stretched and modified to fit a variety of situations in which the idea of absolute power is questionable. The patrimonial nature has been stretched in a way that everything can be seen as an asset today – even in cases where there is a social interest. In fact, presently, we usually tend to define a property right when the use/control of a resource can be divided from an ultimate property entitlement and is lent for profit. In this way, we can, for example, conceive of some property rights on financial contracts which are nothing other than some conditional promises.

However, research from the law side also moved in the direction of the legal position of the individual beyond pure property rights. After Reich (1964, 1990b), we are more aware of the conventional and interdependent nature not only of what we buy and sell, but also of all economic socially defined engagements. Therefore, all arrangements involve some right or duty, admissible and not admissible behavior that have some relevant economic value and a technology allowing certification. Reich underlined how in what we often group into the category of services; a growing share of our transactions concern relevant stocks of value (present or future) embodied in social arrangements such as insurances, pension funds, pension entitlements from repartition schemes, universal health services and other club-form collective arrangements able to supply flows of value (which are not necessarily traded in a market). Reich (1964) has, in this way, stressed that most flows of value depend on an organized society and its administrative arrangements, including conventional accountancy systems. The only stock of capital behind these arrangements is organizational and is embedded in social trust. From the legal perspective, the set of external rules prevail compared to purely individual property rights of the subject, defined as an actor-good relationship. This fact not only questions the idea of commodity as the foundation of economic activity; it also questions the related economic idea of the strict relationship between markets and property rights (Vandevelde 1980).

The idea of *non-interference* or *excludability* usually connected to property rights is, in fact, very broad and depends on both technology and legal arrangements (Katz 2008). But today, excludability does not univocally imply property, and if we broaden these categories too much, we abandon any reference to the legal idea of property as a real right. Moreover, excludability includes the flow of services from administrative arrangements consequent to the legal position that an individual occupies in them. Alchian (1977) and Alchian and Demsetz (1972) are correct in affirming that our property is totally dependent on general consent and on duties of non-interference.[12] But this is a criterion that encompasses a wide set of legal entitlements, including all *new property* as defined by Reich (1964, 1990a, 1990b).

A final element that broadens and weakens the founding industrialist elements of economics is the transformation of goods into some "paid-for experience" kind of service. This phenomenon is connected to what Rifkin (2000) has called the *era of access*. Rifkin has demonstrated how less and less we hold the property of goods we enjoy. Goods are increasingly sold in the form of access to some experience. E-books and TV streaming are typical examples, but also restaurants are turning to this philosophy by means of rapidly evaporating licenses to provide a specific sensory experience. Therefore, fewer actors are reciprocally exchanging property rights on resources; on the contrary, property is firmly in the hands of a part, which sells a rapid glimpse of it to the other part. This is often achieved by recourse of license, which is not a property right, although there is a tendency to extend the characteristics of the latter to the former. The capitalistic process is increasingly developing in the sense of producing stocks of goods for a broadly defined entertainment and enforcing barriers to their enjoyment. They tell you that you share goods, but, in fact, the stock of goods

12 Is it such a robust view when most of our wealth depends on the specific interference of others?

is more and more concentrated in the hands of a few global organizations, and you just have access to some of their services in a kind of property-less society.[13] The consequence is that, in the final step of consumption, there is no real right involved, and the notion of access is much more appropriate than that of exclusion. Excludability without property is, therefore, the trending form of goods, and the idea of commodity is becoming less relevant.[14]

All this means that individual legal positions are quite complex. They depend much on the organizational environment and include a wide array of rights/duties, including also real rights. But if we aim at understanding how the economy interacts with law to shape the present-day economy we should understand how rules shape rights/duties and the large variety of new property that is created in this way, and that is the object of economic transactions. Therefore, with regard to transaction-cost economics, rules not only reduce transaction costs, but also shape the very object of our desires and the technology to enjoy it.

7. Conclusion: toward an economics of entitlements

Law and Economics is a fundamental field of study which needs some attention regarding the epistemological problems that the encounter of the two disciplines poses. Economics tends to assume very simplified abstract categories supporting its analytical vocation. Law, on the other hand, suffers from historical incrustations that prevent a clear view of the new categories needed to fit the changing ways of production and consumption. The result is a certain convergence toward the transfer and stretching of old categories, as in the case of property rights, which unfortunately loses sight of important aspects concerning the social and ethical dimension of the law.

Legal scholars looking for some less obsolete way of dealing with present-day problems may find in mainstream economic reasoning a deceiving friend. The case of the theory of choice and its static and elusive nature has been examined with particular attention on the model of man adopted. The economic theory of choice tends to flatten and force into commensurable dimension heterogeneous elements that should be treated differently. Finally, economic choice requires simplified categories, suggesting the difficulty of including legal elements, particularly rules, without sensibly changing their nature. Therefore, the suggestion is to exploit economics for the inputs it can reliably supply to legal reasoning and avoiding the fascination of generalized simplificatory consequentialist reasoning in legal issues.

If we would like to make sense of contemporary trades, we should refer to and develop the concept of *legal position*, as well as that of *entitlements*. In this sense, we can say that individuals have some entitlements that are socially or relationally

13 Once proletarians had no means of production. Today, they do not even have the property of what they consume.

14 I have the fear that all this risks producing a society of proletarians.

acknowledged. This requires an evolution of both legal and economic instruments. Coase (1960) rightly proposed the idea of *legal position*, which has not been developed by economists in the sense of being able to interact with legal studies. The foundational role of rules and the relational dimension of rules and rights have not been developed much in the analysis of markets. On the contrary, Law and Economics has turned back to a commodity view of exchanges that is insufficient to understand the present-day economy, and it assures little contact with the reasoning of law.

Economics need not be as dull as described in this contribution; all these issues could be mastered by an institutionalist approach to Law and Economics. But we should be aware that it suffers from an industrialist legacy in the theorization of markets. This has consequences for the definition of goods and in their evaluation. It also prevents a good understanding of goods in the era of access. In turn, it is also responsible for the confusion between the legal and technical nature of exclusion. Law is not an instrumental barrier granting exclusion to others' enjoyment but a foundational element in the definition of markets. The latter are shaped by legal elements, and prices arise in different ways according to the specific devices that give form to economic interaction.

Finally, property rights are one of the categories now stretched to cover many new goods and situations. This has made them lose the characteristic of *real rights*. Economists tend to supply innovative and simplified definitions which find no support in legal theory. The confusion of possession and property can produce difficulties of understanding for people with a minimal knowledge of the law. On the other hand, as already pointed out in the early modernity, the economist's focus is to develop the notion of some absolute right defining the legal position of man, protecting the *suum* in a situation of vanishing materiality.

References

Alchian, Armen A. 1965. "Some Economics of Property Rights." *Il Politico* 30: 816–829.

Alchian, Armen A. 1977. "Some Implications of Recognition of Property Right Transaction Costs." In Karl Brunner (ed.), *Economics and Social Institutions: Insights from the Conferences on Analysis and Ideology*. Boston: Martinus Nijhoff, pp. 234–255.

Alchian, Armen A., and Harold Demsetz. 1972. "Production, Information Costs, and Economic Organization." *American Economic Review* 62(4): 777–795.

Allen, Douglas W. 2015. "On Hodgson on Property Rights." *Journal of Institutional Economics* 11(4): 711–718.

Anderson, Elizabeth S., and Richard H. Pildes. 2000. "Expressive Theories of Law: A General Restatement." *University of Pennsylvania Law Review* 148(5): 1503–1575.

Arruñada, Benito. 2012. "Property as an Economic Concept: Reconciling Legal and Economic Conceptions of Property Rights in a Coasean Framework." *International Review of Economics* 59(2): 121–144.

Backhaus, Jürgen. 1979. "Lawyers' Economics vs. Economic Analysis of Law." *Munich Social Science Review* 1: 1–34.

Barzel, Yoram. 1997. *The Economic Analysis of Property Rights*. Cambridge: Cambridge University Press.

Buckle, Stephen. 1991. *Natural Law and the Theory of Property: Grotius to Hume*. Oxford: Clarendon.

Cartwright, Nancy, and Jhon B. Davis. 2016. "Economics as a Science." In R. Skidelsky and N. Craig (eds.), *Who Is Running the Economy?* London: Palgrave Macmillan, pp. 43–55.

Chan, David K. 2010. "Reasoning Without Comparing." *American Philosophical Quarterly* 47(2): 149–160.

Chapman, Bruce. 1982. "Individual Rights and Collective Rationality: Some Implications for Economic Analysis of Law." *Hofstra Law Review* 10: 455–481.

Coase, Ronald H. 1960. "The Problem of Social Cost." *Journal of Law and Economics* 3: 1–44.

Cooter, Robert. 1998. "Expressive Law and Economics." *The Journal of Legal Studies* 27(S2): 585–608.

Crespo, Ricardo. 2017. "L'ontologie de l'économie selon Aristote et la théorie économique actuelle." In Gilles Campagnolo and Jean-Sébastien Gharbi (eds.), *Philosophie Économique, un État des Lieux*. Paris: Éditions Matériologiques, Collection E-conomique, pp. 259–281.

Cserne, Peter. 2011. "Consequence-Based Arguments in Legal Reasoning: A Jurisprudential Preface to Law and Economics." In Klaus Mathis (ed.), *Efficiency, Sustainability, and Justice to Future Generations*. Dordrecht: Springer, pp. 31–54.

Cserne, Peter, and Akos Szalai. 2010. "On the Necessity of Necessity: An Economic Analysis of Contracts Concluded in a Situation of Need." *Silesian Journal of Legal Studies* 2(1): 11–25.

Davis, John B. 2014. "Economists' Odd Stand on the Positive-Normative Distinction: A Behavioral Economics View." In G. DeMartino and D. McCloskey (eds.), *Oxford University Press Handbook on Professional Economic Ethics: Views from the Economics Profession and Beyond*. Oxford: Oxford University Press.

Deakin, Simon, David Gindis, Geoffrey M. Hodgson, Huang Kainan, and Katharina Pistor. 2017. "Legal Institutionalism: Capitalism and the Constitutive Role of Law." *Journal of Comparative Economics* 45: 188–200.

Demsetz, Harold. 1966. "Some Aspects of Property Rights." *Journal of Law and Economics* 9: 61–70.

Dowding, Keith, and Martin van Hees. 2003. "The Construction of Right." *American Political Science Review* 97(2): 281–293.

Ege, Ragip, and Benoit Walraevens. 2011. "G.W.F. Hegel: Toward a Reconciliation." In Ragip Ege and Herrade Igersheim (eds.), *Freedom and Happiness in Economic Thought and Philosophy*. London: Routledge, pp. 183–197.

Engelen, Bart. 2017. "A New Definition of and Role for Preferences in Positive Economics." *Journal of Economic Methodology* 24(3): 254–273.

Epstein, Richard A. 2009–10. "The Disintegration of Intellectual Property? A Classical Liberal Response to a Premature Obituary." *Stanford Law Review* 62: 455–522.

Gärdenfors, Peter. 1981. "Rights, Games and Social Choice." *Nous* 15(3): 341–356.

Greenberg, Joseph. 1990. *The Theory of Social Situations*. Cambridge: Cambridge University Press.

Grey, Thomas C. 1980. "The Disintegration of Property." *Nomos* 22: 69–85.

Hammer, Balz. 2011. "Valuing the Invaluable?" In Klaus Mathis (ed.), *Efficiency, Sustainability, and Justice to Future Generations*. Dordrecht: Springer, pp. 211–235.

Hegel, Georg W. F. 1805–6. Naturphilosophie und Philosophie des Geistes. In *Jenaer Realphilosophie, Vorlesungsmanuskripte zur Philosophie der Natur und des Geistes von 1805–1806*. Hamburg: J. Hoffmeister (ed.), 1969.

Hegel, Georg W. F. 1820. *Philosophy of Right*. Kitchener: Batoche Books, 2001.

Hodgson, Geoffrey M. 2015. "Much of the 'Economics of Property Rights' Devalues Property and Legal Rights." *Journal of Institutional Economics* 11(4): 683–710.

Hutter, Michael. 1978/2017a. "From Pigovian Analysis to Property Rights Theory." *Munich Social Science Review, New Series* 1: 1–10.

Hutter, Michael. 2017b. "Postscriptum: Analyzing Property Rights in the Age of Digital Transactions." *Munich Social Science Review, New Series* 1: 1–10.

Katz, Larissa. 2008. "Exclusion and Exclusivity in Property Law." *University of Toronto Law Journal* 58: 275–315.

Mastromatteo, Giuseppe, and Stefano Solari. 2014. "The Idea of 'Common Good' and the Role of the State in Present-Day Social Economics." *Rivista Internazionale di Studi Sociali* (1): 85–102.

Mathis, Klaus. 2011. "Consequentialism in law." In Klaus Mathis (ed.), *Efficiency, Sustainability, and Justice to Future Generations*. Dordrecht: Springer, pp. 3–29.

Mossoff, Adam. 2003. "What Is Property? Putting the Pieces Back Together." *Arizona Law Review* 45: 371–443.

Nozick, Robert. 1974. *Anarchy, State and Utopia*. Oxford: Basil Blackwell.

Pennington, Kenneth. 1998. "The History of Rights in Western Thought." *Emory Law Journal* 47: 237–252.

Raz, Joseph. 1990. *Practical Reason and Norms*, 2nd ed. Princeton: Princeton University Press.

Reich, Charles. 1964. "The New Property." *The Yale Law Journal* 73(5): 733–787.

Reich, Charles. 1990a. "The Liberty Impact of the New Property." *William & Mary Law Review* 31(2): 295–306.

Reich, Charles. 1990b. "The New Property After 25 Years." *University of San Francisco Law Review* 24: 223–271.

Rifkin, Jeremy. 2000. *The Age of Access: The New Culture of Hypercapitalism, Where All of Life Is a Paid-for Experience*. New York: Tarcher/Putnam.

Schlatter, Richard. 1951. *Private Property, the History of an Idea*. London: Allen & Unwin.

Searle, John. 2005. "What Is an Institution?" *Journal of Institutional Economics* 1(1): 1–22.

Searle, John. 2017. "Money: Ontology and Deception." *Cambridge Journal of Economics* 41(5): 1453–1470.

Sen, Amartya K. 1970. "The Impossibility of a Paretian Liberal." *Journal of Political Economy* 78: 152–157.

Sen, Amartya K. 1997. "Maximization and the Act of Choice." *Econometrica* 65(4): 745–779.

Sen, Amartya K. 2000. "The Discipline of Cost-Benefit Analysis." *Journal of Legal Studies* 29(June): 931–952.

Sen, Amartya K. 2009. *The Idea of Justice*. Cambridge, MA: Belknap Press.

Smith, Henry E. 2012. "Property as the Law of Things." *Harvard Law Review* 125(7): 1691–1726.

Solari, Stefano. 2015. "Individual Rights, Economic Transactions and Recognition: A Legal Approach to Social Economics." In Mark White (ed.), *Law and Social Economics: Essays in Ethical Values for Theory, Practice, and Policy*. New York: Palgrave Macmillan, pp. 41–59.

Solari, Stefano. 2019. "The Recognition of the Other as a Pre-Requisite for Fair Market Prices." In R. Ege and H. Igersheim (eds.), *The Individual and the Other in Economic Thought*. Abingdon, New York: Routledge, pp. 180–193.

Stojanović, Aleksandar. 2019. "Beyond the Pitfalls of Nominalism: A Comparison of Traditional Economic and Legal Institutionalist Approach to Property Rights." In This Volume. . .

Sunstein, Cass R. 1994. "Incommensurability and Valuation in Law." *Michigan Law Review* 92: 779–861.

Sunstein, Cass R. 1995. *Legal Reasoning and Political Conflict*. New York: Oxford University Press.

Sunstein, Cass R. 1996. "On the Expressive Function of Law." *University of Pennsylvania Law Review* 144(5): 2021–2053.

Taylor, Charles. 1982. "The Diversity of Goods." In A. Sen and B. Williams (eds.), *Utilitarianism and Beyond.* Cambridge: Cambridge University Press, pp. 129–144.

Vandevelde, Kenneth J. 1980. "The New Property of the Nineteenth Century: The Development of the Modern Concept of Property." *Buffalo Law Review* 29: 325–367.

White, Mark D. 2017. "Preferences all the Way Down: Questioning the Neoclassical Foundations of Behavioral Economics and Libertarian Paternalism." *Œconomia* 7(3): 353–373.

5 Difficulties of reattachment

Why is property law still a challenge for economic analysis of property rights?

Aleksandar Stojanović

1. Introduction

In a 2015 issue of the *Journal of Institutional Economics*, a debate took place as to whether the economic analysis of property rights (EAPR), one of the most prolific strands of new institutional economics, has adequately treated property law. This issue has been raised before (Merrill and Smith 2001b; Cole and Grossman 2002; Lueck and Miceli 2007), but unlike in those previous cases, this time around, the EAPR authors themselves intervened. They chose to answer the arguments on the inadequacy of their approach. This was then followed by a second round of interventions by the critics, who attempted to clarify their position and push the issue toward a resolution. Throughout the debate, the authors introduced arguments from both legal theory and multiple approaches to economics with the intention of expanding and reforming the EAPR tradition. However, this debate turned into a scattered epistemological discussion on the use of concepts in economic analysis when it is applied to law. That seemed to create more confusion than clarity – both the critics and the defenders of EAPR ended up blaming their counterparts for not understanding the basic concepts and explanatory goals involved. In this chapter, I will approach this debate from the standpoint of the philosophy of interdisciplinarity (PI). PI develops a precise framework for analyzing the interaction between disciplines that maps plural modalities of interdisciplinarity (Mäki 2016). This will help us put the debate over EARP in the context of other possible ways that economics and law could interact.

In the next section 2, we will familiarize ourselves with the EAPR approach and observe how exactly the EAPR authors conceptualized property rights. In the section after that 3, we will turn to the critics of EAPR and their suggestions regarding a more appropriate manner of conceptualizing property rights. We will recapitulate the aftermath of this debate as well. Finally, in section 4, we will analyze the clash between the EAPR authors and their critics using the PI framework. That will help us think about the stakes that the interaction between property law and economic analysis is facing today. We will attempt to understand the difficulties of reattachment – i.e. the pushback that EAPR experienced in its attempt to develop an interdisciplinary study of property law while sticking to a predefined method.

2. The concept of property in the economic analysis of property rights

The economic analysis of property rights has its origins in the works of the fathers of the Law and Economics (L&E) tradition. Central arguments in two of the most influential L&E articles, "The Problem of Social Cost" by Ronald Coase (1960) and "Property Rules, Liability Rules, and Inalienability: One View of the Cathedral" by Guido Calabresi and Douglas Melamed (1972), both use the framework of property rights and transaction costs to shed light on how legal arrangements can lead to more efficient outcomes. However, EAPR as a specific approach became pronounced only with the works of Harold Demsetz and Armen Alchian. In his 1965 "Some Economics of Property Rights", Alchian argued that in the context of scarcity, efficient outcomes can be achieved only if property rights are clearly delineated and enforced as that is the only way to eliminate a destructive competition for control over economic resources. Demsetz's 1967 "Toward a Theory of Property Rights" articulated the argument of "the Tragedy of the Commons"[1] in terms of the possessor's costs of establishing and enforcing property over a commonly held resource that is subject to overuse and underinvestment. In the following decades, EAPR proceeded largely in the direction set by Demsetz. After a number of publications, two landmark publications using his analytical framework emerged: Yoram Barzel's 1997 book *Economic Analysis of Property Rights* and Douglas Allen's 1991 article "What Are Transaction Costs?" In his article Allen provides a precise and explicit conceptualization of the link between property rights and transaction costs, and in the book Barzel uses the EAPR framework to analyze a wide variety of topics such as public domain, contract choice, divided ownership, firm and slavery.

EAPR is founded on the conceptual hybrid that includes both prelegal facts independent of any normativity and property rights recognized by the legal system. Different authors expressed this point somewhat differently. For example, Alchian (1965) defined private property rights in terms of the ability to choose the use of a resource (without affecting property rights over resources that other persons have). Later, Alchian (1977, 238) defined these rights in relation to "the probability that [the owner's] decision about demarcated uses of the resource will determine the use". In the same vein, Barzel (1997, 394) defined a property right as "an individual's net valuation, in expected terms, of the ability to directly consume the services of the asset, or to consume it indirectly through exchange". As he underlines "[the] keyword is *ability*, the definition is concerned not with what people are legally entitled to do but with what they believe they can do". From the standpoint of ability, a legal entitlement to do something with one's possession can seem as an addition that reinforces the existing ability to do that – that doesn't change the nature of one's capacity. That fuses the legal and prelegal fact into the same conceptual hybrid. Barzel is

1 Famously articulated by Hardin (1968).

famous for his distinction between *economic* and *legal* property rights. According to him (Barzel 1997, 3) the term "property rights" carries two distinct meanings in the economic literature: "One . . . is essentially the ability to enjoy a piece of property. The other, much more prevalent and much older, is essentially what the state assigns to a person". He decides to designate the first "economic property rights" and the second "legal (property) rights". Later Barzel (1997, 3) goes on to explain that "economic rights are the end (that is, what people ultimately seek), whereas legal rights are the means to achieve the end. Legal rights play a primarily supporting role." Finally, Allen (2014, 4) claims that, in his view, "Following others, economic property rights are defined as the ability to freely exercise a choice".

EAPR authors introduce this conceptual hybrid that establishes the uniformity across prelegal facts independent of any normativity and property rights recognized by the legal system as it affects the utility-maximizing economic agent. In one of the examples, Allen (2015, 712) considers "someone walking down a city street late at night". According to him, the person might choose to "take a short-cut down a dark alley [but] if, after three steps into the darkness the pedestrian sees the shadow of a shady character lurking up ahead, the fact that he has the legal property right to walk through the alley is quite irrelevant for what he does next" (Allen 2015, 712). What will be relevant to the person is what EAPR proponents define as economic property rights. As Allen (2015, 712) argues, "the explanation for why the walker turns around and spurns the alley for a longer route rests on the set of realistic choices held at that moment [and it is] the economic rights count for behaviour". Barzel (2015, 720) considers a similar example in which, even though a company is the legal owner of a brand name, in practice, "the public expropriated the term, using it generically as a term in common use, essentially depriving the company of the brand name's value". Barzel (2015, 720) notes that the EAPR framework has a lot of pertinence as it explains that "although the state recognizes the brand name . . . the company's legal ownership over the name is of little value as it essentially has no economic rights over it". The point of making the distinction in the precise way that EAPR makes it has to do with the way that economic rights can be backed by law (to some degree) and become legal property rights, but in many cases they are not, for reasons that they are either illegal or do not have to do with law at all:

> When legal rights are granted and enforced, it enhances the corresponding economic rights. Whoever actually drives the car over which I have legal rights has economic rights over it, be it myself, a person I authorized to use it, or a thief, though if it is a thief, the state will help me recover it. A Jewish Hassid diamond trader has the economic rights over the value of expensive diamonds he just passes to another Hassid with a promise to pay guaranteed by a handshake. Indeed, in case of dispute, they are likely to resolve it not by the state court, but via their rabbi.
>
> (Barzel 2015, 720)

There is a particular goal that EAPR authors try to achieve in defining the concepts in the way they do. As Merrill and Smith (2001b, 376) point out, their world "consists of a multitude of assets, each of which has multiple attributes. Some of these attributes are the subject of specific contracts. However, because of positive transaction costs, the attributes of assets will never be fully reflected in contracts . . . [and] Barzel describes attributes not captured by contracts as being in the 'public domain'".

Thus, Merrill and Smith (2001b, 376) argue that "Barzel treats someone who has the ability to capture attributes of assets in the public domain as a type of residual claimant". Focusing on residual claimants implies paying close attention to how, when and to what effect legal titles follow possession and control in economizing with resources. As Barzel (2015, 719) claims, "Legal rights are neither necessary nor sufficient for economic rights. For the sufficiency, suppose Congress grants me ownership over an accurately delineated chunk of the Pacific Ocean. This secures my legal rights, but what good are these rights without (costly) naval protection? As for necessity, suppose two neighbours fully recognize and respect the border separating their properties even though its legal delineation is fuzzy. Nevertheless, these neighbours will use their border resources efficiently".

When the conceptual framework based on the lack of differentiation between nonlegal and legal relationships to objects of possible possession is coupled with a carefully conceptualized set of transaction costs,[2] this can lead to interesting insights about negotiation and contracting among rational agents. Also, it can be useful in approaching the cases of the emergence of legal titles as has been famously done by Demsetz and others. Finally, the EAPR framework fits especially well in an analysis that focuses on the relationship between a possessor's actions and the enforcement of law. In particular, compliance can be approached by inserting the probability of enforcement within the welfare function that possessors of assets maximize.

3. Limits of present conceptualization of property

In a 2015 article, Geoffrey Hodgson launched a thorough critique of this economic conceptualization of property rights. His criticism drew on the issues that were brought up by both lawyers and economists who commented on EAPR over the years. In approaching the EAPR understanding of property rights, Hodgson (2015a, 3) first notices that what is conceptualized as an economic property right is not in line with ordinary language. In ordinary language, the term "right" implies something "morally correct, just, or honourable" or

2 One of the advantages of this approach comes from the fact that following Barzel and Allen, EAPR authors do not treat transaction costs as elements of friction in neoclassical economic models but as strictly related to property rights: these costs are thought to exist only in cases when the initial delineation of property rights affects reaching Pareto optimal outcome.

"a moral or legal entitlement to have or do something". According to him, "Alchian and subsequent scholars have removed morality from the picture and downgraded the role of law, from being the source of legitimate authority concerning rights to one means among others for enforcing possession and control" (Hodgson 2015a, 3). The problem here is that, in establishing the uniformity of the prelegal fact of possession and the legal institution of property, EAPR authors use the term "right" to describe the prelegal element.

Hodgson (2015a, 11) identifies the foundation of this approach with the general intuition that the "structure of property rights" refers primarily to a set of constraints upon, and incentives and disincentives for, specific individual behaviors. This diagnosis resonates with the argument put forward recently by Di Robilant and Syed (forthcoming). They identify a fundamental problem with the L&E approach to property as the tendency to omit the legal-architectural issues (what property is) related to property law and rush into substantive issues (how property emerges and what incentive structure it implies) that involve cost-benefit analysis. The problem here is that, by approaching property rights within the conceptual space defined by the prelegal fact of possession, EAPR authors never consider whether these rights might involve a completely new level of (institutional) reality that would create interactions that are not rooted in the interactions around possession.

Hodgson's criticism of this way of approaching property is summarized in the following passage:

> When von Mises and Alchian referred to property, they reduced it simply to the fact of possession or control. Likewise, when Barzel and Allen refer to "economic rights" they simply mean possession or control. My objection to these accounts is illustrated by the case of a thief who manages to steal an item and retain control of it. According to von Mises and Alchian, this would become the thief's "property". According to Barzel and Allen, the thief would have established an "economic right" to the stolen goods.
>
> (Hodgson 2015b, 736)

There are three notable elements of this argument that relate to both legal and economic arguments made against EAPR. The first one has to do with adjudication and enforcement. According to Hodgson, the general problem of this approach consists in using the concept of a right to describe a prelegal fact and downplaying the issue of legitimate legal rights. As he reminds us, "possession is foremost a relation between a person and a thing [which] does not amount to legal ownership [while] . . . the term 'property' should be reserved for cases of institutionalized possession with legal mechanisms of adjudication and enforcement" (Hodgson 2015ab, 6). Institutionalized possession and compliance with it are not only a matter of instrumental rationality of utility-maximizing individuals. Hodgson refers to the "possibility that law may be sometimes followed for non-instrumental reasons, simply because it is a legitimate, just or moral course of action" (2015a, 14) and shows that this point becomes problematic from the standpoint of economic analysis as well. Modern behavioral economists substitute this "narrow model of wholly self-interested behaviour. . . [of] . . . individuals maximizing monetary payoffs. . . [with the] . . . the notion of other-regarding, 'social preferences'" (Hodgson 2015a, 13). Although Hodgson's argument regarding behavioral economics addresses a limitation that is not exclusively present in EAPR, we can notice that property as a legal institution involves issues of legitimacy of laws that will determine the relationship of both the possessor and third parties to these property rights. In situations of competing and contested social orders (Fitzpatrick 2006), there may be a multiplicity of legal property rights involved – and the choice among them can be based on culture, ideas of legitimacy etc., rather than on instrumental reasons.

The second element of the argument has to do with the legal account of the bundle character of property. Property involves "multiple different types of possible right that can be either the right to use a tangible or intangible asset (*usus*), the right to appropriate the returns from the asset (*usus fructus*), the right to change a good in substance or location (*abusus*), the right to the capital derived from the use of the good as collateral, the right to sell a good (alienation), and several other rights or limitations or a combination of those" (Hodgson 2015a, 7, following Hohfeld 1917; Honoré 1961). EAPR treats property as a monolith (i.e. a singular indivisible right) instead of considering that it is a bundle made up of a diverse set of possible rights. An approach that avoids this problem would follow Di Robilant and Syed's suggestion mentioned earlier: substantial issues related to property can only be established if clarity is reached with regards to the prior legal-architectural aspects. In a more adequate account, the economic agent would consider different types of rights that can be bundled together instead of asking himself whether he should acquire "property rights" (as an undifferentiated unit) over some resource that he could otherwise only possess. In EAPR accounts these actors do not consider different possible bundles of rights for what they (or others) possess (Smith 2017). The lack of a legal-architectural account leads EAPR authors to overlook a choice that economic actors face when dealing with property rights. Indeed, these differentiated bundles will, in turn, influence behavior in different ways. For instance, we consider a possession differently if we have the right to sell it than if we have the right to returns from its use.

The third element of the argument has to do with the *in rem* character of rights that is relevant for both legal and economic analysis. The inability of EAPR to account for the specificity of property as a set of rights as opposed to the prelegal fact of possession leads to further lack of recognition of the specific type of rights that property involves in contrast to other legal institutions. Hodgson (2015a, 6) only notes in passing that property generally involves *in rem* rights as opposed to *in personam* ones that we find in contracts – a central concern for others who criticized EAPR for its insensitivity to the legal character of property rights.[3] As Arruñada explains, rights *in personam* are only valid against specific persons, *inter partes*, [while] rights *in rem* are valid against all individuals, *erga omnes*.[4] The inability of EAPR to account for the *in rem* character of property rights leads its proponents into problems with conceptualizing the relation and interaction of contract and property.[5] The main difficulty here stems from the fact that possession as a prelegal fact is not defined by the relationship between the possessor and anyone else while property is defined precisely by that: unlike contract which implies only rights against a specific person, it is a right against everyone. Conceptualizing possession as an (economic) property right completely disregards that and leads to confusion in differentiating contract and property and understanding the relationship between the two. Among the many good illustrations of the problems caused by not recognizing the *in rem* character of property rights, we will present two. The first one can be found in Merrill and Smith (2001b, 377), who show how Barzel "starts with contractual exchange and then defines 'property' as those attributes left over after all maximizing contracts that are possible within transaction-cost constraints have been exploited". That parallels their previous explanation of how EAPR authors understand property not as a baseline but as a residuum of value. The problem here is, as Merrill and Smith (2001b, 377) notice, that one cannot enter into contracts over the use of resources without some baseline to determine who contracts with whom – which is defined by property law. The second illustration has to do with Demsetz's analysis of property identified with rules of exclusion (Smith 2002, 454) that emerge among utility-maximizing commoners when confronted with negative externalities from the intensifying use of commons. Smith (2002, 455) argues that besides the rules of exclusion, property can imply rules of governance, which are similar to (but not identical with) what we find in contracts. In exclusion, decisions about resource use are

3 Arruñada (2012), Fitzpatrick (2006), Merrill and Smith (2001a, 2001b). Of course, Merrill and Smith show that, besides the pure cases, there is a wide space in between, and that, for example, common property is legally realized through *in rem* rights that, to a certain extent, specify the parties that have duties toward the owners.

4 Merrill and Smith (2001a, 783) recapitulate Hohfeld's (1919) analysis of the specificity of *in rem* rights in contrast to *in personam* rights: they are characterized by both an indefinite class and a large number of duty holders; they attach to persons through their relationship to particular things rather than to persons as persons; they are numerous and indefinite in two directions – not only does each *in rem* right give rise to a large and indefinite number of duty holders but each duty holder also holds such duties against a large and indefinite number of right holders; finally, they are always claims to abstention by others as opposed to claims to performance on the part of others. In addition, one and the same patrimonial (private law) right may have both obligational and proprietary aspects to it, depending on which person relations we look at – the obligational ones appear between the parties, the proprietary ones in relation to third parties. For example, in the transfer (assignment) of claims, questions between the transferor and transferee are obligational, but questions between the transferee and, say, the transferor's creditors are proprietary. More generally, modern property law mostly focuses on "dynamic" questions of disposition of rights and the exchange of rights (especially third-party conflicts), whereas EAPR seems to have a much more static perspective.

5 Merrill and Smith (2001b); this has its origin in Coase and Hohfeld.

delegated to an owner who, as a gatekeeper, is responsible for authorizing and monitoring specific activities with respect to the resource. To set up such rights, rough proxies like boundaries and the *ad coelum* rule are used.[6] These exclusion rules are used when the audience (of duty holders) is large, and the simplicity of these rights reduces the processing costs that would be high for such a large and anonymous audience. However, when we are dealing with smaller groups that have an interest in the use of the resource, property can be articulated through governance rules. These are introduced as they "pick out uses and users in more detail, imposing a more intense informational burden on a smaller audience of duty holders" (Merrill and Smith 2001a, 385) and, while the number of users is reasonably small, allows them to coordinate their use to achieve desirable outcomes. In short, to conceive of property rights as rights in a uniform manner is problematic as it does not match empirical reality where they are distinguishable from rights established in contracts and, for that reason, imply very different regimes of influencing interaction over resources.[7]

★ ★ ★

In answering these criticisms, proponents of EAPR focus on the semantic implication of Hodgson's criticism. To begin with, they admit the apparent contrast of their definitions of property rights to those that can be found in dictionaries. Barzel (2015) even goes on to express his regret that, as it happens, once definitions get established within a certain academic milieu, it is very hard to change them. All this is to say that even if the desired terminological change could occur, it would not make a difference when it comes to the analysis performed on the basis of the definition of property rights as exclusive possession.

The main argumentative strategy EAPR authors follow in interpreting the criticism is this. To think that property rights involve more than possession implies putting the substantive findings of EAPR analysis into question. The reader is presented with a trade-off: if you accept the criticism of EAPR's conceptual framework, you automatically dismiss its findings. There seems to be no one who is really willing to go as far as dismissing EAPR's substantive findings. In sum, the proponents of EAPR closely follow the strategy that was already noticed by Merrill and Smith (2001a, 775f). When confronted with evidence that "[their] notions [of property] may be incomplete, [they] often retreat by saying that the 'economic' definition of property is different from the 'legal'

6 The *ad coelum* rule implies that the owner of a plot of land owns everything below and above the land, up to the sky and below the earth to its core.

7 In a way Barzel acknowledged that (1997, 4), though not as something problematic, when he stated: "[a]t the heart of the study of property rights lies the study of contracts". The same approach can be found in Cheung (1970). EAPR authors end up treating property as purely a basis for contracting, as a possessor can relate to determine other parties with regards to control over the possession (either by exchanging it, offering services etc.) or assuming that possession necessarily becomes backed by exclusionary rules.

definition". As Merrill and Smith notice, that is supposed to absolve them of any obligation to explain the function of the legal institution involved.

This strategy makes the significance and benefit of the criticisms of EAPR quite ambiguous. The crucial question is whether the framework used in EAPR analysis is deficient in the precise way that Hodgson accuses it of being and what limitations to the possible findings this entails. Presenting the issues raised by critics through the trade-off mentioned earlier causes this crucial question to be ignored.

EAPR scholars try to delimit this "economic" context of property as something that can be adequately approached without considering the legal specificities related to it. Outside of this economic context, they seem to be willing to admit the relevance of definitions different from the ones they use (Barzel 2015). But what exactly is relevant within that context? Barzel argues that the problem boils down to distinguishing what is "useful for affecting behaviour", and he admits that he considers "economic rights (by whatever name) as useful, whereas [he doesn't] view as useful Hodgson's understanding of what either kind of rights is" (Barzel 2015, 4). The following argument by Barzel is particularly illustrative of his attitude:

> Whereas the term "economic rights" may be ill chosen, the substance behind it – its role in affecting behaviour – is basic. Such a role is largely absent from rights as viewed by Hodgson (though he vacillates about this). . . . Generalizing, a person in possession of an asset will maximize its value to him by choosing the appropriate form of protection. One form of protection, of course, is establishing legal rights.
>
> (Barzel 2015, 722)[8]

As Hodgson (2015b, 743) rightly notices, the crux of this argument lies in its nominalist attitude. The validity of concepts used in analysis stems from their usefulness for a predefined explanatory purpose. Beyond that, the question of how we define the concepts is only an exercise in naming. Thus, using "property right" to describe factual possession and control may well be ill chosen, but the idea that a property right granted by law should be the object of economic analysis only insofar as it is relevant to a generic utility maximizing agent with (or without) factual possession and control is not put into question.

The interactions that EAPR successfully analyzes are quite prevalent, and its framework has shown the ability to analyze the regularities that exist in those interactions. For that analysis it does not seem necessary to recognize the fact that (property) rights do not exist in a prelegal context. But critics are

8 When EAPR authors write about the establishment of legal property rights, they do not have in mind the establishment of a property rights system. They assume that system to already be in place. The economic analysis of the establishment of property rights systems is tackled by Robert Sugden (2004).

suggesting that there are other types of interactions that can only be analyzed if we recognize that fact. They suggest that interactions analyzed by EAPR are an inseparable part of a wider set of interactions that do not necessarily follow the same regularities. These interactions can only be identified (and hopefully successfully analyzed later on) if the analytical framework is adapted to recognize the right-character of property. Only if that adaptation is made can it be expected that these interactions will be defined precisely enough – with regards to different bundles that are involved, different opportunities for contracting that they entail and agents' relationships to different authorities based on culture and legitimacy. Only after this can any inquiry about the regularities in interactions among economic agents begin in a meaningful way.

The debate between the EAPR authors and their critics has left open many questions, and it is not even clear which of the two parties, after the first exchange of arguments, bears the burden of proof. In particular, EAPR has not shown that these other interactions are irrelevant or that they can be analyzed without the recognition of the right-character of property. At the same time, as much as critics have shown that phenomena exist that seem to contradict the construction of EAPR's analytical framework (in particular the conceptual hybrid between prelegal possession and property rights), they have not performed a full-blown analysis of these phenomena within a new framework synthetizing the conceptual changes that they suggested. In that sense, maybe the most important take-away from the debate between EAPR authors and their critics is to become sensitive to the novelty in the analysis that is going to be performed in the coming years.

4. Toward an amended concept of property

It is surprising how little has been achieved in the debate between the EAPR authors and their critics. One would have thought that after decades of expansion of the research area of EAPR, its proponents would have considered the issues brought up by critics as opportunities to push their analysis further in previously unexplored areas. One could argue that this development was hindered, first, by the fact that these issues were visible only through a more sophisticated legal analysis (which EAPR refused to engage with) and, second, that they would have required the economic analytical framework to be adapted substantially (which EAPR was also unwilling to do). In this section, I want to argue that the underwhelming outcome of the debate is deeply linked with the disciplinary nature of EAPR as an endeavor of economists. This invites one to interpret this debate from the standpoint of philosophy of interdisciplinarity (PI). Through accumulated comparative work on interdisciplinary exchanges across fields, PI offers a new perspective, that of the philosophy and sociology of science, to situate the character of EAPR as interdisciplinary, its internal dynamics and its potential for change.

A distinctive trait of PI as a meta-theoretical approach is that it abandons the traditional question of how disciplines could be unified on the basis of the connection between their domains of inquiry (Grüne-Yanoff and Mäki 2014, 52). This section will follow that dictum. Still, for the purpose of understanding how both lawyers and economists could criticize EAPR, a highly developed interdisciplinary project combining law and economics, and why EAPR authors showed little appreciation for suggestions about where the project could be taken, we will consider the issue of the connection between these domains shortly.

At first glance, one notices that if economics is concerned with how goods are exchanged in markets and property law defines how individuals can own goods, the connection between them is a very intimate one: markets presuppose some sort of definition and protection of control rights over goods. Additionally, in trying to understand how, throughout history, ideas about property law and the economy, namely legal theory and economics, grew apart, one immediately notices that, at the time when economics emerged as an independent discipline, property was very much an object of economic analysis. For Adam Smith (1776, Book I, Chapter X, Part I), property rights are important as only through that legal institution can the allocation of labor occur according to the interest of the laborer and the potential profitability that will motivate the employer to improve his "stock of capital" (Richards 2004, 355). Another example of how early economists considered property can be found in the work of Frederic Bastiat who explained that only due to the existence of the institution of private property can the technological advancement be mobilized for the increase of common wealth.

It is curious then how some two centuries later, not only contemporary economics itself, but also the specific strand that attempts to offer "a unified theoretical structure to deal with exchange, rights formation and organization which traditional economic theory assumes away" (Barzel 1997, 15) is deemed to be "ignorant of property law" (Lueck and Miceli 2007, 187). Without attempting to make a rigorous analysis of why this separation between economics and property law occurred, we can notice how the role of economics changed over this period. In the time of Smith and Bastiat, economics was only emerging as a subdiscipline in lawmaking. Smith (1776, Book IV) defined it as "a branch of the science of a statesman or legislator [with the twofold objective of providing] a plentiful revenue or subsistence for the people. . . [and] to supply the state or commonwealth with a revenue for the publick services". As time passed, economics moved away from Smith's attempt to carve out how specific elements of lawmaking impact wealth creation, in the direction of "intellectual territory that was previously deemed to be outside the discipline's realm" (Lazear 2000, 99). According to one view on the topic,[9] this invasion became possible through the substitution of its original goal defined by disciplinary domain with

9 This view was defended by Alain Marciano during his course on the history and methodology of Law and Economics in Turin in February 2017 within the program Institutions, Economics and the Law.

the one defined by its method. Economic method was conceptualized as "a study of any human behaviour as a relationship between ends and scarce means which have alternative uses" (Robbins 1932, 15), "combin[ing the] assumptions of maximizing behaviour, stable preferences, and market equilibrium, used relentlessly and unflinchingly" (Becker 1976, 5).

Curiously, it is in the context of the expansion of the economic method to fields that were previously considered to belong to separate disciplines that some economists decided to approach the issue of property rights. EAPR authors directly heeded Coase's call for economists to "study the influence of the legal system on the working of the economic system" (1996, 104). Coase referred to the connection between the two domains, claiming that "it is hardly possible to discuss the functioning of a market without considering the nature of the property right system" (Coase 1994, 45–46). But unlike Coase, who had a Smithian outlook and thought that economics has a subject matter namely, "the study of the working of the economic system, a system in which we earn and spend our incomes" (Coase 1994, 93), EAPR authors approached property rights with the intention of applying the supposedly universal economic method. For that reason, any observation on how legal institutions can incentivize economic behavior that could contest that method seemed both unapproachable and uninteresting. We should understand the emergence of critical voices in this context. Indeed, after decades of successful EAPR exploration of the legal-economic terrain where the light of dominant economic method could shine, the existence of an unexplored dark side of the complex legal embedding of the economic process has become more and more apparent and the necessity to explore it more and more pressing. Yet, as section 3 has shown, this change hasn't happened yet. We want to understand why.

⋆ ⋆ ⋆

Having this in mind, we can now turn to the PI analysis of EAPR. PI focuses on analyzing interdisciplinary exchanges that occur when "objects employed or developed in one discipline are used to solve problems of another discipline" (Grüne-Yanoff and Mäki 2014, 55). Grüne-Yanoff and Mäki (2014, 55) situate these exchanges within a classification based on distinguishing the agent (who performs it), the object (what is exchanged) and the problem (for what purpose) involved in the exchange. From that standpoint, an interdisciplinary exchange can be exportation, importation, transfer collaboration, genuine collaboration, new field generation and parallel development. Exportation and importation are cases of interdisciplinary transfer as the agents who pursue this exchange belong to only one of the disciplines involved and retain either the method or the object of research while transferring the other from the other discipline. The other four are cases of collaboration where agents from both disciplines jointly (or parallel to each other) pursue the exchange.

If we try to situate EAPR within this classification, we can see that it is a case of exportation. Authors are economists who use the tools of economic analysis to approach what Smith (2017, 2) defines as the private law problem: namely the problem of potentially conflicting complex horizontal interactions among actors as they are reconciled by the law. It is interesting to notice that, as an example of exportation, Grüne-Yanoff and Mäki (2014, 55) use the economics of the family. They explain how a model of reproductive choice was developed using economic models of optimization under constraints, "calibrating it for the value of a child and for opportunity costs characteristic of various countries" (Grüne-Yanoff and Mäki 2014, 55).

For EAPR to achieve its goal, the concept of property rights had to be adapted to the method of traditional economic analysis. This is an exportation as the economic method is not adapted itself. It is applied in the same form that it usually is. The benefit of this approach was that it expanded the set of choices considered in economic analysis. EAPR considered individuals that decide not only among different objects that would satisfy their preferences but also whether to only possess them or to own them. EAPR provided a novel tool for thinking about the legal problem as it allows legal practitioners to consider the legal institution of property as it appears to an economic agent within his set of preferences, thus supplementing what is explicitly accounted for within law.

In this context, one might interpret the responses of EAPR scholars to critics as part of a conservative pushback (EAPR pushback) reacting to the innovation through exportation of the economic method. The argument that there exists a trade-off between appreciating the criticism and affirming the findings of EAPR analysis follows this path to a large extent. According to that interpretation, the critics introduce legal concepts that are not adapted to economic analysis in order to show that this type of analysis is inadequate. In this reconstruction, their goal is to protect the turf of legal theorists. The point of the proponents of EAPR is that the conceptual adaptation had to be made for the economic method to produce the findings that it did.

However, PI provides another way to understand the criticism of EAPR. Critics can be interpreted to argue that the research agenda pursued by EAPR authors can be modified by incorporating a more Smithian type of economic analysis of wealth creation that would, in turn, involve a more comprehensive consideration of property rights. In PI terms, this means that critics consider the possibility of the interdisciplinary project between economics and property law being a genuine collaboration instead of exportation. In the case of property, genuine collaboration implies that lawyers and economists together apply a mix of legal theory and economic analysis to the private law problem of potentially conflicting complex horizontal interactions among actors as they are reconciled by the law (Smith 2017, 2).

If we follow this line, the EAPR pushback against criticisms stems from the difference between the two modes of interdisciplinary exchange, exportation and collaboration. The EAPR pushback is based on the argument that the "legal-economic reality" that critics are trying to introduce is not analyzable within EAPR's "conventional disciplinary style and standard practice" (Grüne-Yanoff and Mäki 2014, 57). Critics could, in that context, be interpreted as putting out a proposal for collaboration between lawyers and economists that would delve into the more complex legal-economic reality than the one that EAPR economists recognized – also using new tools of economic analysis that were not available at the time when EAPR emerged. It is important to notice that even if the argument of the critics is an anti-nominalist one – namely, that analytical concepts such as property right have to account for the legal nature that those rights have – their argument has the character of a proposal.

Of course, such a proposal needs to be more than just a case of wishful thinking so that it can, in turn, serve as a complement to their criticism. The final question to resolve the debate is then whether the critics have provided evidence that they propose something viable and valuable. There are three elements that correspond to the previously presented criticism that could serve as evidence in that regard.

First, the insistence of critics on the fact that the legal system and, to that extent, property rights have a normative foundation could prove valuable in performing a rigorous analysis of interactions and conflicts over resources in developing country contexts. EAPR indeed presupposes the absence of conflict among multiple enforcement mechanisms and correlative norms (that usually characterizes developed economies, Hodgson 2015b, 7–9) and ignores the fact that actors deciding how to behave regarding resources are more inclined to comply with some norms rather than others.[10] Fitzpatrick (2006) argued that the traditional economic approach to law lacks the resources to analyze developing country contexts in this regard. Steps toward a rigorous analysis of the role of normativity in legal compliance have been made e.g. by Tyler (2006), although without accounting for the presence of competing norms. Thus, there are reasons to hope for a more rigorous economic analysis to address the following question: in the context of competing normative systems and correlative enforcement mechanisms, when do actors tend to interact toward wealth creation, and when do they not?

Secondly, the recognition of the *in rem* character of property rights would allow an economic analysis of interactions in which legal rights conflicts over resources can be resolved using different types of rules within the same system. This would allow a rigorous analysis of complex trade-offs between societal goals. Arruñada has already performed substantial exploration in this direction. For example, he takes the case in which an agent exceeds his legal powers when selling a good to an innocent third party (Arruñada 2012, 5). Law can apply a rule favoring the *in rem* right, according to which "no one can transfer what he

10 Examples of this include the case of palm oil plantations in Indonesia, where the rights of investors cannot be protected by the state but can be by regional power groups (Fitzpatrick 2006); the case of the so-called Islamic State, when parts of the population chose to have their land rights registered and protected by terrorist groups instead of the state (De Soto 2014) and, more generally, post-colonial environments, where due to their continuity with colonial authorities, the tribal population expresses distrust for state institutions and relies instead on the local customary legal system.

does not have, they rule to have the sold good returned to the 'original owner', and the innocent third party wins a mere claim against the agent. . . [The] owners will feel secure with respect to this contingency, because this outcome maximizes property enforcement, but it worsens the information asymmetry suffered by all potential third parties with respect to legal title" (Arruñada 2012, 5). However, law can apply a different type of rule that would favor an *in personam* right according to which "the sold good stays with the third party and the principal only wins a claim against the agent. [This, in turn,] will minimize information asymmetry for potential third parties, but will also weaken property enforcement, making owners feel insecure" (Arruñada 2012, 5). Arruñada's analysis traces the harms and benefits of treating property rights on the basis of one or the other type of rules:

> Enforcing [this type of] rules thus obviates the information asymmetry usually suffered by third parties and encourages them to trade. In so doing, [these rules] transform the object of complex transactions into legal commodities that can be traded easily, thus extending the type of impersonal transaction that characterizes modern markets [but at the same time, they] weaken the principals' property rights, endangering investment and specialization in the tasks of principals and agents.
>
> (Arruñada 2012, 5)

A study by Dari-Mattiacci and Guerriero (2015) takes this insight further and performs a comparative analysis of more than seventy jurisdictions showing what considerations, beyond the immediate efficiency-based ones, explain the variance in the legal regimes. Finally, a more developed bundle-of-rights view of property proposed by critics would be able to overcome the one-dimensional concept of value capture that EAPR pursued. This, in turn, would enable an analysis of choices over layered entitlements. Depending on the kinds of interests agents have, their interactions could lead to the adoption and division of different types of bundles of rights over the same resource. Such an analysis would go along the lines of what Ostrom (2010) analyzed as well as including relevant third parties as Calabresi and Melamed (1972) have shown in the cases of inalienability.

* * *

When dealing with a proposal for "genuine collaboration" à la Grüne-Yanoff and Mäki (2014, 56), we should have in mind that it can be very close to "parallel development". What interdisciplinary collaboration really involves is an opening of the space for a plurality of uses of a jointly developed method. Taking the case of synthetic biology as an example, they emphasize that "having different uses of the concept of noise in mind, different synthetic biologists, largely according to their disciplinary origin, prefer different models and associate different practices with them" (Grüne-Yanoff and Mäki 2014, 56). In that context, it should be noticed that EAPR is usually regarded as part of a wider research agenda of New Institutional Economics (NIE). Indeed, many of the insights that reinforce the criticism of EAPR come from NIE-related authors. The essential issue here is that, unlike the broad and heterogeneous research program of NIE that it contributes to, EAPR itself relies on a strictly defined set of assumptions and a research focus on property rights. A proposal for a more collaborative project that modifies EAPR by using NIE insights is precisely a proposal for a way that these insights can be synthetized with existing EAPR insights into a more rigorous framework – and that could still potentially be done in a multiplicity of ways.

It is also important to notice in this context, as Grüne-Yanoff and Mäki (2014, 58) remind us, that "not all interdisciplinary exchanges succeed epistemologically, and many of those that do succeed do not involve integration". Thus, if the proposal of the critics to modify EAPR is heeded, it could lead to both collaborative practices and new forms of transfer. If one values EAPR as the right way to bring economics and law back together, this might be treated as a weakness and another proof of the problematic character of the criticism. Yet PI enables one to think otherwise. It could be argued that, if these approaches can explore the inherent connections that exist between property law and the economy in different ways, equally rigorous as EAPR and without excluding each other, that could only be regarded as an added value. Which stance one takes toward the future and the past at this transitional and uncertain point when one continent has been explored but many others worth exploring might be within our reach could as well depend, as Fichte famously said, on what kind of person one is.

References

Alchian, Armen A. 1965. "Some Economics of Property Rights." *Il Politico* 30: 816–829.

Alchian, Armen A. 1977. "Some Implications of Recognition of Property Right Transaction Costs." In K. Brunner (ed.), *Economics and Social Institutions: Insights from the Conferences on Analysis and Ideology*. Boston: Martinus Nijhoff, pp. 234–255.

Allen, Doug W. 1991. "What Are Transaction Costs." *Research in Law and Economics* 14: 1–18.

Allen, Doug W. 2014. "The Coase Theorem: Coherent, Logical, and Not Disproved." *Journal of Institutional Economics*: 1–12.

Allen, Doug W. 2015. "On Hodgson on Property Rights." *Journal of Institutional Economics* 11(4): 711–717.

Arruñada, Benito. 2012. "Property as an Economic Concept: Reconciling Legal and Economic Conceptions of Property Rights in a Coasean Framework." *International Review of Economics* 59(2): 121–144.

Barzel, Yoram. 1997. *Economic Analysis of Property Rights*. Cambridge: Cambridge University Press.

Barzel, Yoram. 2015. "What Are "Property Rights" and Why Do They Matter? A Comment on Hodgson's Article." *Journal of Institutional Economics* 11(4): 719–723.

Becker, Gary S. 1976. *The Economic Approach to Human Behavior*. Chicago: University of Chicago Press.

Calabresi, Guido, and A. Douglas Melamed. 1972. "Property Rules, Liability Rules, and Inalienability: One View of the Cathedral." *Harvard Law Review*: 1089–1128.

Cheung, Steven. 1970. "The Structure of a Contract and the Theory of a Non-Exclusive Resource." *Journal of Law & Economics* 13: 49–67.

Coase, Ronald H. 1960. "The Problem of Social Cost." *The Journal of Law and Economics* 3: 1–44.

Coase, Ronald H. 1994. *Essays on Economics and Economists.* Chicago: University of Chicago Press.

Coase, Ronald H. 1996. "Law and Economics and AW Brian Simpson." *The Journal of Legal Studies* 25(1): 103–119.

Cole, Daniel H., and Peter Z. Grossman. 2002. "The Meaning of Property Rights: Law Versus Economics?" *Land Economics* 78(3): 317–330.

Dari-Mattiacci, Giuseppe, and Carmine Guerriero. 2015. "Law and Culture: A Theory of Comparative Variation in Bona Fide Purchase Rules." *Oxford Journal of Legal Studies* 35(3): 543–574.

De Soto, Hernando. 2014. "The Capitalist Cure for Terrorism, the Wall Street Journal." www.wsj.com/articles/the-capitalist-cure-for-terrorism-1412973796, last accessed March 22, 2019.

di Robilant, Anna, and Talha Syed. forthcoming. "Hohfeld in Europe and Beyond: The Fundamental Building Blocks of Social Relations Regarding Resources." In Shyamkrishna Balganesh, Ted Sichelman, and Henry E. Smith (eds.), *The Legacy of Wesley Hohfeld: Edited Major Works, Select Personal Papers, and Original Commentaries.* Cambridge: Cambridge University Press.

Fitzpatrick, Daniel. 2006. "Evolution and Chaos in Property Rights Systems: The Third World Tragedy of Contested Access." *The Yale Law Journal*: 996–1048.

Grüne-Yanoff, Till, and Uskali Mäki. 2014. "Introduction: Interdisciplinary Model Exchanges." *Studies in History and Philosophy of Science*, Part A 48: 52–59.

Hardin, Garrett. 1968. "The Tragedy of the Commons." *Science* 162(3859): 1243–1248.

Hodgson, Geoffrey M. 2015a. "Much of the 'Economics of Property Rights' Devalues Property and Legal Rights." *Journal of Institutional Economics* 11(4): 683–709.

Hodgson, Geoffrey M. 2015b. "What Humpty Dumpty Might Have Said About Property Rights – and the Need to Put Them Back Together Again: A Response to Critics." *Journal of Institutional Economics* 11(4): 731–747.

Hohfeld, Wesley N. 1917. "Fundamental Legal Conceptions as Applied in Judicial Reasoning." *The Yale Law Journal* 26(8): 710–770.

Honoré, Antony M. 1961. "Ownership." In Anthony G. Guest (ed.), *Oxford Essays in Jurisprudence.* Oxford: Oxford University Press, pp. 107–147.

Lazear, Edward P. 2000. "Economic Imperialism." *Quarterly Journal of Economics* 115(1): 99–146.

Lueck, Dean, and Thomas J. Miceli. 2007. "Property Law." In A. Mitchell Polinsky and Steven Shavell (eds.), *Handbook of Law and Economics*, vol. 1. Amsterdam: Elsevier, pp. 183–257.

Mäki, Uskali. 2016. "Philosophy of Interdisciplinarity: What? Why? How?" *European Journal for Philosophy of Science* 6(3): 327–342.

Merrill, Thomas W., and H. E. Smith. 2001a. "The Property/Contract Interface." *Columbia Law Review*: 773–852.

Merrill, Thomas W., and H. E. Smith. 2001b. "What Happened to Property in Law and Economics?" *The Yale Law Journal* 111(2): 357–398.

Ostrom, Elinor. 2010. "Beyond Markets and States: Polycentric Governance of Complex Economic Systems." *Transnational Corporations Review* 2(2): 1–12.

Richards, Howard. 2004. *Understanding the Global Economy*. Thousand Oaks, CA: Peace Education Books.

Robbins, Lionel. 1932. *An Essay on the Nature and Significance of Economic Science*. London: Macmillan.

Smith, Adam. 1776. *An Inquiry into the Nature and Causes of the Wealth of Nations*, 2 vols. London: Strahan and Cadell.

Smith, Henry E. 2002. "Exclusion Versus Governance: Two Strategies for Delineating Property Rights." *The Journal of Legal Studies* 31(S2): 453–487.

Smith, Henry E. 2017. "The Economics of Property Law." In Francesco Parisi (ed.), *The Oxford Handbook of Law and Economics*. Oxford: Oxford University Press.

Sugden, R. 2004. *The Economics of Rights, Co-Operation and Welfare*. Basingstoke: Palgrave Macmillan.

Tyler, T. R. 2006. *Why People Obey the Law*. Princeton, NJ: Princeton University Press.

Part III

Interdisciplinarity in normative reasoning

Moral theory, economic theory and adjudication

6 Value pluralism and the foundations of normative Law and Economics

The case of threshold deontology[1]

Patricia Marino

In this chapter, I explore issues related to value pluralism as a case study of how debates in Law and Economics can profitably engage with ethical theory. By "value pluralism", I mean the idea that there are various distinct values, such as benevolence, justice and liberty, not reducible to a single overarching value. In the "Law and Economics" movement, economic reasoning is used not only descriptively, to explain and predict the effects of particular laws, but also normatively, to recommend laws based on their consequences. As in consequentialist ethical theories like utilitarianism, economic approaches to the law evaluate consequences by aiming at some form of "efficiency" – that is, we try to maximize well-being or goodness in one way or another.

In one sense, value pluralism would seem to pose an obvious challenge to the use of economics in legal reasoning. Often, consequentialism is seen as an essentially "monistic" normative approach, since it involves maximizing one value rather than attempting to honor or reconcile multiple values. Many of the long-standing objections to consequentialism rest on its seeming inability to accommodate values beyond benevolence, such as justice and fairness. If laws are being proposed and evaluated for their consequentialist efficiency, they would seem to inherit the same problem of being unable to incorporate, at a fundamental level, a range of important values. On the face of it, we do seem to value pluralistically, so crafting laws that simply maximize efficiency seems to require us to neglect or even violate some cherished values such as justice – a particularly striking example in the legal context.[2]

1 Early versions of this paper were presented at the MetaLawEcon Workshop on Law and Economics (2017), the Canadian Philosophical Association Annual Meeting (2017), the Workshop in Methodology in Applied Ethics, Georgetown University (2017), the Association for the Study of Law, Culture, and the Humanities annual conference (2017), and the Brooklyn Law School Faculty Workshop Series (2017); I am grateful to the participants for their insightful questions and comments. My thanks also to Rosalind Abdool, Jonathan Dewald, Uri Leibowitz, Govind Persad, and Nelson Tebbe for helpful discussion of the issues, and to Péter Cserne and Magdalena Małecka for their excellent comments on an earlier draft.

2 For a general discussion of plural values and the Law and Economics movement, see Nussbaum (1997).

But various matters here are complex. For one thing, the nature of value pluralism and the extent to which it is incompatible with consequentialist theories are contested. In cases where multiple values recommend conflicting obligations or considerations, values must be weighed or balanced against one another. To avoid arbitrariness, it is suggested, one always needs a monistic "meta-theory" in the background to justify these comparisons. Also, some consequentialist theories are proposed as being, themselves, pluralistic: as long as we're weighing and comparing values anyway, why not say the thing to do is maximize the good and give an analysis in which "the good" has multiple aspects? Recently, it's been argued that seemingly nonconsequentialist moral theories can be "consequentialized": for any set of moral judgments, we can find a consequentialist theory that entails those very same judgments.[3]

In what follows, I draw on research in ethical theory, including my own work on value pluralism and moral reasoning (Marino 2015), to explore how these issues play out in one particular Law and Economics context: debates over Eyal Zamir and Barak Medina's (2010) *Law, Economics, and Morality*. In contrast to typical approaches in Law and Economics, Zamir and Medina propose honoring plural values through "moderate deontology", in which there are obligations to promote the good overall, but there are also deontological constraints – constraints which are to be overridden when thresholds are met. Echoing debates in ethical theory, critics have charged that moderate deontology rests on arbitrary judgments and that addressing this problem of arbitrariness requires a monistic meta-theory, ultimately causing moderate deontology to collapse into a version of consequentialism.

While Zamir and Medina have aptly defended their approach, I'll suggest that drawing further on ethical theory allows for a stronger defense of moderate deontology and a deeper analysis of issues concerning plural values in the Law and Economics context. I begin, in section 1, with some background, explaining what value pluralism is and how it relates to various forms of deontology. In section 2, I draw on my previous work to examine how coherence and justification function in the relevant contexts. In section 3, I explain Zamir and Medina's moderate deontology, some challenges to that view raised by critics and Zamir and Medina's responses. In sections 4 and 5, I show how drawing on ethical theory allows for illuminating and, in some cases, stronger responses to these challenges. Among my other aims, I hope to show the fruitfulness of bringing disciplinary discussions in ethical theory and in Law and Economics into dialogue with one another.

3 Sources and texts are cited later. A related issue is that economic approaches to efficiency are sometimes more subtle than straightforward maximization: typically, consequences are evaluated for forms of cost-benefit analysis such as "Pareto efficiency", in which no one could be made better off without making someone worse off, or "Kaldor-Hicks efficiency", in which the benefits to those who gain outweigh the costs to others. Since the Law and Economics texts I am discussing are focused on other issues, I won't be discussing these distinctions here.

1. Value pluralism, forms of deontology, conviction ethics and coherence

I start in this section with some preliminary discussion of value pluralism and its expression in deontological moral theories. To say that values are plural is to say that there are various, genuinely distinct values, not reducible to one another or to some "super-value" (Mason 2008). It is often noted that the way we value in ordinary life seems "pluralistic" in this sense. As Thomas Nagel (1979) notes, not only do we care about various different kinds of things, but even the form of moral concerns we encounter varies. For example, some obligations are to specific people and arise because of specific past actions or relationships, some form constraints on our behavior due to rights everybody has, some are directed toward general benevolence toward all existing beings and some arise out of particular projects of our own. Familiar values seem to exemplify multiplicity. We care about honesty, but also about not hurting others. We care about abstract values such as fairness, but we also care more about our friends and family than about others. We care about human rights, but we also care about bringing about the collective good. Values like justice and efficiency seem to represent distinct goods, resisting expression in terms of a unifying value. In contexts of value pluralism, competing considerations can conflict: if a person must lie to keep a promise, say, then honesty may recommend promise-breaking while fidelity recommends deception. In such cases, deciding what to do is often a matter of prioritizing among conflicting concerns.

Some recent research from anthropology and sociology supports the common idea that the way we value is pluralistic and that, for people around the world, there are a number of common but distinct moral values. In his explanation of this research, Jonathan Haidt argues that there are roughly five basic items: harm/care (helping others and not hurting them); fairness/reciprocity (treating others with justice, not cheating them, honesty); in-group/loyalty (commitment to protecting one's community); authority/respect (respect for, and obedience to, those in positions of authority) and purity/sanctity (cleanliness, chastity, temperance in desires).[4]

In contexts of value pluralism, one approach to moral reasoning is to begin with a set of intuitions or considered judgments and try to bring them into coherence with one another – as in the method of reflective equilibrium (Rawls 1951; Daniels 2018). As Geoffrey Sayre-McCord (1985) says, methods of moral reasoning that appeal to our intuitions are aptly considered "conviction ethics", because we begin our moral reasoning not with just any intuitions, but rather with a set of considered convictions that represent what we take to be our best moral judgments (see also Scanlon 2003). If we are working with principles, as in deontological approaches, the idea is that we work back and forth among our considered judgments – such as, you ought to keep this particular promise – and

4 See also Haidt and Joseph (2004) and Haidt and Joseph (2007); for discussion, see Marino (2015).

the general principles we endorse – such as, promise-keeping is generally morally required – seeking an acceptable coherence among these.

On the face of it, applying coherence reasoning in contexts of value pluralism, we should expect to end up with a moral theory with multiple moral principles – principles such as "keep your promises", "don't lie", and "don't harm others" – grounded in various values and leading to potentially conflicting obligations. This is because (1) if values are indeed plural, then we'll need a range of principles reflecting these plural values and (2) such multiplicity is indeed necessary, because the reasons we give for the moral judgments and the principles we endorse will not ultimately be reducible to a single kind of consideration. To say that beneficence and justice are fundamentally different is to say that they resist expression in terms of a single value, and thus the principles behind our judgments will not be reducible either. When various considerations apply in a given case, the principles we endorse will potentially conflict; if values are plural, the proper activity in such a case is weighing considerations against one another rather than seeking out a more general point of view from which our principles can be seen to follow. That is, we have to prioritize our cares, rather than unifying them.[5]

I'll call moral theories with multiple principles "pluralist deontological" theories. The best-known example of a moral theory that is pluralist in this sense is that of the early twentieth-century ethicist W. D. Ross, who argues for principles grounded in seven or so different kinds of obligations: there are duties of fidelity, such as promise-keeping; of reparation, as when one has done something wrong; of gratitude; of justice; of beneficence; of self-improvement; and of not inflicting harm (Ross 2002 [1930]). A more contemporary example of a pluralist deontological theory is the practical theory of principlism in bioethics. In presenting their pluralist version of "principlism", bioethicists Beauchamp and Childress (2009) argue for a multiplicity of principles grounded in four distinct values: respect for autonomy, non-maleficence, beneficence and justice. In pluralist theories, when principles recommend mutually incompatible actions – e.g. a person ought to keep an appointment and ought to help an accident victim but cannot do both – we must determine which obligation is most pressing or whether the two are in equipoise.

2. Pluralist deontology, coherence and justification

When it comes to understanding pluralist deontology and its epistemological aspects, two important challenges are (1) to interpret "coherence" appropriately for contexts of value pluralism and (2) to give an account of how, in cases of moral conflict, we can determine which moral obligations or consideration override others. In recent work, I've tried to address these matters, and I give a

5 Of course, this is "on the face of it" because there can be further arguments in favor of unifying principles. I address such arguments below.

summary of that discussion here.[6] With respect to coherence, I've argued that the typical understanding of that concept in moral philosophy is inappropriate in pluralist contexts. It is typical to interpret coherence as involving a norm of "systematicity" – that the principles of a theory be as few and as simple as possible.[7] A norm of systematicity would entail favoring unified, single-principle theories such as utilitarianism, in which the right action is the one that produces the most happiness or well-being overall. It might seem that even if values are plural, we should systematize as much as possible. That is, we might say that (1) whenever there are multiple principles, we make trade-offs between the goal of reducing the number and that of fitting with our considered judgments, and (2) systematicity functions as a tie-breaker: in cases in which two theories fit equally well with our considered convictions, we ought to prefer the more systematic one.

But, as I've argued, systematicity is unjustified and inapplicable in contexts of value pluralism (Marino 2015, ch. 3). If values are plural, then there is no reason to prefer more systematized and unified theories; single-principle theories would be less justified than pluralist ones. Let's take a moment to look briefly at the reasoning behind this claim. The preference for unified theories is usually justified epistemologically by appeal to the fact that the beliefs in more unified sets support and explain one another better than those in less unified, more pluralistic ones. For example, David Brink says that "insofar as a moral theory explains the connections among moral considerations and arranges them in a systematic fashion, as unified theories do, it makes our beliefs more coherent and better justified", and that because it "places a premium on systematic explanation . . . coherentism . . . favours unified over nonunified or fragmented moral theories" (Brink 1989, 250). In a similar vein, Shelly Kagan talks about the importance of finding moral explanations – knowing not only that something is so but why it is so. Kagan says we need understanding, and this means having explanations to the extent possible. With respect to the adoption of principles that are themselves not justified by a more fundamental and general principle, Kagan says that "even though explanations may "have to come to an end somewhere", there is "no license to cut off explanation at a superficial level" (Kagan 1989, 13–14). And later: "An adequate justification for a set of principles requires an explanation of those principles – an *explanation* of why exactly these goals, restrictions and so on, should be given weight and not others. Short of this, the principles will not be free of the taint of arbitrariness which led us to move beyond our original *ad hoc* shopping lists (Kagan 1989, 13, emphasis in original). The common complaint is that pluralist deontology gives us an "unconnected heap of

6 Patricia Marino, *Moral Reasoning in a Pluralistic World.*

7 For endorsements of norms like systematicity, see, e.g., David Brink, *Moral Realism and the Foundations of Ethics* (Cambridge University Press, 1989), p. 250, Shelly Kagan, *The Limits of Morality* (Clarendon Press, 1989), p. 13, and Brad Hooker, *Ideal Code, Real World* (Oxford University Press, 2000), p. 21. For discussion, see below, and also my *Moral Reasoning in a Pluralistic World.*

duties", and the hope is that greater systematicity will lead to better explanations and thus improved justification and deeper understanding.[8]

But I claim that this way of supporting systematicity relies on claims that are questions begging or worse in the context of value pluralism. The problem, in a nutshell, is that the relevant claims about understanding and justification are true only if we have independent reason to think that the more systematized a theory is, the more likely it is to be correct or on the right track. This makes sense only if it is justified by implicit appeal to independent reasons for thinking that more unified theories are better and, thus, independent reason for thinking values are more unified than our considered judgments would suggest. But if we believe values are plural, there are no such independent reasons.

To see this more concretely, notice that an explanation isn't worth much unless it's a good explanation. To know why something is so, you need not just a more general explanatory principle that explains it, but also a reason to think the explanation is a good one. And even when we have a generality that seems to explain something more specific, knowing when that explanation is a good one can be complex. For example, if I were to propose to explain why this cat is black by saying that all cats are black, then I obviously have neither increased justification nor improved understanding, because the "explanation" appealed to is false. If I were to propose to explain why the economy was failing in 2009 by appealing to the general principle that the economy generally fails when the American Football Conference wins the Super Bowl (and the Steelers won that year), then I also have neither increased justification nor improved understanding – even though the correlation in question is real. Though there is a correlation between the economy and the Super Bowl, that correlation doesn't depend on any actual causal regularity; the generalization is accidental. To know why something is so, it's not enough to have a general principle that explains it; we have to have some reason to think the explanation is a good one.

This means that we have no reason to prefer the explanations in systematized moral theories unless we have independent reason to think that they are good explanations. Take, for example, the obligations of truth-telling and the prevention of harm. With value pluralism in the background, we might explain these by appeal to two distinct principles, grounded in the distinct values of honesty and non-maleficence. In a more systematized theory, we might explain both in terms of a single value, such as the promotion of the overall good, showing how lying leads to harms. To say that increased systematicity yields increased understanding and justification, we would have to have reason to believe that the latter are better explanations. But on what could such a reason be based? If values are plural, there is no reason to think that the explanations in more systematic theories are better than the ones in theories with more principles. This means we have no reason to prefer more systematic theories, either in cases of trade-offs

8 For the phrase "unconnected heap of duties", in connection with Ross, see McNaughton (1996). For a similar approach, see Brad Hooker's (2000) defense of unification.

with intuitive acceptability or when systematicity is used as a tie-breaker: in each case we have no reason to think the explanations – and thus moral reasons – in the more systematic theory would be better, and they may well be worse.

Other times, the problem with pluralist deontology and the need for systematicity are framed in terms of avoiding conflict. Multiple moral principles often conflict, and then we face the problem of determining which obligation outweighs the other. In monistic versions of consequentialism, such as utilitarianism, this problem does not arise: in the rare case where the same amount of well-being is produced by two different actions, we can simply choose whichever we want. But, as has been noted, this feature of monistic consequentialism is not due to its having a single principle, since single-principle theories can generate conflict all by themselves. For example, the single principle "keep your promises" can itself lead to conflicting obligations: you might, for instance, promise to give twenty dollars to A and twenty dollars to B and then find that a thief has stolen most of your money, leaving you with only enough to pay one. In the single-principle theory containing only this principle, we would still face the problem of how to judge which obligation overrides the other. What this shows is that insofar as single-principle theories avoid engendering conflicts, it is not only because they have only one principle; it is also because of the form of that principle. So, for example, in monistic consequentialist theories like hedonistic utilitarianism, there are no moral conflicts, not because there is a single principle, but because that principle is a certain kind of maximizing principle rather than a principle specifying particular obligations.

As an alternative to forms of coherence that involve systematicity and to address the problem about judgments in cases of conflict, I have argued for an approach I call "pluralist coherence"; instead of focusing on unity and systematicity, the basic idea is to aim at principled compromises among conflicting values. One relevant norm is what I call "case consistency" – which means judging morally similar cases similarly when there are no morally significant differences between them. Case consistency is a common way of reasoning morally. For example, in the abortion debate, it is typical to hear interlocutors accuse one another of being "inconsistent": of not treating similarly cases that are like one another in morally relevant features.

For a person's moral beliefs to be case consistent is for them to judge in accordance with what they take to be morally significant similarities and differences. This is obviously a complex matter, but a paradigmatic example of case inconsistency might be found in framing effects, where people judge cases differently only because of the words used in the description of otherwise identical cases. Typically, the words used in a description would not seem a morally significant difference if the situation described is the same.

A set of principles and judgments can be case inconsistent in at least two ways. First, the principles can be structured so that they apply in different ways to cases that have no morally significant difference between them. "Telling a lie at home is wrong" and "telling a lie outside is permissible" are case-inconsistent principles, as long as one regards "being at home" versus "being outside" as an intrinsically morally insignificant difference, as I take it most of us would. Second, in cases of conflict, judgments about one's overall obligation can be made in case-inconsistent ways. If I judge that I ought to stop and help accident victims instead of keeping a promised appointment when I dislike the person I am meeting with but ought to keep my appointment instead of helping accident victims when I like the person I am meeting with, then I have a set of principles and judgments that is case inconsistent from any point of view which takes the "liking" clause to introduce a morally insignificant difference.

With respect to judgment in cases of conflict, both Ross and Beauchamp and Childress say that in such cases, we must use our judgment to "balance" competing considerations. In the approach of pluralist coherence, we also must use our judgment to determine relative weights of various obligations and considerations, but the crucial difference is that these judgments are then subject to consistency demands and are not made on a case-by-case basis. When principles conflict, our judgments about overall obligations are subject to the same demands of judging in accordance with what we take to be morally significant similarities and differences. In this approach, judgments about the relative stringency of various obligations and judgments about what is and what is not morally significant are understood along the same lines as other moral judgments: they are based on considered convictions and subject to demands for case consistency and are thus revisable in the back-and-forth method of reflective equilibrium. Because people direct and prioritize values differently in fundamental ways and because they endorse different judgments about what is and what is not a morally significant difference, it follows from this framing that there can be multiple internally coherent moral systems that do not agree with one another.

3. Moderate deontology in Law and Economics: explication and objections

The previous sections provide, at best, a rough and cursory overview of pluralist deontology and pluralist coherence, but let's move on to examine the intersections with Law and Economics. As mentioned earlier, Zamir and Medina's *Law, Economics, and Morality* makes use of "moderate deontology" – an approach that combines deontological thresholds with consequentialism. In taking up this approach, the authors agree with other proponents of the Law and Economics movement that consequences should be considered and that measuring them is relevant, but they argue that we should also incorporate constraints: there are some acts, like killing, that should not be evaluated solely on a maximizing basis. In developing these ideas, Zamir and Medina distinguish a "foundational" from a "factoral" level of theorizing: the former has to do with what values ultimately matter, and the latter has to do with the factors that determine the morality of an act, their relative weight and their interaction – this has more to do with decision procedure. A theory like rule-utilitarianism might be monistic at the foundational level but associated with a procedure that is a version of moderate deontology – if, say, following that procedure brings about the most well-being overall. Zamir and Medina develop and defend moderate deontology as a theory at the factoral, or decision-making, level.

To put consequences and constraints together, Zamir and Medina appeal to the idea of a threshold: in this approach we follow familiar deontological principles – e.g. those against killing and harming others, lying and breaking promises, but we are justified in contravening these principles when consequences warrant.[9] For example, in the case where we must decide whether to shoot down a plane of citizens that has been hijacked for use as a weapon, threshold deontology pushes us to go beyond a consideration of harm to ask whether the good that will result from breaking the rule against killing reaches the threshold at which that action can be justified. Moving away from frameworks in which "efficiency" of one kind or another is the only aim, Zamir and Medina use the idea of the threshold to propose a more nuanced way that evaluation of consequences can play a role in the legal context. Their book then develops explications of how moderate deontology, or "threshold deontology", can be put to use in crafting policy and laws.

While "moderate" or "threshold deontology" is distinct from "pluralist deontology", I believe the former could be usefully seen as an example or expression of the latter. As long as our multiplicity of principles include one that demands promoting the overall good, the moral considerations in play will be the same, and the threshold question can be understood as the question of how to judge, in cases of conflicting principles, what overrides what. This is not to say that the idea of threshold deontology should generally be subsumed into pluralist deontology – the specific expression in terms of thresholds may be particularly apt and useful for certain contexts. But, as I will argue below, from an abstract theoretical point of view, seeing threshold deontology as a kind of pluralist deontology can help in analyzing and addressing some criticisms of the former view.

In ethical theory debates, two common and connected criticisms of approaches like pluralist deontology are (1) that they are unacceptably arbitrary and (2) that, in their proper form, they ultimately collapse into consequentialism. As we'll see, objections to Zamir and Medina's moderate deontology have paralleled these.

In contexts of ethical theory, the arbitrariness objection goes like this: deontological pluralism renders our moral conclusions hopelessly arbitrary because they rest on judgments: we must make judgments about how stringent or weighty various considerations are, we must make judgments about what overrides what and we must make judgments about what is and is not a morally significant difference. In section 2 earlier, we discussed Kagan's idea that cutting off explanation at an overly superficial level may leave our judgments lacking adequate justification. Theories that engender conflict, as well, require judgment in cases of conflicting obligations, and it's often said that this use of judgment is arbitrary

9 For more on "moderate deontology" in ethical theory, see Brennan (2009).

in a problematic way. In their bioethics theory of principlism, Beauchamp and Childress appeal to the idea of "balancing" conflicting considerations to decide what is most important to do overall. In response, critics like Henry Richardson argue that this kind of balancing is *ad hoc.* What often happens, Richardson says, is that since we have opinions about what the right outcome should be overall, instead of assigning weights to various obligations, we improperly work backward – "reading off" the weights from our judgments about what to do. This, he says, is inappropriate because it means the weights aren't assigned in an independent way but, rather, are being built back in to get the outcome we want (Richardson 2000; see also Richardson 1990). Without a deeper theory telling us how our principles are connected to one another, we have at best an *ad hoc* shopping list of morally relevant considerations.

Even proponents of deontological pluralism sometimes admit concerns about arbitrariness as substantive problems, going on to argue that the other advantages of deontological pluralism, such as its plausibility, outweigh them as defects. For example, Beauchamp and Childress (2009) suggest that if a systematized theory could be found that would fit adequately well with our intuitions, that theory would be preferable to "a heap of obligations and values unconnected by a first principle" (p. 396). The problem, they suggest, is simply that no systematized theory fits well with our commonly shared ways of valuing.

Critics of Zamir and Medina's threshold deontology have similar complaints about arbitrariness. In a review of Zamir and Medina's book, Avihay Dorfman (2011) says that while appealing to "intuitions" might seem a reasonable way to begin moral thinking and ensure that the morality we are using is connected to commonly held moral beliefs, morality cannot get off the ground without theory. And theory, he says, requires systematicity: within moderate deontology alone, it is "impossible to understand our intuitions in any systematic way so as to solve the conflicts that might – indeed, will likely – arise from the need to balance between the different components of this theory in general and in each and every particular case (say, between the deontological commitment to treat people as equal, on the one hand, and as free agents, on the other)" (2011, 66). Without a "systematizing" theory in the background, the judgments of moderate deontology are arbitrary and cannot be justified.

Likewise Larry Alexander (2000, 2011), drawing on work by Anthony Ellis (1992), argues that the problem with threshold deontology is that the setting of the threshold is always arbitrary. How can we determine when consequences are sufficient to overrule a deontological constraint and when they are not? It is useless to appeal to "judgements", Ellis and Alexander say. What is needed to address the problem is an account of how judgments can be made appropriately. "It is not enough", Ellis writes, "simply to assert that we have to weigh the wrongness of the action against the badness of the consequences of refraining from it. That is not the solution, but the problem. What we need an account of is how that weighing can be carried out – an account of what considerations judgment is supposed to be exercised upon, and how that exercise works upon them" (1992, 860).

This first objection about arbitrariness is sometimes linked to a second, about the distinctiveness of moderate deontology. In the ethics context, it's said that what we need in cases of conflict is a principled way of judging what overrides what, and once we have that, we have, effectively, a systematized theory.[10] Moreover, the result can be expressed in the structure of consequentialism. One might endorse a range of values, call the production of this range of values the good, then endorse a consequentialism in which the single principle recommends maximization of the good.[11] For example, G. E. Moore is sometimes thought to have held such a view. More recently, Brad Hooker's (2000) rule consequentialism brings together pluralist values by arguing that they can be systematized and thus brought under a single principle. The objection, then, is that pluralist deontology, properly understood, collapses into consequentialism.

Furthermore, in ethical theory, the relationship between pluralist deontology and consequentialism is complicated by the possibility of consequentializing. In a recent series of papers, a range of philosophers have argued that for any moral theory, one can find a "consequentialist" version of that theory: by assigning to each individual outcome the proper weight, one can find a theory that ends in all the same conclusions about all the same cases while expressing those conclusions as following from the imperative to "maximize" good consequences overall. As Douglas Portmore (2009) puts it in an overview of the procedure: "take whatever considerations that the nonconsequentialist theory says determines the deontic statuses of actions and insist that those considerations determine how their outcomes rank" (p. 330).

Portmore says that the motivation for consequentializing is found in the intuitive appeal of the account of reasons, action and the good that is associated with consequentialism. From the consequentialist point of view, the reasons for and against performing an act are wholly determined by the reasons there are for preferring its outcome to those of alternatives; then the right action for a person is the one she has most overall reason to prefer (Portmore 2009, 333). This, he says, fits with our other beliefs about rationality. Portmore cites Samuel Scheffler as attributing to these factors the "spell-binding force" consequentialism has and its ability to "haunt us" Portmore 2009, 332)[12] In addition, Jamie Dreier (1993) says that there is a "stigma" associated with alternatives, on grounds that they seem to allow us to not do the most good that we can do, which is counterintuitive (for discussion, see Brown 2011). If the best version of a pluralist deontological theory is indistinguishable from a consequentialist theory that is superior, we should adopt the consequentialist theory.

Again, critics of Zamir and Medina raise related points. Dorfman says that once the problem about arbitrariness is addressed, "moderate deontology"

10 For example, Sayre-McCord (1985) argues that overcoming conflicts requires seeking out a monistic theory (pp. 171–172). For discussion, Marino (2015, 28–33).

11 My thanks to Uri Leibowitz, who mentions this possibility in a 2017 review of Marino (2015).

12 Philippa Foot (1985) also uses the "haunting" metaphor.

collapses into a version of consequentialism: to judge appropriately in cases of conflict requires comparing values along a single measure and thus requires a monistic meta-theory; once we realize this, we are better off moving explicitly to "humane consequentialism" – which maximizes value but is sensitive to the various sources of value. Thus, as in debates over pluralist deontology in ethics, the charges are that moderate deontology is "arbitrary" and "incoherent": it is arbitrary to insist on using intuitions in the absence of systematized moral theory, and it is incoherent to describe the theory as moderate deontology when it really collapses into a version of consequentialism.

Zamir and Medina (2011) respond effectively to these objections, partly by pointing out that they often fail to appreciate the distinction between the factoral and foundational levels (p. 111). In what follows, however, I will explore the idea that drawing on ethical theory and engaging more with the foundational level may result in a fruitful and ultimately even stronger defense of moderate deontology.

With respect to arbitrariness, Zamir and Medina point out that as long as we're endorsing a theory that aims to incorporate multiple values, we're always going to encounter the same difficulty about how to weigh considerations against one another. Any theory honoring multiple values has the problem, but given the other advantages of such theories overall – and especially how preferable they are with respect to fitting with commonly held moral views – we should accept the arbitrariness problem in order to reap these other benefits. While there may be plausible alternatives to moderate deontology at the foundational level, Zamir and Medina explain, its main rivals at the factoral level – namely, act-consequentialism and absolutist deontology – are "far more problematic" (2011, 111). Echoing Beauchamp and Childress's thought that deontological pluralism is flawed but the best that we can do, they write that "Faced with the 'Scylla' of extreme consequentialism, which is willing to sacrifice anything and anyone in order to achieve the general good, and the 'Charybdis' of absolutist deontology, with its refusal to consider aggregate good at all, the choice – of moderate deontology" – is clear (2011, 125–126).[13]

With respect to the incoherence charge, Zamir and Medina argue that there is a basic difference between weighing considerations against one another and maximizing a good – even when the good is understood to involve various possibly conflicting values. "The difficulty with these attempts", they say, "is that even those consequentialist theories that do pay heed to values such as autonomy, human dignity and basic liberties, do so in the wrong way. They treat these values as goods that should be maximized, rather than as constraints on maximizing the good" (2011, 116). In particular, consequentialism cannot accommodate agent-centered restrictions – that is, restrictions that concern the specific relationship of the action to the person performing the action.

13 The metaphor is from Larry Alexander. We saw earlier that Beauchamp and Childress say something similar.

"Moderate deontology", they point out, "prohibits the intentional killing of a baby, even when there is no doubt that this is the only way to prevent her father from intentionally killing two other babies. Consequentialists, taking an impartial outlook, view such a prohibition as 'utterly irrational' as it results in more intentional killings overall" (2011, 116). So moderate deontology is preferable to consequentialism at the factoral level because it makes sense of the idea that a person is specially responsible for what she does herself.

4. The arbitrariness objection

We've seen how challenges to Zamir and Medina's moderate deontology in Law and Economics debates are similar to those leveled at pluralist deontology in ethical theory debates, especially with respect to arbitrariness and incoherence. The next two sections explore the fruitfulness of developing the relevant interconnections further.

Let's look first at arbitrariness. In their response to this objection, Zamir and Medina point out – correctly, in my opinion – that the same problem arises for any pluralistic normative theory (or, more precisely, for any pluralistic normative theory that does not "accord one factor an unqualified lexical priority over the others" (2011, 125). However, I think there is a stronger response available, and this response can be seen more clearly when we view threshold deontology as an instantiation of a pluralist deontology and engage with the foundational as well as factoral levels. From that perspective, we can see why it's not just that other pluralistic theories are "arbitrary" as well. Instead, we can say that pluralist theories have no more problem with arbitrariness than monistic single-principle ones.

To see this, we have to get into deeper questions about methodology and justification. In the ethical theory context, single-principle theories like consequentialism are often justified through a process like the one already described, in which we start with our considered convictions and use something like reflective equilibrium to try to bring them into coherence. Brad Hooker, for example, justifies his rule consequentialism by arguing that his single principle does the best job unifying and systematizing the various duties entailed by Ross's list of principles: the strategy applies coherence to our considered convictions.

I claim that when monistic single-principle theories are justified by appeal to convictions and coherence, pluralist deontology has no greater problem with arbitrariness than single-principle theories do. The interpretation of coherence as case consistency, mentioned earlier, asks us to use our judgment to evaluate the relative weights of various moral considerations and to bring those into coherence with one another. In the context of conviction ethics, this is the same way all our moral beliefs are evaluated and justified. So, *contra* Ellis, appealing to "judgments" in this context is appropriate: if the method of reasoning is conviction ethics, then appealing to judgments and trying to bring them into coherence is the way we bring justification to *all* of our moral judgments and conclusions. So it is appropriate to use it in cases of assigning weights and balancing. Analogous remarks apply to Richardson's complaint about methodology and "reading off" the various weights. In the context of conviction ethics, reading off the relative weights of obligations from our judgments about what should override what in the given circumstances is an instance of the same methodology – bringing coherence to considered convictions – and so is unproblematic. (For a more detailed argument, see Marino (2015, 99–101).)

It may seem that monistic single-principle theories are still better than pluralist ones because they reduce the need for judgment: in case of a difficult dilemma or conflict or question about the threshold, a monistic single-principle theory may allow us to calculate an answer where the pluralist must make a role for judgment about the answer. But I think that, at least in the absence of more powerful justificatory considerations, this is mistaken. It is not better to have an answer one can calculate than an answer that requires judgment unless we have some reason to believe that the calculated answer is the right one. Using numerology on the letters in a moral question involves calculation rather than judgment and yields an objective answer based on this calculation. But any answers derived this way would wrong because they aren't based on the right kinds of moral considerations. Unless we have independent reason to believe the monist single-principle theory is more accurate in general, its answers are no less arbitrary and may well – as in the case of numerology – be worse.

What might those independent reasons be? If we begin from the assumption that values are plural, then as we saw in section 1, a monistic single-principle theory is not more accurate than a pluralistic one; rather, it is less accurate, yielding explanations based on false generalizations. Even if we are agnostic about value pluralism, we still don't have positive reason to trust monistic single-principle theories more. In fact, given the widespread acknowledgement that the way we value in practice is generally pluralistic, it seems we would need reason to believe that we're making a widespread mistake in order to conclude that systematizing would lead us in a good direction.

In the absence of these independent reasons, a preference for monistic single-principle theories must rest on "judgments" similar to the ones denigrated in pluralist and threshold theories. For example, some forms of utilitarianism rest on considered convictions about the moral relevance of happiness or preference satisfaction or whatever. They also must appeal to some judgments about how to generalize – rejecting, for example, familiar Kantian intuitions about the importance of the separateness of persons in favor of stressing the importance of the similarity of preferences or utils. This means that not only do monistic single-principle theories rely on "judgment" the way pluralistic theories do, they often do so in ways that reject some of our most familiar and widely shared values in favor of others. So – again, at least in the absence of strong independent reasons to believe in value monism – they are no less arbitrary than pluralist theories and perhaps more so.

This shows that as long as we are using coherence methods like reflective equilibrium, pluralist and moderate deontology have no more problem with arbitrariness than single-principle alternatives do. In a different direction, it is sometimes claimed that consequentialism has another form of justification that doesn't depend on considered convictions or judgments at all. Peter Singer (2005), for example, argues that consequentialism has a "rational" foundation that does not depend, as deontological theories do, on intuitions or judgments.[14] A full discussion of this topic is beyond the scope of this chapter, but there are reasons to be skeptical of this claim. For example, in a critical analysis, Joakim Sandberg and Niklas Juth (2011) argue that Singer's own method of justification relies on intuitive judgments: for example, judgments about what does and does not constitute a morally significant difference are needed to explain why we should universalize over our interest satisfaction in the way Singer's consequentialism tells us to do. Furthermore, different versions of consequentialism appeal to different notions of well-being and thus of what, exactly, should be maximized; to say why one candidate for maximizing is better than another plausibly requires appeal to judgment as well. And as long as judgment comes into the picture, the same problems of justification and arbitrariness come into play.

This shows how engaging with the foundational level helps explain more deeply why pluralist deontology and, by extension, moderate deontology have no greater problem with arbitrariness than rival theories do.

5. The incoherence objection

With respect to the possibility that moderate deontology collapses into monistic consequentialism, the heart of Zamir and Medina's response is that while this could be true at the foundational level, it is not the case at the factoral level, as shown by the fact of agent-centered restrictions. I'll argue here that (1) looking at ethical theory gives us a wider perspective and further resources for answering the incoherence objection, and also (2) the consequentializing possibility complicates Zamir and Medina's responses in ways that show the importance of (1).

As noted, when plural values have been prioritized, it is possible to represent them through a single-principle version of consequentialism. I claim that, in addition to agent-centred restrictions, there are two other considerations in favor of pluralist deontology, related to dilemmas and to pragmatics.

Let's look first at dilemmas. In a case where honoring one value requires performing action A and honoring another requires performing action B, and A and B are mutually incompatible, a theory with multiple principles allows us to say that both acts are obligatory, so that whatever we choose, something suboptimal has happened. While there is long-standing debate on how to interpret the formal status of moral dilemmas, there are reasons to adopt an ethical framework in which dilemmas play a role. One reason dilemmas are thought

14 In the law and economics context, a similar strategy is used by Louis Kaplow and Steven Shavell (2002). For a philosophical discussion of this part of Kaplow and Shavell's book, see Adler (2005).

to be significant is that they play a certain role in our moral lives: they leave a "remainder" or "residue", reflecting that even when we have acted for the best, a duty has been breached, and something that ought to have been done was not. In ethical theory, the remainder can be understood as alerting us that things are not as they ought to be and motivating us to change our lives and institutions so that dilemmas are less likely to arise in the future (Marcus 1980; Marino (2001). In legal theory, the idea of a remainder has also been linked to the idea that in cases of conflict, where exercising a right can also mean breaking a law, there can be obligations of compensation and amends (Finkelstein 2001).

The idea that remainders play an ethically significant role, originally articulated by Ruth Marcus in the 1980s, has been called a "mutuality principle" by bioethicist Joseph DeMarco (2005). For example, DeMarco describes a dilemma in which parents want to refuse a life-saving blood transfusion for their child on religious grounds. Respect for parental autonomy means honoring their wishes, but respecting the rights of the child means rejecting them. DeMarco says that even if we agree with the outcome of Beauchamp and Childress's "principlism" – that the rights of the child are overriding in such cases – the mutuality principle points to the importance of investigating and eventually developing alternative treatments, treatments that, because they do not require transfusions, would allow us to honor both values at once. In legal theory, an analogous view of conflicting rights has been articulated by Claire Oakes Finkelstein (2001), who argues for the importance of remainders (she calls them residues). If I promise to give each of two people a banana, and I only have one, I have a conflict of obligations; but, plausibly, if I can compensate the bananaless person in some equivalent way, I ought to do so. Without the remainder, we lose the sense that in cases of conflict a duty has been breached; if no duty has been breached, then "compensation, apologies, and any other way of making amends are all unnecessary" – this does not fit, she says, with the way we regard duties of compensation in such cases (Finkelstein 2001, 295).

For remainders to play these roles, dilemmas must be real in some sense, rather than being explained away – by, for example, saying that only the most stringent obligation is our actual obligation or by adding exception clauses to our principles.[15] With a multiplicity of principles, the possibility of conflict, what it represents and the possibility of taking dilemmas to be real are all immediate. Since the roles of the remainder concern the decision-making aspect of moral thinking, their importance concerns not only the foundational level of morality but the factoral level as well.

Even when maximizing single-principle theories reflect multiple values, it is difficult to see how they can capture these ideas about conflicts and dilemmas. As we've seen earlier, this is not so much because they are "single-principle" theories, but rather because of their maximizing form. Suppose autonomy,

15 Ross's idea of "*prima facie*" duties is an example of the former; Henry Richardson's "specification" approach is an example of the latter. See discussion in Marino (2015).

justice, liberty etc. are different values, and we weigh them against one another into a single property of "goodness", and then we articulate a single-principle requiring us to maximize the good or follow the rules that would do so. In that case, when we maximize the good or follow the rule, we've done what we ought: there is no sense of a remainder or residue.[16] In the transfusion and banana cases, as long as we've maximized the good by respecting the rights of the child, maximizing consequentialism renders obscure the sense that, no matter what action is undertaken, an obligation was unmet. Pluralist deontology fits with and helps explain the relevant aspects of moral conflict and the role it plays in our lives.

Moving beyond dilemmas, a second relevant consideration has to do with the process of weighing and the possibility of disagreement. As is often emphasized in the debates over moderate deontology, people may disagree over where to set the threshold. As deontological pluralism makes obvious, determining the weight of various values is a difficult problem – and it is a problem about which we may expect to find a range of different answers and substantive disagreement from one person to another. As I've argued, some moral disagreement is plausibly explained by differences in how to balance conflicting values (Marino 2015). Two people might each value truth-telling and promise-keeping but disagree about what to do when keeping a promise requires telling a lie – because they prioritize these values differently. Differences in prioritization would lead to different judgments about thresholds as well.

Because it puts the weighing process front and center, the framework of principle pluralism facilitates our engagement with one another about these differences. For example, the people who disagree about promise-keeping and lying may, at first, know only that they disagree: one says the promise must be kept; the other says the truth must be told. If they frame their thinking in terms of maximizing goodness, their disagreement will be constructed in an unilluminating way – as one over whether one thing is most "good" or another thing is most "good". But if they frame their thinking in terms of multiple values and moral conflict, an exchange demanding reasons will bring to light the reasons for their disagreement: they respect similar principles but disagree over prioritization in the given case. Again, this pragmatic point about how to facilitate moral debate has to do primarily with the factoral, or decision-making, level since it has to do with the framing of ethical theories rather than their ultimate foundation.

These points about dilemmas and pragmatics gain importance when we consider how the consequentializing possibility complicates Zamir and Medina's response about agent-relativity and the difference between weighing and maximizing. In consequentializing, weights are assigned to individual outcomes so that the moral conclusions are identical to those of the deontological theory. In

16 Typically, if the rules of rule-consequentialism conflict, one's overall obligation is simply to perform the action that will maximize best consequences in the particular situation.

this approach, any set of moral judgments, including those with agent-centred restrictions, can be produced through a consequentialist theory.

Here, the points about dilemmas and pragmatics become especially important. With respect to dilemmas, as Portmore (2009) points out, there are some subtleties, but consequentializing does not allow for the kind of dilemmas most pertinent to the issues mentioned earlier. The subtleties arise because consequentializing can allow for "prohibition dilemmas" – in which no matter what one does, one has acted wrongly. This is because it is formally possible to assign ranks to outcomes (in a way that is dependent on which actions are undertaken) in such a way that, no matter what a person does, there is another action whose outcome has a higher rank (Portmore, 339–340). However, consequentializing is incompatible with "obligation" dilemmas – the dilemmas in which there are two conflicting obligations.[17] Plausibly, this is the kind of obligation most relevant to the mutuality principle and the thoughts about compensation and amends.

With respect to the pragmatics of moral decision-making, the most important here is the fact, noted already by others, that the consequentializing strategy makes it obscure how we are to explain why our moral judgments are what they are. If our moral judgment is that baby killing is not allowed, even if it would prevent other infant deaths, then from the point of view of pluralist or moderate deontology, we have a simple explanation of why: there is a principle against it, and either the principle isn't overridden or the relevant threshold has not been met. This is an explanation we can use and appeal to in other contexts and justifications. Once we have consequentialized, what are we to make of such explanations?

As Andrew Schroeder (2017) argues, this point about explanations can make a difference pragmatically since it may affect the way we reason. Using the example of debate over whether measuring DALYs (disability-adjusted life years) should incorporate distributive considerations, Schroeder argues that framing the issues in terms of consequentialism distorts them. From the consequentialist point of view, the "simpler" and default assumption is that distributive considerations should not factor in. Schroeder gives an example of how this leads one consequentialist to ignore distributive factors despite the fact that most people do "take distribution to be important in some way". This pragmatic point suggests another way that, at the factoral level, a framing of deontological pluralism, and thus moderate deontology, could be better than a consequentialist framing, even when the latter is available.

17 Portmore argues that obligation dilemmas are generally conceptually impossible for formal reasons, but I think his argument is question-begging in its definition of "obligation". There are various ways to formulate obligation dilemmas so that contradictions do not arise. For an overview, see McConnell (2018).

Conclusion

In exploring the ways that debates in Law and Economics might engage with ethical theory, I have shown how similar issues and debates tend to arise and also how bringing the two domains into dialogue with one another can allow for illuminating discussion. More specifically, focusing on the example of Zamir and Medina's moderate deontology, I've argued that framing this view as an expression of pluralist deontology and drawing on discussions of value pluralism, coherence, epistemology and justification in the ethics context allows for a fruitful engagement, especially with respect to charges of arbitrariness and incoherence. Moderate deontology has no more problem with arbitrariness or incoherence than rival theories do, and drawing on ethical theory helps us understand why.

References

Adler, M. 2005. "Review of *Fairness Versus Welfare*." *Ethics* 115: 824–828.

Alexander, L. 2000. "Deontology at the Threshold." *San Diego Law Review* 37(4): 893–893.

Alexander, L. 2011. "Deontological Constraints in a Consequentialist World: A Comment on *Law, Economics and Morality*." *Jerusalem Review of Legal Studies* 3: 75–90.

Beauchamp, T. L., and J. F. Childress. 2009. *Principles of Biomedical Ethics*, 6th ed. Oxford: Oxford University Press.

Brennan, S. 2009. "Moderate Deontology and Moral Faps." *Philosophical Perspectives* 23(1): 23–43.

Brink, D. O. 1989. *Moral Realism and the Foundations of Ethics*. Cambridge: Cambridge University Press.

Brown, C. 2011. "Consequentialize This." *Ethics* 121(4): 749–771.

Daniels, N. 2018. "Reflective Equilibrium." In Edward N. Zalta (ed.), *The Stanford Encyclopedia of Philosophy* (Fall Edition), https://plato.stanford.edu/archives/fall2018/entries/reflective-equilibrium/

DeMarco, J. P. 2005. "Principlism and Moral Dilemmas: A New Principle." *Journal of Medical Ethics* 31(2): 101–105.

Dorfman, A. 2011. "Humane Consequentialism: A Critical Note on Eyal Zamir & Barak Medina, *Law, Economics, and Morality* (2010)." *Jerusalem Review of Legal Studies* 3: 54–74.

Dreier, J. 1993. "Structures of Normative Theories." *The Monist* 76(1): 22–40.

Ellis, A. 1992. "Deontology, Incommensurability and the Arbitrary." *Philosophy and Phenomenological Research* 52(4): 855–875.

Finkelstein, C. O. 2001. "Two Men and a Plank." *Legal Theory* 7(3): 279–306.

Foot, P. 1985. "Utilitarianism and the Virtues." *Mind* 94(374): 196–209.

Haidt, J., and C. Joseph. 2004. "Intuitive Ethics: How Innately Prepared Intuitions Generate Culturally Variable Virtues." *Dædalus*, Fall: 55–66.

Haidt, J., and C. Joseph. 2007. "The Moral Mind: How Five Sets of Innate Intuitions Guide the Development of Many Culture-Specific Virtues, and Perhaps Even Modules." In P. Carruthers, S. Laurence, and S. Stich (eds.), *The Innate Mind*, vol. 3. Oxford: Oxford University Press.

Hooker, B. 2000. *Ideal Code, Real World: A Rule-Consequentialist Theory of Morality*. Oxford: Oxford University Press.

Kagan, S. I. 1989. *The Limits of Morality*. Oxford: Clarendon Press.

Kaplow, L., and S. Shavell. 2002. *Fairness Versus Welfare.* Cambridge, MA: Harvard University Press.

Leibowitz, U. 2017. "Review of Moral Reasoning in a Pluralistic World." *Ethics* 127(3): 792–797.

Marcus, R. B. 1980. "Moral Dilemmas and Consistency." *The Journal of Philosophy* 77(3): 121–136.

Marino, P. 2001. "Moral Dilemmas, Collective Responsibility, and Moral Progress." *Philosophical Studies* 104(2): 203–225.

Marino, P. 2015. *Moral Reasoning in a Pluralistic World.* Montreal: McGill-Queen's University Press.

Mason, E. 2008. "Value Pluralism." In Edward N. Zalta (ed.), *The Stanford Encyclopedia of Philosophy* (Fall Edition), http://plato.stanford.edu/archives/fall2008/entries/value-pluralism/

McConnell, T. 2018. "Moral Dilemmas." In Edward N. Zalta (ed.), *The Stanford Encyclopedia of Philosophy* (Fall Edition), https://plato.stanford.edu/archives/fall2018/entries/moral-dilemmas/, section 5.

McNaughton, D. 1996. "An Unconnected Heap of Duties?" *The Philosophical Quarterly* 46(185): 433–447.

Nagel, T. 1979. "The Fragmentation of Value." In his *Mortal Questions.* Cambridge: Cambridge University Press, pp. 128–141.

Nussbaum, M. C. 1997. "Flawed Foundations: The Philosophical Critique of (a particular type of) Economics." *The University of Chicago Law Review* 64(4): 1197–1214.

Portmore, D. W. 2009. "Consequentializing." *Philosophy Compass* 4(2): 329–347.

Rawls, J. 1951. "Outline of a Decision Procedure for Ethics." *The Philosophical Review* 60(2): 177–197.

Richardson, H. S. 1990. "Specifying Norms as a Way to Resolve Concrete Ethical Problems." *Philosophy & Public Affairs*: 279–310.

Richardson, H. S. 2000. "Specifying, Balancing, and Interpreting Bioethical Principles." *The Journal of Medicine and Philosophy* 25(3): 285–307.

Ross, W. D. 1930/2002. *The Right and the Good.* Edited by Philip Stratton-Lake. Oxford: Clarendon Press.

Sandberg, J., and N. Juth. 2011. "Ethics and Intuitions: A Reply to Singer." *The Journal of Ethics* 15(3): 209–226.

Sayre-McCord, G. 1985. "Coherence and Models for Moral Theorizing." *Pacific Philosophical Quarterly* 66(1–2): 170–190.

Scanlon, T. M. 2003. "Rawls on Justification." In Samuel Freeman (ed.), *The Cambridge Companion to Rawls.* Cambridge, New York: Cambridge University Press, pp. 139–167.

Schroeder, S. A. 2017. "Consequentializing and Its Consequences." *Philosophical Studies* 174(6): 1475–1497.

Singer, P. 2005. "Ethics and Intuitions." *The Journal of Ethics* 9(3–4): 331–352.

Zamir, E., and B. Medina. 2010. *Law, Economics, and Morality.* Oxford: Oxford University Press.

Zamir, E., and B. Medina. 2011. "*Law, Economics, and Morality:* A Response to Critiques." *Jerusalem Review of Legal Studies* 3: 107–146.

7 Economic consequences as legal values

A legal inferentialist approach

Fabrizio Esposito and Giovanni Tuzet

1. Introduction

There was a time when explaining the content of the law was, in some sense, a priority for the economic approach to law. We refer to the 70s and 80s of the last century and, more precisely, to Posner's efficiency hypothesis of the common law. Posner attracted much attention to the economic approach to law by exploring "the hypothesis that common-law rules and institutions tend to promote economic efficiency", with "economic efficiency" to be understood as "wealth maximization" (Posner 1979, 285). Ironically, at the time it was fashionable to distinguish between the positive approach of Posner and the Chicago School in opposition to the normative approach of Calabresi and the New Haven School.[1] This is ironic because the now-mainstream approach of the Chicago School over the years abandoned its positive aspirations and became normative all the way down. The abandonment of the positive approach is typically explained by pointing out its significant methodological shortcomings (see Garoupa, Ligüerre and Mélon 2017, 14–21; Bridgeman 2009, 355; Kraus 2001, 420). In particular, it can be objected that many purported positive explanations are advanced by cherry-picking the *explananda* and are fundamentally disinterested in actual legal reasoning and argumentation.

This chapter gives reason to economists of law to revive the explanatory, positive project pioneered by Posner. To do so, the chapter does three things: (1) it discusses two limitations of the view that norms are desirable because of their economic consequences; (2) it finds the second of those limitations particularly challenging and (3) it offers legal inferentialism as an alternative (and better) approach. So, in sum, we suggest a methodology for explanatory economic projects of the content of law firmly grounded in legal inferentialism, in that legal inferentialism fixes semantic problems (problems about the meaning of legal texts in particular) and points out the axiological and economic assumptions of law. Notice that we do not promise to offer a conclusive solution to axiological disagreements by semantic arguments; rather, we will use legal

1 On the distinction between the Chicago and New Haven Schools, see Esposito (2017b).

inferentialism to address the semantic ambiguity of "economic consequences", in certain legal contexts at least, and to point out the value choices that explain[2] legal content in those contexts.

Our method does not provide conclusive axiological and normative justification but makes values explicit. Reconstructing in inferential terms some disputes about legal meaning delivers information about legal content and values. Then it is open for economists (or anyone else, for that matter) to engage in critical discourse about that.

Only to the extent that the law's claim to authority is morally justified (Raz 1979), the institutional fact that the law selects certain economic consequences as relevant (and ignores others) is a conclusive moral reason in favor of this or that meaning of "economic consequences". This is the broader theoretical background where we can place Calabresi's penetrating discussion of Posner's efficiency hypothesis. Calabresi (1983) made two points. He shared the concerns about the proof of the hypothesis – going as far as labeling it a "sophistry". He nevertheless noted the appeal of the hypothesis from a legal point of view: "if the common law is a legitimate source of law, and if over the centuries it has predominantly served a given goal, it is not silly to assert that any judicial failure to serve that goal, unless clearly required by the legislature, is criticisable" (Calabresi 1983, 87–88). Those who accept the law's claim to authority have a reason to take research elucidating the animating values (mapping the "normative DNA") of the law seriously. They can comply more easily in this way. Likewise, those who are skeptical of or even reject the claim to authority have a reason to take research elucidating the animating values (mapping the "normative DNA") of the law seriously to show its undesirable mutations and need of reform, lobbying, protest, disobedience etc.

In this inquiry, we will build on some previous research on the relationship between total and consumer welfare. One of us has been working on the claim that *consumer-welfare maximization* can be an alternative axiological foundation for an economic approach to law; this appears to be particularly relevant for the legal community because it explains better than total-welfare maximization the content of economic law, especially in the EU (see Esposito 2013, 2016, 2018; Esposito and Grundmann 2017; Esposito and De Almeida 2017). For current purposes (and in the lack of a better name), we shall call this claim "the consumer-welfare hypothesis", in opposition to the traditional "total-welfare hypothesis". It is a new and alternative efficiency hypothesis of the law, having

2 In this chapter, we use the term "explanation" and its cognates in a way that is consistent with its use in the philosophy of action as "the explanation of intentional actions in terms of the agent's reasons for acting" (Wilson and Shpall 2012). Explanations and justifications are thus intertwined in this use. This use is also found in natural language, of course. For example, if I think you wronged me, I can ask you interchangeably "Why did you do it?", "Can you explain yourself?", "Can you justify yourself?". A similar use is enshrined in the so-called "comply or explain" regulatory approach, where a certain rule must be followed unless reasons are given to explain (and justify) the departure from the rule.

consumer welfare instead of total welfare as its maximand. A bit more precisely, the consumer-welfare hypothesis holds that by assuming that the microeconomic rationale of the market mechanism is the maximization of consumer instead of total welfare, we can account for the legal arguments involved in the practice of economic law, at least in the EU.

The other of us has been working in the field of legal argumentation and interpretation, contributing in particular to the discussion on *legal inferentialism*. The general idea of this approach is to understand and determine legal content in terms of inferential relations between terms, expressions and sentences used in legal practice. In particular, it is the practice of legal interpretation and argumentation that shows the correctness conditions of the use of legal terms, expressions and sentences. So, in previous works, Canale and Tuzet have used Robert Brandom's model of scorekeeping to show how the meaning of a legal provision is fixed in a pragmatic interaction between different speakers (see Canale and Tuzet 2005, 2007, 2008, 2009, 2010; cf. Brandom 1994, 2000). Also these ideas are discussed in more detail later. At this early stage, one aspect of the inferentialist approach is worthy of emphasis. In inferential terms, conceptual content is determined in the linguistic practice of a community of speakers, who fix the meaning of the relevant terms by accepting certain inferences as correct and others as incorrect. For instance, whether "intent" in a criminal context encompasses *oblique* intention (namely unwanted but foreseen consequences of an act) is an issue that can be addressed and answered by keeping score of the relevant inferences.

The chapter is structured as follows. Sections 2 and 3 set the stage by detailing the basic analytical models used in economic analysis of (legal) norms and in the theory of legal argumentation. Section 4 takes stock and shows that if economic consequences have to have any bearing on legal argumentation, they must be used in the argumentation developed about norms. The main problem then becomes understanding which economic consequences are legally relevant. Section 5 describes the consumer-welfare hypothesis and its relationship with mainstream literature. As both the traditional total-welfare hypothesis and the consumer-welfare one have an economic pedigree, a reason must be given for choosing one maximand over the other in economic analysis. This choice is particularly difficult for those economists who consider the justification of value choices as external to economic research. Legal inferentialism offers a solution to these economists. Section 6 introduces legal inferentialism and explains how it allows us to establish which hypothesis between the total- and the consumer-welfare one fits better with legal practice. This shows which efficiency hypothesis works better as animating value (normative DNA) of the analyzed legal materials. For illustrative purposes, this method is applied to the relation between the concept of consumer weakness and the prohibition of unfair terms in consumer contracts in the case law of the Court of Justice of the European Union (CJEU). Section 7 concludes by pointing out the extent of our claim and directions for future research.

2. The consequentialist foundations of the economic approach to norms

A basic idea of the economic approach to legal norms is to look at these as incentives to perform certain forms of conduct. If these incentives have a minimum of effectiveness, they have an impact on the conduct of their addressees and produce some economic consequences.

Now, for a better understanding of this mechanism, we find it useful to consider the logical structure of legal norms. Legal norms generally have a *conditional* logical structure (von Wright 1963; Alchourrón and Bulygin 1971; Navarro and Rodríguez 2014): they are constituted by an antecedent part representing a form of conduct and a consequent ascribing a legal consequence to that conduct. If a certain conduct is performed, a certain legal consequence ought to follow. Logically speaking, the antecedent is descriptive of a form of conduct while the consequent is normative in that it prescribes what ought to follow from that conduct. Typically, the legal consequence is a *sanction* on those who perform the regulated conduct.

When the sanction is negative (e.g. a fine), it has the apparent role of an incentive not to perform the regulated conduct. When it is positive (e.g. a fiscal deduction), it provides an incentive to perform the conduct. If such norms are effective, they play a role in the decision-making of the law's addressees. The addressees take the norms into account when they determine how to act. In this way, legal norms produce (or contribute to the production of) economic consequences. For instance, law's addressees perform certain transactions that are legally encouraged because of their beneficial effects. In other terms, the ascription of legal consequences to certain forms of conduct causes (or contributes to the causal determination of) certain economic consequences.

Bearing all this in mind, we introduce the *foundational scheme* of an economic approach to law, with C for conduct, S for sanction, EC for economic consequences, $\Rightarrow_n$ meaning that between C and S there is a normative (legal) implication, and $\Rightarrow_f$ meaning that between $(C \Rightarrow_n S)$ and EC there is a factual (causal) implication:

(1) $(C \Rightarrow_n S) \Rightarrow_f EC$

Proposition (1) requires some comment. First, remember that implication $\Rightarrow_n$ means that, according to the law, S ought to follow when C is the case, while implication $\Rightarrow_f$ predicts that EC will follow given the norm. Second, the concept of economic consequence is ambiguous in an important sense. On the one hand, economic consequences can be consequences in the economy. For example, variations in the GDP, employment rate, import-export ratio etc. On the other hand, "economic consequences" can stand for "consequences calculated with some economic method". For example, one can estimate the effect of a merger between firms A and B on price, quality and quantities of the goods exchanged in the market where they operate. This meaning often overlaps with the previous one, but sometimes it does not. For example, an economic consequence could be calculated with a noneconomic method (e.g. a philosophical claim about welfare), or a noneconomic consequence could be calculated with an economic method (e.g. an economic analysis of the judicial system). For example, the libertarian economist Harold Demsetz (1969) famously charged legal scholars with committing the "nirvana fallacy", which consists of ignoring the enforcement costs[3] of legal norms.

As we discuss in more detail in section 5, the total- versus consumer-welfare disagreement is exactly a disagreement about which economic consequences have to be included in the foundational scheme. In other terms, it is a semantic disagreement about what "economic consequences" means in the context of the economic analysis of legal practice. Solving this disagreement helps identify the animating values (normative DNA) of this practice.

We give to proposition (1) the somewhat pretentious name "foundational scheme" because it establishes the implication between norms and some notion of economic consequences and because this implication is at the core of all the questions economic analysts of law typically ask. Both the ideas of predicting the economic consequences of a norm and of measuring these consequences presuppose the existence of the factual implication schematically represented by proposition (1). Also, the normative analyses of economists presuppose this factual connection. Norms are evaluated for their capacity to *cause certain economic consequences.*

Such consequentialist normative analyses presuppose a further premise: namely, a *relation of preference* between different norms in light of their economic consequences. This preference can be specified at the legislative level, as a preference for the enactment of an economically better regulation, or at the judicial level, as a preference for the interpretation of a legal provision that results in an economically better norm. Let N1 be the norm $C \Rightarrow_n S$, EC_{N1} the expected economic consequences if norm N1 is in force, EC_{N2} the expected economic consequences if a different norm N2 is in force, p an operator expressing a preference relation between different states of affairs and $\Rightarrow_i$ the implication between preferred consequences and the interpretive outcome consisting in a preference relation p between the two norms (N1 and N2); then an argument from economic consequences can be written as follows:

(2) $(EC_{N1}\ p\ EC_{N2}) \Rightarrow_i (N1\ p\ N2)$

Proposition (2) establishes an interpretive legal implication on the finding that the economic consequences are preferable if N1 instead of N2 is in force. In other terms, it is desirable to have N1 because the economic consequences are more valuable when N1 is in force than when N2 is in force. For current purposes, proposition (2) is particularly important because, as we shall see next, it expresses

3 Enforcement costs can be distinguished in direct and indirect costs. Direct costs are the costs related to the functioning of the legal system, such as the salaries of police officers, judges, court clerks, litigators etc. Indirect costs are other costs caused by the legal system, such as the costs deriving from over- and underenforcement of a norm. A *locus classicus* of this analysis is Calabresi (1970).

a type of consequentialist argument that is often used in legal practice.[4] To see this, we now turn to the analytical model of legal reasoning and argumentation.[5]

3. The analytical model of legal argumentation

Analytical philosophers typically divide legal arguments into two broad categories: arguments about *norms* and arguments about *facts*. Arguments about norms aim at justifying (or contesting) the construction, identification and validation of norms as legal norms. In a legal dispute, the participants typically start from a legal provision like a code article, which is in need of *interpretation*, or of being contextualized to the legal system it belongs to. Arguments about facts, instead, aim at justifying (or contesting) the reconstruction or representation of the relevant facts.

Once the facts are found and the relevant norms are pointed out, the decision-makers need only apply the latter to the former. Some analytical approaches to this subject claim that this kind of application consists, logically speaking, in a deductive inference. According to the traditional model of the "judicial syllogism" (Beccaria 1764), decision-makers are to deduce the legal consequences in the case from the facts and the applicable norms. Following the syllogism model, the relevant norm constitutes the major premise of the syllogism, the relevant fact constitutes the minor premise and the legal consequence of them constitutes the conclusion of the inference. The literature calls "internal" the justification of the conclusion provided by the deductive structure of the inference and "external" the justification of the premises of it. Interpretive arguments provide the external justification of the major premise, and evidentiary arguments provide the external justification of the minor premise of the syllogism (see Alexy 1978; Wróblewski 1992).

Now, interpretive arguments usually make appeal to the "canons of interpretation", or the "interpretive directives", which can be used in a given legal system. Research on legal interpretation provides a list of such devices. A standard taxonomy of the interpretive directives divides them into textual, systemic and consequentialist arguments (see MacCormick and Summers 1991; Bengoetxea 1993, 218 ff.; Beck 2013, 187 ff.). *Consequentialist arguments*, in particular, are those according to which a norm is justified in the light of the consequences that it brings about. At this point, it is interesting to recall proposition (2): $(EC_{N1}\ p\ EC_{N2}) \Rightarrow_i (N1\ p\ N2)$. In essence, proposition (2) expresses more formally the same idea of the consequentialist argument given in natural language in the

4 From a logical point of view, the scheme of (2) can be taken as an interpretive directive and, therefore, as a norm itself but also as a proposition about an interpretive and normative implication; we use it in the latter sense.

5 Just a terminological note: "reasoning" refers to the inference performed, e.g. by a judge or court, while "argumentation" refers to the public activity of giving and asking for reasons. To capture the features of legal practice, the latter is better, but of course, it is an inference-governed activity.

previous sentence. The main difference is that proposition (2) is strictly focused on economic consequences, while consequentialist arguments allow for considerations about consequences in general. It then follows that proposition (2) expresses a particular type of consequentialist argument, the argument from economic consequences. And the interpretive directive upholding this argument, simply put, would be something like this: *interpret provisions so as to bring about the best economic consequences.*

In some legal systems (or subsystems), *some arguments prevail*, that is, they are preferred over the others. For instance, textual arguments, such as the argument from literal meaning, usually prevail in criminal law over other arguments because they put more constraints on judicial interpretation and decision-making and therefore better protect the rights of criminal defendants. Every time a system has an interpretive directive that dictates the preference for one argument over another, such a directive can be called a second-order directive, whereas the arguments in the ranking are first-order interpretive directives.[6] Second-order directives establish, more in detail, the systemic preference criteria about first-order directives. More precisely, they concern the precedence of some argument when they require it to be used before others are, and they concern the prevalence of it when they require that, in case of conflict between interpretive outcomes generated by different arguments, one argument be given more weight or strength.[7]

In light of the considerations of this section and the previous one, it is possible to identify the first limit of normative economic analysis: it cannot rest with the simple eulogy of consequentialist arguments for other arguments compete with them in legal practice.

4. First limit: What about the other first-order interpretive directives?

Consequentialist arguments can conflict with other arguments used in legal interpretive practice. The fundamental scheme of economic analysis outlined in section 2 shows that economists of law typically focus their attention on the relation between economic consequences and legal norms. When their analysis is normative, they take economic consequences as the criterion for evaluating the law and suggest reforms when needed. In so doing, their argumentation is *not that far from legal practice* as one might think. Indeed, the role of economic consequences is discussed in the study of legal reasoning and argumentation, in

6 Tedeschi (1979) calls "the law of laws" the set of norms about norms (concerning interpretation, analogy, custom, the regulation of precedent, retroactivity etc.).

7 Cf. MacCormick and Summers (1991, 530). The precedence relation is usually accompanied by the idea that the subsequent arguments need not come into play if the precedent ones are sufficient to settle the issue.

particular in connection to consequentialist arguments.[8] For current purposes, we take it for granted that consequences that are *prima facie* extralegal[9] can be incorporated into legal argumentation and therefore become legally relevant consequences. For example, price stability is a consequence of the economic context and is, therefore, *prima facie* an extralegal one. It is, however, clear that in EU law, it is legally relevant pursuant to Article 3(3) of the Treaty of the European Union. This suffices to conclude that, according to EU law, price stability is indeed legally relevant. Thus, we find it analytically appropriate to distinguish three things here: legal consequences *stricto sensu*, *prima facie* extralegal consequences (which are later found to be legal consequences) and extralegal consequences *stricto sensu* (consequences that are later not found to be legally relevant).

In this context, it is illuminating to discuss the idea of adding a *jurisprudential preface* – as proposed by Craswell (1993) and endorsed by Cserne (2011, 50) – to the consequentialist interpretive arguments of mainstream economists of law. The jurisprudential preface would inform the audience that the arguments of mainstream economics of law can be taken into account with the proviso that it remains to be settled what their argumentative power in a court of law is (Craswell 1993, 293). This preface is, indeed, necessary because, as we said earlier, consequentialist arguments are first-order interpretive directives, but second-order directives are needed to solve conflicts between the various first-order interpretive directives. Unfortunately, the jurisprudential preface strategy begs the question "Which economic consequences are legally relevant?"

So, the limit of the economic approach to law which consists in its preference for the first-order interpretive directive from economic consequences requires a second-order interpretive directive which gives preference to this directive over others. Obviously, this second-order directive is in need of a justification.

5. Second limit: Which economic consequences matter? A difficult question for the economists of law

In this section we emphasize an additional limit of the preference for the first-order interpretive directive from economic consequences. The critique we are interested in exploring is that the first-order interpretive directive from economic consequences must be specified with regard to which economic consequences matter. Three reasons justify this emphasis. The first is that in legal

8 Remember that we do not want to deny that other arguments can also be relevant. We simply find it appropriate for the purposes of this chapter to limit the analysis to these forms of legal argument. On the role of textual arguments, see Papayannis (2013, 73–74) and Esposito (2017a, 103–105).

9 See Cserne (2011) and Carbonell (2013) for a discussion and further references on the distinction between legal and extralegal consequences.

practice there is currently wide disagreement on which second-order interpretive directives are justified.[10] Accordingly, with regards to the limit identified in section 4, the economists of law are in good company on this point, and moving to them a critique that applies to legal practice in general would be unfair. Economists of law can plausibly deflect that critique to specialists in legal argumentation. The second reason is that the critique we discuss here and in the following section applies even if a convincing justification for such second-order interpretive directive is given. Suppose in fact that economists of law come up with the justification that, in case of conflict, the argument from economic consequences prevails; they would still owe us an argument about which economic consequences matter. The third reason for the emphasis is that economists with an inclination to pursue positive analysis (in the following, economists with positive inclinations) feel discomfort with problems they perceive as normative, given their reluctance to engage in normative and axiological discourse. Later on, we will argue that legal theory and, in particular, legal inferentialism can help economists in addressing the problem.

The critique we are interested in can be taken as a semantic one: the argument from economic consequences is not clear enough because the meaning of "economic consequences" is ambiguous. This is a serious problem because if it is not clear enough, it cannot be operationalized in a rigorous way. A particularly significant aspect of this problem for the economics of law relates to the meaning of "allocative efficiency". Economists of law take for granted that the market is an allocative efficient institution because it maximizes total welfare. At most, the question is how to measure this welfare. This is a very important question indeed, especially as behavioral research has powerfully challenged standard economic methods based on revealed preferences (cf. Beshears et al. 2008). There is, however, another and perhaps even more fundamental disagreement about the meaning of "allocative efficiency" that any normative economic approach to law must address: namely *whether the maximand is total or consumer welfare.* Recall proposition (2): $(EC_{N1}\ p\ EC_{N2}) \Rightarrow_i (N1\ p\ N2)$. In the context of proposition (2), this disagreement implies that depending on what the maximand is, the content of proposition (2) will be different because the meaning of EC will be different.

The semantic critique is, in other terms, that as there is disagreement on whether the maximand for the efficiency analysis of market allocations is total or consumer welfare, this disagreement implies the formulation of different arguments from economic consequences. In other words, it is unclear whether the animating value (normative DNA) of the (sub)system of law under consideration is total or consumer welfare. Thus, one needs a second-order reason to prefer one maximand over the other. This is a challenging limit for normative economics of law for two reasons. The *first* reason is that both arguments are entitled to the label "argument from economic consequences" because economists use, in fact, one or the other. The *second* reason is that the reliance

10 See, for example, Dolcetti and Ratti (2013).

on economic methods does not offer to the economists of law a specific set of argumentative tools to adjudicate between these two criteria. In fact, the one under consideration is an axiological disagreement, and economists with positive inclinations try to avoid these disagreements as much as possible. This section articulates at greater length the two reasons that make this limit particularly challenging for normative economics of law. The next section will show how the economists of law can rely on legal inferentialism to address this limit.

By now, it should be clear that unless an answer is given to the semantic question about the meaning of "economic consequences" in a legal context, interpretive arguments assuming that the maximand is total welfare beg the question as to whether the outcome would have been different had the maximand been consumer welfare. This is so because the economic consequences that are relevant when deciding what market-related state of affairs is more desirable can be measured either in terms of total welfare or in terms of consumer welfare.

Let us put some flesh to the bones of the first reason making the semantic critique particularly challenging: namely that, from an economic point of view, the maximand can be either total or consumer welfare. The case in favor of this reason made here is limited, perhaps tentative even, but one of us has dealt with it at much greater length elsewhere (see Esposito and De Almeida 2017; Esposito and Grundmann 2017; Esposito 2018, 159–261). Traces of the consumer welfare maximand can be followed along the history of economic thought all the way down to Adam Smith, who wrote that:

> Consumption is the sole end and purpose of all production; and the interest of the producer ought to be attended to, only so far as it may be necessary for promoting that of the consumer. The maxim is so perfectly self-evident, that it would be absurd to attempt to prove it.
>
> (Smith 2007 [1776], 426; see also 85, 162–163, 318)

In recent times, principal-agent theory sometimes takes the welfare of the principal as maximand (see Esposito 2018, 90–93). This line of modeling fits nicely with the idea of consumer sovereignty as articulated by William Hutt, who wrote that:[11]

> [T]he only test of the desirability of a given flow of production is the utility to consumers. . . [while] the sacrifices and discomforts of the producers

11 Hutt (1940, 70). See also Hutt (1936, 311): "in replacing the idea of economic welfare by that of consumers' sovereignty, we have not destroyed the significance of most utility studies. . . . We have, however, introduced a concept which greatly enhances the realism of economic theory. . . . Incidentally, it brings economic science much more vividly into relation with political science". Buchanan, in his homage essay to Hutt, defines consumer sovereignty as the criterion according to which "[v]alue to consumer of final products and services . . . may be used to make the distinction between voluntary agreements that pass the ultimate value test and those that do not" (Buchanan 1988, 6).

(or, for that matter, the happiness and satisfactions they derive from their work) are of no relevance whatever from the point of view of total welfare.

Occasionally, economists of law describe economic models as having total welfare as maximand where they actually have consumer welfare as maximand. For example, Shavell (2007, 156), in the analysis of product liability, writes:

> Let c be the direct production cost per unit of a firm's product, x the cost of care per unit of the product, s the quantity of the product produced and consumed, and u(s) the utility consumers obtain from the product. Then social welfare is $u(s) - s[c+x+p(x)h]$, where the term in brackets is the production cost, cost of care, and expected harm suffered by strangers per unit.

It is, in fact, patently evident that, if the only positive value in Shavell's equation is "the utility consumers obtain", one might well say that Shavell's equation is about consumer rather than total welfare. While limited, these examples show that we can and do model market relations as having the goal of maximizing consumer instead of total welfare. Accordingly, consumer welfare maximization is not a noneconomic goal, as often repeated by competition lawyers with an economic background (see Ayal 2014; Kaplow 2012; Cseres 2007; Monti 2007; Averitt and Lande 1997). This finding leads us to the second reason supporting the relevance of our semantic critique to the unspecified normative appeals to "economic consequences".

The reluctance of many economists to make and justify value judgments is well known. Pareto efficiency, for example, is highly regarded by many because it rests on an ordinalist measurement of preferences. Similarly, the success of Kaldor-Hicks efficiency among economists derives from the possibility of making objective welfare judgments based on the variations of surplus. The philosophers of economics Alexandrova and Haybron (2011, 96; 2013, 169) describe the commitments underpinning mainstream economic research as epistemological and normative minimalism. In short, economists exalt the rigor and parsimony of mathematical modeling and try to minimize their normative commitments. Economists of law, by and large, have long shared and applauded these features of economic research (see, for example, Cooter 2011; Schwartz 2011; Scott 2013; Posner 2015; Rubin 2017).

A problematic implication of this reluctance to make value judgments is that the economists of law sometimes fail to acknowledge their own implicit value judgments (for similar discussions, see Ogus 2010; Geistfeld 2013; Calabresi 2016, 131 ff.). For example, in his celebration of Posner's intellectual production and abilities, Sunstein (2016) writes that:

> Posner's main goal has been to use economic tools to identify the real-world consequences of different legal rules. . . . Posner thinks that courts should reject families' effort to shut down a cement factory if the health benefits turn out to be lower than the total economic costs.

It is evident that there is something wrong with this statement if it fails to distinguish between positive and normative discourse. The statement by Sunstein suggests that the formulation of an argument from economic consequences is part of a positive discourse. However, the previous discussion in this chapter shows clearly that this cannot be right. When referred to judicial reasoning, an argument from economic consequences is an interpretive argument and, as such, is in need of a normative justification. The circumstance that economists of law often fail to acknowledge when they are undertaking axiological commitments or making value judgments implies – rather clearly in our view – that *a fortiori* they are not in a comfortable position to solve such axiological disagreements.

A more instructively puzzling account of the normative foundations of the economics of law is given by Sanchez-Graells. In his clear introduction to the economics of law, Sanchez-Graells (2018, 170) explains that "the normative dimension of the economic analysis of law . . . ultimately rests on the pursuit of economic efficiency as a proxy for the maximization of social welfare", which, he acknowledges, is an axiologically controversial criterion. However, the author also holds that the aims of the economics of law is "ensur[ing] that the legal system is both effective in achieving its goals (which are by no means predetermined by the law and economics approach), and efficient in doing so". Sanchez-Graells makes explicit the tension between the commitment to the second-order preference for interpretive arguments from economic consequences and the aim of pursuing legally determined goals. This tension is more instructive because the opposition is between the normative commitment of the economist of law to an efficient allocation of resources and the social fact that the law pursues goals that might well be different from allocative efficiency.

Going back to the semantic critique according to which one has to justify which economic consequences matter, applied in particular to the meaning of "allocative efficiency", we hope the reader sees now clearly how strong a limit it is for normative economics of law. In fact, if economists of law want to perform positive instead of normative analyses and, at the same time, wish to formulate interpretive arguments from economic consequences, they must find a positive way to address our semantic critique. Legal inferentialism offers a solution, as the next section explains.

6. How legal inferentialism can help economists with value choices

The previous section has articulated the limit for normative economics represented by the semantic critique to the argument from economic consequences. This first-order interpretive directive begs the question of which economic consequences matter. At the same time, it was seen that the significance of this limit derives in particular from the reluctance of some economists to address and justify their axiological assumptions with normative discourse.

This section proposes to economists of law to adopt legal inferentialism as a method for the analysis of legal discourse. We are confident that many economists can find legal inferentialism appealing in light of their commitment to positive analysis and their reluctance to engage in normative discourse to justify their axiological assumptions. To them, finding that a piece of law has in fact such-and-such animating value (normative DNA) should be a good enough reason to incorporate this animating value in the normative assumptions of their analysis. More precisely, our proposal is (a) to perform an inferentialist analysis of legal discourse to identify the axiological assumptions that fit better with the reasons given in legal argumentation and then (b) to use the results of this inquiry to justify the selection of one version of the argument from economic consequences. The justification so offered relies on a set of social facts – the reasons found in certain legal documents – which can be rigorously analyzed with an inferentialist approach. Note that this method can be applied to both axiological and descriptive assumptions. An example of descriptive assumption is whether EU consumer law takes the view that consumers are fully or boundedly rational. It is, however, for axiological assumptions that legal inferentialism is particularly appealing to economists of law. As noted in section 1, the authority claimed by law implies the normativity of legal reasons. Accordingly, the animating values (normative DNA) of the law are not mere social facts but reasons given in a practice claiming authority. Those accepting this claim to authority will find these animating values to be parameters of correct behavior. Those rejecting this claim have a better understanding of the target of their critique.

Relying on legal inferentialism, economists of law can formulate a specific argument from economic consequences and justify that certain economic consequences, but not others, matter. This can be done by showing that those economic consequences matter within the legal materials applicable to a certain behavior. They are, in other words, part of the animating values (normative DNA) of that law and behavior. In this way, economists delegate to the legal system the selection of the axiological assumptions and focus on the identification of the best means to achieve the legally given goal. Before illustrating how legal inferentialism helps economists with an account of value choices, a few additional words on legal inferentialism are advisable, especially for the reader unfamiliar with this approach.

The general idea of *legal inferentialism* is to determine legal content in terms of inferential relations between terms, expressions and sentences used in legal practice (see especially Canale and Tuzet 2005, 2007). In particular, the ascription of meaning to a legal provision can be seen as the act of assessing the *correctness conditions* of the use of legal terms or expressions that figure in the provision. Determining what a legal expression means is to fix under what conditions the expression is correctly used in the linguistic practice which is called legal argumentation and adjudication. As far as an inferential approach to content is concerned, these conditions have an inferential nature and can be made explicit in legal argument: the meaning of a legal expression can be seen as the set of its correct inferential relations in a discursive practice. Let us now conceive of legal argumentation and interpretation in inferentialist terms. In inferentialist terms, legal argumentation and interpretation have to deal with the inferential relations of legal terms, expressions and sentences and, more in particular, with the *deontic statuses* expressing such content in a scorekeeping practice. These deontic statuses determine the inferences that can be treated as correct in the context of legal argumentation and interpretation. For example, if in a criminal case the prosecution is committed to the claim that "intent" means also *oblique* intention (namely, unwanted but foreseen consequences of an act; see Williams 1987), this commitment will become an entitlement only when, given the relevant arguments, the decision-maker so establishes in her decision. In legal practice, interpretive arguments are reasons given to justify the transformation of the deontic status of an interpretive statement from a commitment to an entitlement. Recall proposition (2): $(EC_{N1}\ p\ EC_{N2}) \Rightarrow_i (N1\ p\ N2)$. Proposition (2) means that because the economic consequences of N1 are preferable to those of N2, N1 is a preferable interpretation of the relevant legal texts. In inferentialist terms, the function of proposition (2) is to justify the transformation of the deontic status of the preference of N1 over N2 from a commitment to an entitlement. If the argument is accepted, the deontic status of N1 becomes an entitlement. At that point, one is entitled to consider N1 the applicable legal norm within the relevant legal context.

Legal inferentialism can be used to address the semantic critique we moved to the argument from economic consequences without requiring economists with positive inclinations to engage in the type of normative discourse they are uncomfortable with. To do so, legal practice becomes a source of evidence economists can rely upon to justify their axiological assumptions and determine the meaning of "economic consequences" in a given context. More precisely, economists can use legal reasons to transform the deontic status of alternative axiological assumptions from a commitment to an entitlement. This inferential move can be represented as follows:

(3) $LR \Rightarrow_v EC1\ p\ EC2$

In proposition (3), LR means legal reasons, $\Rightarrow_v$ a value implication between these reasons and certain economic consequences, EC1 and EC2 are two possible meanings of "economic consequences". For example, EC1 stands for consumer welfare and EC2 for total welfare. Accordingly, proposition (3) expresses the claim that because of the social fact that the legally relevant economic consequences are those about consumer welfare, economists have a reason to prefer consumer welfare over total welfare as an axiological assumption in their efficiency analyses.

To address the semantic critique, an inferentialist approach walks the following steps: (1) identify a legal *explanandum*, (2) operationalize the disagreement about it in various competing *explanantia* and (3) establish the inferential criteria for deciding which *explanans* has superior explanatory power. The relevance of these steps for addressing the semantic critique becomes apparent once we articulate their relation with proposition (3). Going through these steps gives to the economist the legal reasons needed to select one meaning of "economic consequences": namely the one that fits better with the relevant legal reasons.

The disagreement we focus upon is whether the maximand of allocative efficiency is consumer or total welfare. In other words, we oppose the consumer-welfare hypothesis to the traditional total-welfare one. Given space constraints, we offer a very limited inferential analysis. The warrant provided by the analysis to the competing efficiency hypotheses is thus of limited comprehensiveness.[12] Albeit limited, the analysis is sufficient for our illustrative purposes. First, we select a small but significant *explanandum* (step 1), then we articulate two competing *explanantia*[13] that operationalize the competing efficiency hypotheses (step 2) and we finally discuss why one *explanans* has superior explanatory power (step 3). Building on the content of section 5, one of the competing *explanantia* has total welfare as its maximand, and the other has consumer welfare as maximand.

The *explanandum* is the holding of the Court of Justice of the European Union (CJEU) that unfair terms are not binding on consumers in EU law and the reasoning that justifies this holding.

The two competing *explanantia* have to do with the type of reasons given in legal discourse to justify such consumer law. A line of reasoning consistent with the total-welfare hypothesis sees consumers in need of protection instrumentally. When consumers are not protected, total welfare is reduced. Thus, the harm to consumers matters only in so far as it is of consequence for the reduction of total welfare. In contrast, a line of reasoning consistent with the consumer-welfare hypothesis considers the welfare[14] (or interest) of consumers to be the value justifying consumer protection. The reason for protecting consumers is that they are not able to maximize their own welfare in market relations. According to the consumer-welfare hypothesis, the harm to consumers is relevant without any further need to inquire into the effects of the law on total welfare. These two lines of reasoning can be expressed in two *explanantia* (EX), one based on the consumer-welfare hypothesis (EX1), the other on the total-welfare hypothesis (EX2).

> (EX1): Consumer law is a means to the end of maximizing consumer welfare. Accordingly, consumers ought to be protected only in so far as their protection contributes to the maximization of consumer welfare. In particular, distributive concerns between the parties have justificatory power when they vary consumer welfare.

12 We use the concept of warrant and comprehensiveness consistently with Haack's foundherentist theory of evidence. See Haack (2014, especially 1–26 and 47–77).

13 At least six other competing *explanantia* are useful for the inferentialist analysis aimed to assess the explanatory power of these two efficiency hypotheses with regards to legal argumentation. See Esposito (2018, 169–178).

14 As noted in section 5, the opposition we are considering is compatible with any number of theories about what constitutes welfare.

> (EX2): Consumer law is a means to the end of maximizing total welfare. Accordingly, consumers ought to be protected only in so far as their protection contributes to the maximization of total welfare. In particular, distributive concerns between the parties do not have justificatory power unless they vary total welfare.

The relevant legal reasons can be found in the Court's account of the prohibition of unfair contract terms in consumer contracts set by Directive 93/13/EEC.[15] The account is based on the concept of consumer weakness, which constitutes a recurrent element of the reasoning of settled case law of the CJEU:[16]

> [I]t is settled case-law that the system of protection introduced by the directive is based on the idea that the consumer is in a weak position vis-à-vis the seller or supplier, as regards both his bargaining power and his level of knowledge . . . As regards that weaker position, Article 6(1) of Directive 93/13 provides that unfair terms are not binding on the consumer. As is apparent from the case-law, that is a mandatory provision which aims to replace the formal balance which the contract establishes between the rights and obligations of the parties with an effective balance which re-establishes equality between them.

Some remarks are advisable. First of all, note the clear consequentialist nature of this reasoning. The weakness of consumers causes the unfairness of contractual terms, which implies that the balance between the rights and obligations of the parties establishes an unequal relation between them. Perhaps more importantly, in this argument from the CJEU, the weakness of consumers is connected to two causes of market failure: unequal bargaining power and access to information. Accordingly, this reasoning is rather friendly to economic language, which is incorporated into the explanation of why consumers are in a position of weakness according to EU law. On these grounds, the CJEU explains that to protect consumers unfair terms are not binding on them. Finally, the reference to the equality between the parties can be rightfully taken as a commitment to some idea of equality in exchange. For current purposes, this idea expresses a concern for the

15 Council Directive 93/13/EEC of 5 April 1993 on unfair terms in consumer contracts.

16 *Banco Popular Español SA v Maria Teodolinda Rivas Quichimbo and Wilmar Edgar Cun Pérez and Banco de Valencia SA v Joaquín Valldeperas Tortosa and María Ángeles Miret Jaume*, Joined Cases C-537/12 and C-116/13 (Order), 14 November 2013, ECLI:EU:C:2013:759, [39–40]. *Ex pluribus*, see also: *Océano Grupo Editorial SA v Roció Murciano Quintero* (C-240/98) and *Salvat Editores SA v José M. Sánchez Alcón Prades* (C-241/98), *José Luis Copano Badillo* (C-242/98), *Mohammed Berroane* (C-243/98) and *Emilio Viñas Feliú* (C-244/98), Joined cases C-240/98 to C-244/98, 27 June 2000, ECLI:EU:C:2000:346, [25, 29]; *Elisa María Mostaza Claro v Centro Móvil Milenium SL*, C-168/05, 26 October 2006, ECLI:EU:C:2006:675, [25]; and *Pavel Dumitraş and Mioara Dumitraş v BRD Groupe Société Générale – sucursala Satu Mare*, C-534/15 (Order), 14 September 2016, ECLI:EU:C:2016:700, [29]. On the reasoning of the CJEU, see Bengoetxea 1993; Sarmiento 2012; Beck 2013; Sankari 2013.

distribution of benefits and costs between the weak consumer and the strong seller or supplier, which points in favor of the consumer-welfare *explanans*.

So, the relevant meaning of "economic consequences" is given by the set of inferences that justify, in the Court's view, the prohibition of unfair contract terms. For the sake of analytical clarity, the CJEU's argument can be broken down into three claims:

(CJEU1): an unfair term is caused by a market failure;
(CJEU2): an unfair term makes consumers worse off in comparison to a fair term;
(CJEU3): the consequence of making consumers worse off in comparison to a fair term is the justification for unfair terms not being binding on consumers.

Which *explanans* fits better with this justification of unfair terms regulation between EX1 and EX2? It is rather clear that EX1, the consumer-welfare *explanans*, fits better. Consistently with EX1 and the consumer-welfare hypothesis, the reason given for protecting consumers is that they are not in a position to adequately protect their own interests in market relations. This is one of the relevant inferences. More precisely, EX1 fits perfectly with CJEU1 because the latter places the market mechanism in a causal relation with the fairness of contractual terms. Additionally, the idea that there is a distributive concern in favor of consumers, which is a very distinctive feature of EX1 *vis-à-vis* EX2, is expressed by CJEU2. Finally, CJEU3 is just an instance of proposition (2): $(EC_{N1}\ p\ EC_{N2}) \Rightarrow_i (N1\ p\ N2)$. With respect to CJEU3, EC stands for the consequences of an unfair contractual term for consumers, N1 is the norm according to which unfair terms are not binding on consumers and N2 is the norm according to which these terms are binding on consumers. Accordingly, CJEU3 expresses the inference that making unfair terms nonbinding is justified by the positive economic consequences for consumers it brings about. In light of what was mentioned earlier, the consumer-welfare hypothesis does not need any additional consideration to conclude that it explains the relevant legal materials and their inferential justification given by the Court.

In contrast, for the total-welfare hypothesis to provide an explanation of CJEU1–3 is much more difficult. Taken by itself, CJEU1 can be explained by EX2. The fact that the concept of market failure is connected to the justification of the protection of consumers implies an understanding of fairness consistent with the goal of maximizing total welfare. Fairness is thus instrumentally valuable for the benefits it brings in total-welfare terms (for a clear articulation of this view, see Friedman 1980). But the problem becomes apparent when we consider also CJEU2. The reasoning of the CJEU provides no ground for considering the protection of consumers instrumental to the maximization of total welfare. More precisely, it is hard to reconcile CJEU2 with EX2. Yet this instrumental connection is central to the total-welfare hypothesis. Indeed, this connection could be posited, but the evidence does not support it. In fact, to fit well with EX2, the Court's reasoning should have been more like the following:

> (CJEU2′): an unfair term makes consumers worse off more than it benefits producers in comparison to a fair term.

Note, however, that the Court has not asserted CJEU2′, so the restriction of the concept of an unfair term expressed by the clause "more than it benefits producers" is nowhere to be found. EX2 incurs in the same difficulty with regards to CJEU3. Also in this case, the clause "more than it benefits producers" is needed for providing an appropriate explanation of the Court's argument. The deficiency of the explanatory power of EX2 in relation to CJEU2 and CJEU3 is particularly significant in light of the fact that in CJEU1 the Court has connected the concept of market failure to the concept of unfair contract terms. This connection makes very implausible the view that there is an implicit clause as the aforementioned one in the argument of the Court. Whether it is so implausible to be unacceptable is beyond the scope of this chapter as it is not relevant for current purposes (see Esposito 2018, especially 241–246).

The conclusion of this inferential analysis is that the evidence supports the consumer-welfare hypothesis more than the traditional, total-welfare one. In other terms, the maximand EU consumer law is interested into in light of the evidence considered is consumer welfare. Accordingly, the analysis confers to the consumer-welfare hypothesis an entitlement in relation to its explanation of CJEU1–3.

This establishes the relevant meaning of "economic consequences". As promised, legal inferentialism thus offers a way to address the semantic critique without having to engage in axiological discourse directly. Legal inferentialism gives to economists some legal reasons for assuming consumer welfare as the maximand of their efficiency analysis of consumer contract terms in the European Union, since the argument of the CJEU is better explained by the consumer-welfare hypothesis than by the total-welfare one. These reasons are grounded in the capacity legal inferentialism has of uncovering the animating values (normative DNA) of the law. To the extent one accepts the authority of law, these animating values are normatively appealing. If one does not accept the authority of law, the same finding can be critically engaged with in the context of axiological discourse.

7. Conclusions

This last section recapitulates the flow of the chapter, what it did and did not claim and concludes with some remarks on future research. The starting point of the analysis has been the way in which economists analyze norms. In this regard, section 2 pointed out that economists conceive of norms as a means to bring about economic consequences. Hence, norms are evaluated in their capacity to bring these economic consequences into existence.[17] In section 3, we then moved to legal theory to see what insights can be collected there about the relation between norms and economic consequences. The standard model of legal argumentation conceives of norms as the major premise of a syllogism, with the facts being the minor premise, and the conclusion being the application of the norm to the facts. These premises are justified by way of specific arguments. The arguments justifying norms are interpretive arguments, and they are built in the light of first- and second-order interpretive directives. In this context, it was shown that economists formulate interpretive arguments based on the economic consequences of norms. These arguments are a type of argument from consequences, the argument from economic consequences.

At this point, two limits of the economists' eulogy of the argument from economic consequences were pointed out in sections 4 and 5, respectively. The first limit is that the argument from economic consequences is just one of a variety of first-order interpretive arguments, so that a second-order argument justifying the preference for this argument is needed. For various reasons articulated in the text, we left this issue open and addressed a second problem: namely which economic consequences matter for the formulation of an argument from economic consequences. We stressed the significance of this problem in particular with regards to the maximand to be used in the efficiency analysis of market relations. While normally this maximand is assumed to be total welfare, it might well be consumer welfare. These two alternative maximands lead to two alternative meanings of "allocative efficiency". This ambiguity in meaning animates our semantic critique of the argument.

Section 6 showed how legal inferentialism addresses the semantic critique. This proposal is of particular interest for those economists who prefer not to give a normative justification of value choices. Legal inferentialism compares the explanatory power of the total- and consumer-welfare hypotheses with regards to legal argumentation in a given context. For illustrative purposes, we focused on the argument given by the CJEU to explain why unfair terms are not binding on consumers in EU law. We found that the consumer-welfare hypothesis has superior explanatory power. This finding entitles economists to assume consumer welfare as the maximand in their efficiency analyses of unfair contract terms without the need to provide a normative justification for this value choice. Instead, they can simply say that, consistently with the social fact that this part of EU law fits better with the consumer-welfare hypothesis, they assume consumer welfare as maximand.

In light of what was mentioned earlier, we observe also the following. First, the issue of what economic consequences are legally relevant has important social and legal implications, so it deserves more attention by legal scholars. Second, and conversely, "economic consequences" does not necessarily mean

17 In section 2, this view was named "foundational scheme of an economic approach to law" and expressed with proposition (1): $(C \Rightarrow_n S) \Rightarrow_f EC$.

what mainstream economists think it does. This fact requires more attention by lawyers but also by economists in the choice and justification of the premises of their analyses, arguments etc. This recommendation is particularly important because a mainstream approach can both shift the burden of persuasion to a subjacent one and also claim to have explained a phenomenon by advancing poor explanations. Third, choosing total welfare or consumer welfare as the maximand to evaluate the economic consequences of the law does not challenge in any meaningful way the economists' technique of analysis. It simply changes the maximand.

After having summarized what we claim and why we think it is important, let us emphasize what we do *not* claim. We do not claim that we have established once and for all that it is true that EU consumer law is about consumer welfare maximization. The analysis does not warrant this claim for two main reasons. First, Directive 93/13 is just one component of EU consumer law. Albeit an important one, the analysis has to have a much broader scope to be plausibly extendable to EU consumer law, let alone EU law or consumer law in general. Moreover, we have focused only on the concept of consumer weakness and its relation to the protection of consumers against unfair terms, thereby ignoring many other aspects of the application of Directive 93/13. Second, and perhaps more importantly, the claim is comparative between the total- and consumer-welfare hypotheses. It might well be that a different hypothesis would have superior explanatory power. Additionally, we do not claim that any argument about economic consequences is about consumer welfare. We have simply explored the possibility that in a specific context – EU consumer law – it is. Third and finally, the normative appeal of our inferentialist analysis should not be misunderstood. The analysis identifies the animating values (mapping the "normative DNA") of the *explanandum.* Nothing more, but also nothing less. This normative DNA can be used for different purposes. If one accepts the authority of law, finding that, in a context, the relevant economic consequences are those about consumer welfare is a normative reason to take variations in consumer welfare as a parameter of correct behavior. If one does not accept the authority of law, the same finding can be critically engaged with in order to show that the relevant economic consequences ought to be about something else.

Let us now conclude by pointing out directions for further research. In this regard, we find one consideration particularly significant. We have seen that the explanatory project started by Posner in the 70s of the last century has progressively become unfashionable. However, it is an important research program for legal scholarship. Bearing in mind that moral explanations of legal discourse are customarily offered and debated by legal scholars, we do not see why it should be any different for economic explanations – especially if one considers normative economics as falling within moral philosophy. Additionally, we have shown that if the explanatory hypotheses are spelled out in enough detail, legal argumentation becomes a source of evidence that economists might also want to consider in their theory-building processes. This will ultimately increase the realism of economic analyses and reduce the irritation of doctrinal legal scholars for economic approaches to law. But, more crucially in our view, an explanatory economic project of the content of law firmly grounded in legal inferentialism might well lead to novel and significant contributions to both legal and economic research.

References

Alchourrón, C. E., and E. Bulygin. 1971. *Normative Systems*. Wien: Springer.

Alexandrova, A., and D. M. Haybron. 2011. "High-Fidelity Economics." In J. B. Davis and D. W. Hands (eds.), *The Elgar Companion to Recent Economic Methodology*. Cheltenham: Edward Elgar, pp. 94–120.

Alexandrova, A., and D. M. Haybron. 2013. "Paternalism in Economics." In C. Coons and M. Weber (eds.), *Paternalism: Theory and Practice*. Cambridge: Cambridge University Press, pp. 157–177.

Alexy, R. 1978. *Theorie der juristischen Argumentation: Die Theorie des rationalen Diskurses als Theorie der juristischen Begründung*. Frankfurt am Main: Suhrkamp.

Averitt, N. W., and R. H. Lande. 1997. "Consumer Sovereignty: A Unified Theory of Antitrust and Consumer Protection Law." *Antitrust Law Journal* 65: 713–756.

Ayal, A. 2014. *Fairness in Antitrust: Protecting the Strong from the Weak*. Oxford: Hart Publishing.

Beccaria, C. 1764. *Dei Delitti e Delle Pene*. www.filosofico.net/index024.htm, last accessed November 1, 2017.

Beck, G. 2013. *The Legal Reasoning of the Court of Justice of the EU*. Oxford: Hart Publishing.

Bengoetxea, J. 1993. *The Legal Reasoning of the European Court of Justice: Towards a European Jurisprudence*. Oxford: Clarendon Press.

Beshears, J., J. J. Choi, D. Laibson, and B. C. Madrian. 2008. "How Are Preferences Revealed?" *Journal of Public Economics* 92: 1787–1794.

Brandom, R. B. 1994. *Making It Explicit: Reasoning, Representing, and Discursive Commitment*. Cambridge, MA: Harvard University Press.

Brandom, R. B. 2000. *Articulating Reasons: An Introduction to Inferentialism*. Cambridge, MA: Harvard University Press.

Bridgeman, C. 2009. "Contracts as Plans." *University of Illinois Law Review*: 341–401.

Buchanan, J. M. 1988. "Economists and the Gains from Trade." *Managerial and Decision Economics* 9: 5–12.

Calabresi, G. 1970. *The Cost of Accidents: A Legal and Economic Analysis*. New Haven: Yale University Press.

Calabresi, G. 1983. "The New Economic Analysis of Law: Scholarship, Sophistry, or Self-Indulgence." *Proceedings of the British Academy* 68: 85–108.

Calabresi, G. 2016. *The Future of Law and Economics Essays in Reform and Recollection*. New Haven: Yale University Press.

Canale, D., and G. Tuzet. 2005. "Interpretive Scorekeeping." In R. Guastini and P. Comanducci (eds.), *Analisi e diritto 2005*. Turin: Giappichelli, pp. 81–97.

Canale, D., and G. Tuzet. 2007. "On Legal Inferentialism: Toward a Pragmatics of Semantic Content in Legal Interpretation?" *Ratio Juris* 20: 32–44.

Canale, D., and G. Tuzet. 2008. "On the Contrary: Inferential Analysis and Ontological Assumptions of the a Contrario Argument." *Informal Logic* 28: 31–43.

Canale, D., and G. Tuzet. 2009. "The a Simili Argument: An Inferentialist Setting." *Ratio Juris* 22: 499–509.

Canale, D., and G. Tuzet. 2010. "Inferring the Intention: Or, What Law the Legislature Could Have Intended to Make." *Dignitas* 48–49: 254–272.

Carbonell, F. 2013. "Reasoning by Consequences: Applying Different Argumentation Structures to the Analysis of Consequentialist Reasoning in Judicial Decisions." In C. Dahlman and E. Feteris (eds.), *Legal Argumentation Theory: Cross-Disciplinary Perspectives*, Dordrecht: Springer, pp. 1–19.

Cooter, R. D. 2011. "Maturing into Normal Science: The Effect of Empirical Legal Studies on Law and Economics." *University of Illinois Law Review*: 1475–1483.

Craswell, R. 1993. "Default Rules, Efficiency, and Prudence." *Southern California Interdisciplinary Law Journal* 3: 289–302.

Cseres, K. 2007. "The Controversies of the Consumer Welfare Standard." *The Competition Law Review* 3: 121–173.

Cserne, P. 2011. "Consequence-Based Arguments in Legal Reasoning: A Jurisprudential Preface to Law and Economics." In K. Mathis (ed.), *Efficiency, Sustainability, and Justice to Future Generations*. Berlin: Springer, pp. 31–54.

Demsetz, H. 1969. "Information and Efficiency: Another Viewpoint." *The Journal of Law & Economics* 12: 1–22.

Dolcetti, A., and G. B. Ratti. 2013. "Legal Disagreements and the Dual Nature of Law." In W. J. Waluchow and S. Sciaraffa (eds.), *Philosophical Foundations of the Nature of Law*. Oxford: Oxford University Press, pp. 301–321.

Esposito, F. 2013. "Alcune Note su di un approccio economico ordinalista allo studio del diritto." *Ars Interpretandi* (2): 151–183.

Esposito, F. 2016. "Efficienza paretiana ed efficienza allocativa: Considerazioni teoriche per giuseconomisti." *Materiali per una storia della cultura giuridica* (1): 225–236.

Esposito, F. 2017a. "Alcune note sui disaccordi teorico-interdisciplinari del diritto con l'economia." *Rivista Internazionale di Filosofia del Diritto*: 91–177.

Esposito, F. 2017b. "How the Behavioural Turn in Law and Economics Vindicates the New Haven School." *Oeconomia* 7(3): 375–406.

Esposito, F. 2018. *Law and Economics United in Diversity: Minimalism, Fairness, and Consumer Welfare in EU Antitrust and Consumer Law*. Fiesole: European University Institute.

Esposito, F., and L. De Almeida. 2017. "A Shocking Truth for Law and Economics: Consumer Welfare Explains the Internal Market for Electricity Better Than Total Welfare." In K. Mathis and B. Huber (eds.), *Energy Law and Economics*. Cham: Springer, pp. 101–133.

Esposito, F., and S. Grundmann. 2017. "Investor-Consumer or Overall Welfare: Searching for the Paradigm of Recent Reforms in Financial Services Contracts." *EUI Law Department Research Paper Series* 5.

Friedman, D. 1980. "In Defense of Thomas Aquinas and the Just Price." *History of Political Economy* 12(2): 234–242.

Garoupa, N., C. Gómez Ligüerre, and L. Mélon. 2017. *Legal Origins and the Efficiency Dilemma*. London: Routledge.

Geistfeld, M. A. 2013. "Fault Lines in the Positive Economic Analysis of Tort Law." In J. H. Arlen (ed.), *Research Handbook on the Economics of Torts*. Cheltenham: Edward Elgar, pp. 149–168.

Haack, S. 2014. *Evidence Matters: Science, Proof, and Truth in the Law*. Cambridge: Cambridge University Press.

Hutt, W. H. 1936. *Economists and the Public Interest: A Study of Competition and Opinion*. London: Jonathan Cape.

Hutt, W. H. 1940. "The Concept of Consumers' Sovereignty." *The Economic Journal* 50: 66–77.

Kaplow, L. 2012. "On the Choice of Welfare Standards in Competition Law." In D. Zimmer (ed.), *The Goals of Competition Law*. Cheltenham, UK: Edward Elgar, pp. 3–26.

Kraus, J. S. 2001. "Reconciling Autonomy and Efficiency in Contract Law: The Vertical Integration Strategy." *Philosophical Issues* 11: 420–441.

MacCormick, N., and R. S. Summers, eds. 1991. *Interpreting Statutes: A Comparative Study*. Aldershot: Dartmouth.

Monti, G. 2007. *EC Competition Law*. Cambridge: Cambridge University Press.

Navarro, P. E., and J. L. Rodríguez. 2014. *Deontic Logic and Legal Systems*. Cambridge: Cambridge University Press.

Ogus, A. 2010. "Law and Economics in the Legal Academy, or, What I Should Have Said to Discipulus." *University of Toronto Law Journal* 60: 169–175.

Papayannis, D. M. 2013. "Spiegazione funzionale e analisi concettuale: Sull'incidenza dei modelli economici nello studio della pratica giuridica." *Ars Interpretandi* (2): 69–109.

Posner, R. A. 1979. "Some Uses and Abuses of Economics in Law." *The University of Chicago Law Review* 46: 281–306.

Posner, R. A. 2015. "Norms and Values in the Economic Approach to Law." In A. N. Hatzis and N. Mercuro (eds.), *Law and Economics: Philosophical Issues and Fundamental Questions*. London: Routledge, pp. 1–15.

Raz, J. 1979. *The Authority of Law: Essays on Law and Morality*. Oxford: Clarendon Press.

Rubin, E. L. 2017. "From Coherence to Effectiveness: A Legal Methodology for the Modern World." In R. van Gestel, H-W. Micklitz, and E. L. Rubin (eds.), *Rethinking Legal Scholarship*. Cambridge: Cambridge University Press, pp. 310–350.

Sanchez-Graells, A. 2018. "Economic Analysis of Law, or Economically-Informed Legal Research." In D. Watkins and M. Burton (eds.), *Research Methods in Law*, 2nd ed. London: Routledge, pp. 170–193.

Sankari, S. 2013. *European Court of Justice Legal Reasoning in Context*. Amsterdam: Europa Law Publishing.

Sarmiento, D. 2012. "The Silent Lamb and the Deaf Wolves: Constitutional Pluralism, Preliminary References and the Role of Silent Judgments in EU Law." In M. Avbelj and J. Komárek (eds.), *Constitutional Pluralism in the European Union and Beyond*. Oxford: Hart, pp. 285–317.

Schwartz, A. 2011. "Two Culture Problems in Law and Economics." *University of Illinois Law Review*: 1531–1549.

Scott, R. E. 2013. "The Promise and the Peril of Relational Contract Theory." In J. Braucher, J. Kidwell, and W. C. Whitford (eds.), *Revisiting the Contracts Scholarship of Stewart Macaulay. On the Empirical and the Lyrical*. Oxford: Hart, pp. 105–139.

Shavell, S. 2007. "Liability for Accidents." In M. Polinsky and S. Shavell (eds.), *Handbook of Law and Economics*, vol. 1. Amsterdam: Elsevier, pp. 139–182.

Smith, A. 2007. *An Inquiry into the Nature and Causes of The Wealth of Nations*. Hampshire: Harriman House (original edn. 1776).

Sunstein, C. R. 2016. "Listen, Economists!" *New York Review of Books*, November 10, 2016, www.nybooks.com/articles/2016/11/10/listen-economists/, last accessed June 15, 2018.

Tedeschi, G. 1979. "The Law of Laws." *Israel Law Review* 14: 145–163.

von Wright, G. H. 1963. *Norm and Action. A Logical Enquiry*. London: Routledge & Kegan Paul.

Williams, G. 1987. "Oblique Intention." *Cambridge Law Journal* 46: 417–438.

Wilson, G., and S. Shpall. 2012. "Action." *Stanford Encyclopedia of Philosophy*, https://plato.stanford.edu/entries/action/#ExpAct, last accessed January 30, 2019.

Wróblewski, J. 1992. *The Judicial Application of Law*. Dordrecht: Kluwer.

8 Is economic analysis of law relevant in Italian case law?

Some remarks about consequentialism and equity

Silvia Zorzetto

Introduction

The aim of this chapter is to outline whether and to what extent judges in European civil law systems, such as Italian judges, are familiar with the economic analysis of law (hereinafter, "EAL"). In more precise terms, the key issue of the analysis is whether and how judges rely on EAL in adjudication and whether and how EAL influences the way judges work and reach their decisions.

The method applied herein belongs to the analytical jurisprudence approach.[1] This chapter provides a meta-jurisprudential description and a critical clarification.[2] It does not argue either in favor of or against the use of EAL in legal reasoning, nor does it propose a model of adjudication.[3]

As will emerge over the course of the chapter, contemporary Italian case law may be deemed paradigmatic of a widespread approach which is not limited to Italy in particular, nor to the legal tradition of civil law.[4] The majority of the selected examples belong to private law, in particular to contract law and torts, mostly the latter. Together with property law, these are two classical fields of investigation in EAL. In short, I am confident that the case law considered in these pages is instructive beyond a specific legal system or area, providing a significant indication of the role of EAL in courts.

Needless to say, the extent of economic analysis of law is broad and without clear-cut boundaries. Extensive literature has also been advanced to investigate its presumptive origins and its ample developments throughout the nineties.[5] Many scholars and legal philosophers have also noted that EAL not only

1 For an introduction, see, e.g., (Postema 2011; Coleman, Himma and Shapiro 2004).

2 From a methodological standpoint, an essential reference of the present essay is found in Schauer (1999–2000).

3 As in every analysis, this one at least implicitly relies on a model of adjudication, which is a preliminary condition to identifying the object of any analysis. About this topic, see Chapter 7.

4 Concerning the European legal systems and the classical fields of contracts and torts from an extensive and broad body of literature see, e.g., Schäfer and Ott (2005) and Mathis (2014).

5 The literature is plentiful; for instance, see the recent history by Butler and Klick (2018); concerning the numerous methodologies and different approaches that EAL comprises, see, e.g., (Ulen 2017; Kornhauser 2017; Parisi 2005).

examines the intersection of law and economics, but also deals with a multitude of studies concerned with ethics and meta-ethics, political theory and general philosophy.[6] However, I think that a review of such vast and diverse schools of thought and trends around the world is not necessary for the purposes of this investigation. As the analysis will show, usually the references to EAL in Italian case law are, in effect, so generic and indefinite that they do not reveal any correlation with a specific tendency of EAL.

Here are the ideas I wish to discuss.

Firstly, although legal scholars mention EAL quite frequently, this approach – as developed and applied by its supporters – is still generally unknown to judges. Ever since its origin, EAL has moved beyond national legal boundaries, eventually becoming a worldwide movement. Without doubt, it has been a factor in the macroscopic pattern of "legal migration", "legal transplantation" and, thus, of "legal globalization", which has been increasingly relevant in recent decades.[7] However, notwithstanding the global diffusion of its doctrines, it is dubious that EAL has a substantial impact on adjudication. In fact, interaction and dialogue between jurists and economists is still uncommon in many legal systems, the Italian one included.

Secondly, this analysis tests the hypothesis that EAL is an essential vehicle for bringing economic ideas and concepts into judicial discourse and concludes that this is not the case. In fact, the vast majority of references to EAL in courts appears mainly incidental and peripheral: that is to say, they do not appear to play a determining or conclusive role in the legal reasoning that justifies the decisions.

It is instructive to recall some of the factors that contribute to explain why courts sometimes appear inhospitable to economic reasoning (Breyer 2009, F125). First and foremost, of course, we find the rule of law doctrine, which leads judges to an institutional preference for the administration of the law as an autonomous domain governed by certain predetermined rules. Then there is a certain tunnel vision present among both economists and lawyers that inhibits each from taking full account of the other's discipline and relative differences. This second point more directly explains why economic reasoning does not play a greater role in legal decisions (Breyer 2009, F125). Third, it is typical of lawyers and judges to embrace a conservative attitude and distrust toward novelty, especially whenever the "transplanted" approaches, such as the economic ones in our case, are contested or not firmly established in their own field. Fourth, the confidence of judges in EAL normally fluctuates because "economic reasoning does not automatically welcome the use of bright-line rules": that is to say, "it often concerns gradations with consequences, while judges seek clear distinction in kind" (Breyer 2009, F125). In addition, economic reasoning is

6 For a general introductory overview, see, e.g., Hatzis and Mercuro (2015); White (2008, 2015); Zamir and Medina (2010).

7 I refer to the insightful analysis of Schauer (2000).

thoroughly complicated and costly if we consider not only initial training and knowledge, but also empirical and social surveys, which in each case are fundamental for construing the relevant, feasible economic models and calculi. A further reason for the mistrust of judges in EAL includes the misconception that it involves an insidious, unpalatable ideology (Coleman 1984, 661). This objection is present in an overwhelming manner in many cases. But we should consider that no legal method can be free from ideologies, and, as mentioned, EAL is one of the methodologies whose philosophical, ethical and political assumptions and premises have been rather extensively and critically examined.

Thirdly, in several cases, the function of references to EAL or economics appears to be to hide the real line of reasoning, which is based on a variety of reasons that do not pertain to economic assessments. This does not mean that judges neglect economic considerations, and the same may be said of lawyers. Generally, there is close attention to economic issues in legal processes and in the practice. Economic concerns are likely to be among the most considered, albeit implicit, motivators of adjudication. What is worth noting is that references and arguments related to costs, benefits, welfare, efficiency, externalities etc. are not usually formed into refined economic models and theories. They rather entail teleological or consequentialist thought and take, therefore, the form of consequentialist arguments. In other words, the analysis of case law supports the hypothesis that most of the arguments ascribed to EAL are nothing more than a subset of the group of arguments based on and/or oriented toward consequentialism, which is and has always been deeply embedded in legal thinking.[8]

As a final point, the application of EAL reveals the extent to which judges generally employ eclectic justifications, pursuing both legal and policy goals.[9] In this respect, although the judicial use of EAL is usually combined with a variety of other methodologies, the consequentialist approach often proves to be prevalent, so a consequentialist approach often underpins references to EAL. In many cases, however, the final decision does not seem to rest on consequentialism[10] but on an equitable basis, involving a general balance of values.[11] Sometimes EAL in the law in action – far from being a vehicle of economic rationality or of utilitarianism based on universalizability[12] – opens the door to idiosyncratic

8 Concerning the consequentialist "essence" of economic analysis of law, see, e.g., Mathis (2012). A critical opinion is expressed, for instance, by Tribe (1985). On the success of consequentialist arguments in the Italian tradition, see, e.g., Cariello (2015). The literature on consequentialist arguments in legal reasoning is broad; some contributions that are relevant for the present analysis are those of Cserne (2011); MacCormick (1994); Carbonell (2011); Feteris (2005).

9 A valuable analysis is outlined by Baum (1994).

10 For a general introduction, see, e.g., Hooker (2016).

11 Concerning the relationships between efficiency and equity, see, e.g., Polinsky (2011); Farber (2003); Sanchirico (2001).

12 The link between utilitarianism and universalizability is contested. For instance, the debate between R. M. Hare and J. L. Mackie (see Mackie (1984) and Hare (1984). Pettit affirms that a plausible link between utilitarianism and universalizability exists if we assume reasons as "agent-relative reasons of preference" (Pettit 1987, 75). On this issue, see also Harrison (1952–1953).

value-laden judgments that do not have any genuine underpinning economic criteria or calculations. In this respect, EAL functions as a corrective to law, akin to common sense and equity,[13] by which I mean *aequitas* or *epieikeia*.[14] The examples presented in the next paragraphs will provide evidence for this hypothesis.

1. A case study: uses of EAL in Italian courts

The relevance of EAL in courts is a contentious issue among legal scholars around the world, especially in civil legal systems where it has taken hold.[15] In many cases, there is a significant gap between the theoretical debate and the proposals of its uses and the effective influence of EAL on law in action.

As mentioned in the introduction, my analysis of case law focuses on a selection of ten examples derived from Italian judgments awarded in the last decade by the Italian Court of Cassation, which is the highest national court. I noted at the beginning that the cases demonstrate certain practices on the part of judges that are not limited to the Italian civil domain considered.[16] I will briefly present each case by comparing the references to EAL in the decisions with the mainstream references found in Law and Economics literature concerning the relative subject matters.

1.1. Public offering for shares purchase on capital markets and loss of opportunities

The first example deals with *public offering (IPO) for shares purchase on capital markets*. In particular, it concerns the breach of the duty to launch a public offering by majority shareholders, which violates the right of minority shareholders under Italian law.[17]

In the opinion of the court:

> [T]he aim of the legislator of pursuing the public interest through a more efficient functioning of the market dynamics is often carried out through

13 Although it is a highly controversial topic, many authors challenge the stance of a trade-off between equity and efficiency; my analysis follows these criticisms. About the debate, some classical references in favor of the possible compatibility of efficient and fair goals and outcomes are found, for example, in Varian (1974) and Sen (1987). See also Chavas (1994).

14 See, e.g., Bushlack (2015, 94–95); D'Agostino (1977); Lefebvre (1963).

15 See, e.g., Mattei (1994); Ogus (2001).

16 Due to the limit in scope, I will provide only a brief sketch of each case. For a more general overview of the state of the art in Italy, see, e.g., Pardolesi (2003); Pardolesi and Tassone (2005); Pardolesi (2015); Villa (2015).

17 See Court Cass. Civ. Sec. I, judgment 4–4–2016, no. 6504, in database Utet giuridica; Court Cass. Civ. Sec. I, judgment 10–8–2012, no. 14392, ibid. All quotations of legal decisions are my translations from Italian into English.

> the preservation of specific subjective situations. It is increasingly clear that, in areas such as this, there is constant interaction between individual interests and the general interest of the market, the integrity and proper functioning of which are inseparably connected with the adequate protection of subjective positions . . . The presence of market protection tools does not imply per se that individual interests, which are possibly involved in the affair, are excluded from the sphere of protection. On the contrary, as shown by the evolution of competition law and the well-known accepted principle of protection of subjective positions "downstream" of the prohibited anticompetitive agreements . . . it is considered normal that the market legislation now provides forms of private enforcement; that is to say, that the pursuit of public interests can also be carried out through the deterrent effect of remedies operated by individuals in their own personal interest.[18]
>
> The complaints of the petitioners concerning the absence of a legal basis of the so-called "theory of the division of the banquet" cannot be substantiated in terms of mutual, equitable, compensatory, *economic analysis of law*, and normative perspectives . . . The compensatory content, which consists in the request for compensation as result of the failure to complete the IPO, is the *loss of opportunity* to implement a *cost-effective disinvestment* at the moment when the obligation should have been performed. For such purposes, the assessment of damages will certainly have to take into account all the elements on the basis of the *actual economic value of the loss of opportunities* as explained by the judgments of this Court of 2012. The participation of the minority shareholders into the majority premium therefore is not a favour, but a legal right implemented through the instrument of IPO. Further, it is not necessary to invoke the economic analysis of law to understand how capital gains achieved by controlling shareholders has an economic origin beyond the legal one, which is instead common to all shareholders inasmuch as they are participants in the same collective enterprise; these shareholders must therefore be able to benefit from the ability to monetise or confirm one's investment in optimal conditions in a logic of the market's good functioning and attraction of investors to the equity investment.[19]

Therefore, in the judges' opinion, the right of the minority shareholders to be compensated by the majority shareholders who do not fulfill the duty to launch an IPO is justified on the basis that each stakeholder has the right to exploit all potential chances that might exist on the stock exchange market. This idea is based on the assumption that such a market works according to its internal logic and that it can achieve a level of optimal functioning if the mechanism of buying and selling shares is ruled by law. The proper functioning of the market is a public good that should be achieved by governing the behavior of economic

18 See Court Cass. Civ. Sec. I, judgment 10–8–2012, no. 14392, in database Utet giuridica.

19 See Court Cass. Civ. Sec. I, judgment 4–4–2016, no. 6504, in database Utet giuridica.

agents and, in particular, by imposing sanctions on the behavior of the majority stakeholders who violate the rights of the minority. The references both to EAL and to private enforcement seem only ancillary and do not play a central role in the judgments, and judges here believe that the market is a normative and not a natural environment. In particular, the references to EAL and private enforcement neglect the standard EAL consideration of the substantive point.[20] For our purposes, it suffices to recall that no consideration is given here by the judges to the whole argument of the so called "tender pressure", the "freezing out" of minorities or "tunneling" analyses found in EAL literature. As is well known, EAL scholars examine the problem of choice distortions generated by IPOs and debate which remedies can allow for a rational choice by both sellers and buyers and, hence, transactions based on a market "fair value". There is no trace of this discussion here.

1.2. Joint and several liability or several-only liability and creditor's interests

The second example regards the justification of *joint and several liability or several-only liability*,[21] which is an issue in which Italian courts sometimes mention EAL in order to argue in favor of either the former or the latter. While the topic has been carefully analyzed by EAL scholars with reference to tort liabilities and in cases of settlement agreements,[22] in Italian case law the paradigmatic cases deal with the discipline of liabilities in a commonhold.

The Supreme Court of Cassation states as follows:[23]

> The co-owners of a building unit located in a commonhold are bound, jointly and severally, to the commonhold to pay communal expenses, either because the obligation of contributions rests on the joint holders of the storey or of the portion of the storey as something unique and because the communal residents themselves represent, towards the commonhold, a set, or

20 See, for instance, Bebchuk (1987); Johnson et al. (2000); Gilson and Gordon (2003); Tucci (2008, 26–27).

21 The alternative arises in situations where the claim results from the actions of multiple parties. See Kornhauser and Revesz (2000). Under several-only liability, the creditor can recover from a losing debtor only the share of compensation attributable to that debtor. In contrast, under joint and several liability, if the creditor litigates against multiple debtors and prevails against only one, he/she can recover his/her compensation from that debtor. If the creditor prevails against all debtors but some are insolvent, he/she can recover his/her compensation from the solvent debtors. Finally, if the creditor prevails against all debtors and all are solvent, he/she can still choose to recover his/her full judgment from anyone or to recover a portion from each. Thanks exclusively to the right of contribution, the debtor that has paid a disproportionately large share of the creditor's claim as result of the application of joint and several liability has the right to obtain compensation from a debtor that has paid a disproportionately small share of the claim.

22 A traditional reference is to the studies carried out by Kornhauser and Revesz since the 90s, e.g., Kornhauser and Revesz (1993, 427–493, 2009, 427–493).

23 See Court Cass. Civ. Sec. II, judgment 21–10–2011, no. 21907, in database Utet giuridica.

by virtue of the general principle dictated by art. 1294 Civil Code (according to which, in case of plurality of debtors, solidarity is assumed) . . . The rule of passive solidarity was introduced by the Civil Code of 1942 as a result of the commercialisation of civil obligations in order to strengthen them, in the implementation of obligations, in order to increase the creditor's opportunities to see his interest satisfied . . . There is a "community of interests" from which, in fact, "most debtors . . . bounded towards one debt . . . are linked intimately" (civil code report, n. 597). On the contrary, the function of indivisibility should be captured in the need to ensure the unity of performance, given the unsuitability of its subject matter to be divided into portions, suitable to keeping the same economic function proportionately of the entire performance. And since the justification of passive solidarity does not consist in the need to protect the entire performance of an obligation relating to a thing or a fact that is not susceptible to division, but to strengthen the opportunities for the creditor to achieve the performance, being it divisible or indivisible, it shall be excluded that the indivisibility of the obligation constitutes a necessary feature . . . It follows that the natural divisibility of monetary obligations of the joint owners of a flat located in a commonhold to contribute to communal expenses does not preclude solidarity among the co-holders.

On the other hand, referring to a precedent decision of the United Section of the Supreme Court of Cassation,[24] the judges confirm the following principle:[25]

The liability of the co-owners for the obligations undertaken by the administrator on behalf of the commonhold is only several and not joint in the case of obligations undertaken towards third parties by the representative of the commonhold . . . that for reasons – inter alia – of 'substantive' justice and of *economic analysis of law*, given that 'solidarity would benefit the creditor who, negotiating with the administrator, knows the situation of

24 See Court Cass. Civ. United Sections, judgment 8–4–2008, no. 9148, in database Utet giuridica, which states as follows: "The contract, signed by the representative administrator, on behalf of and in the interest of the represented co-owners and within the limits of the faculties conferred upon him, directly produces effects in respect of the representatives. Once the sentence of the administrator has been obtained, as representative of the co-owners, the creditor can execute individually towards each one, according to their respective shares. In summary, the chosen solution, according to the strict principles of law governing contractual obligations with a plurality of debtors, appears satisfactory with respect to the requirements of substantial justice that emerge from economic and social realities of the commonhold. Solidarity would benefit the creditor who, negotiating with the administrator, knows the situation of the debtor and can take precautions in various ways; but the criterion of several-only liability appears preferable. It does not force the co-debtors to advance sums that are at times quite significant as a consequence of a(n unexpected) choice made unilaterally by the creditor. At the same time, there are no opportune reasons to defer the allocation of debt between the co-owners at the time of redress, rather than implement it at the time of fulfilment".

25 See Court Cass. Civ. Sec. II, judgment 21–10–2011, no. 21907, in database Utet giuridica.

the debtor and can take various precautions', while the several-only liability does not force the co-debtors to advance sometimes highly significant sums as a consequence of a choice (unexpected) made unilaterally by the creditor.

Thus, the several and joint liability regime is considered more appropriate in cases of payments due by the members of the commonhold in favor of the commonhold, while the several-only liability regime is preferred with third parties.

It is interesting to note that the reference to EAL is not genuine:[26] in fact, the precedent of the United Section of the Court of Cassation does not refer to EAL, but rather to substantial needs for justice that emerge from the economic and social realities of a commonhold. In both decisions, the judges refer to economic considerations and the function of legal rules, but those references are vague. The core of the judgment is a comparative evaluation of the positions of the creditor and the debtors that resemble more common-sense assumptions and equitable balancing than economic analysis.

EAL scholars typically investigate whether joint and several liability or several-only liability is a more efficient system of allocation of liabilities from the perspective of each agent and the overall system of transactions. Refined analyses conclude that the two systems seem preferable depending on the costs of transactions that exist in each circumstance, including – for instance – the number of parties involved, the effective possibility to exercise the right of contribution, litigation costs, the solvency of debtors and risk-averseness (Richardson 1999, 86–99). All such considerations are wholly absent from the aforementioned sentence.

1.3. Handling contract and the interests of the agents and users

The third example concerns the debate concerning the nature and the legal qualification of the *handling contract*. Reference is to ground-handling contracts, which cover a wide variety of services required by airlines to operate flights. These services include areas such as maintenance, fuel and freight handling, as well as passenger check-in, catering, baggage handling and transport within the airport. It is governed – *inter alia* – by the European Aviation Safety Agency and International Air Transport Association rules and practices. Within the traditional Italian legal culture, the features of such contracts are unclear as they are a hybrid of multiple services and belong to the international practice of air transport systems. Italian judges refer to EAL to support their position that it is an atypical contract that cannot be assimilated with the contract of deposit in favor of a third party.

26 Specific reference is made to the earlier quotations of Court Cass. Civ. Sec. II, judgment 21-10-2011, no. 21907 in text and of Court Cass. Civ. United Sections, judgment 8-4-2008, no. 9148 in footnote 24.

The Court affirms that:[27]

> [On one hand] the existence of an interest of the sender/beneficiary limited from the start to the custody of the asset does not appear in fact legitimately predicable in terms of an economic and legal reconstruction of the case, on the contrary [the sender/beneficiary shares such interest] with the recipient of the shipment . . . from the initial moment of the execution of the contract and until the final stage of delivery and . . . even if there is no manifestation of entering into an agreement.
>
> On the other hand, the criticism raised by the legal doctrine to the configurability of the case in terms of contract (deposit) in favour of a third party shall be taken into consideration.
>
> An initial argument is founded on the belief, which follows mostly *from the perspective of the economic analysis of law*, that [the hypothesis of contract (deposit) in favour of a third party] would contrast with the need of protection of the interests of the various parties involved in the performance of the transport: the third recipient, unrelated to the stipulation and sometimes unaware of who manages the handling services at the airport where the carrier performs its traffic, would be bound by a contract in whose content he cannot have had any word; the same carrier, in the event of conviction for damages of the sole handler . . . could not invoke the limitation of liability established by international air transport authorities since the action of indemnification would originate from the handling contract and not that of the transport; finally, the same handler claiming on the basis of the alleged contract of deposit could not take advantage of the aforesaid limitations resulting from the uniform law ex art. 30, par. 1 of the Montreal Convention (apart from their inapplicability as provided at the subsequent par. 3),[28] from which it could otherwise benefit if it were held liable in charge of the carrier under tort law.

As the excerpt of the judgment shows, the reference to EAL is cursory and not linked with a true analysis of economic features of handling as is typically found in transport economics.[29] Basically, the Court gives relevance to the interests of

27 See Court Cass. Civ. United Sections, judgment 20–9–2017, no. 21850, in database Utet giuridica.

28 See Convention for the Unification of Certain Rules for International Carriage by Air (Montreal, 28 May 1999) Chapter III – Liability of the Carrier and Extent of Compensation for Damage. Article 30 Servants, agents-aggregation of claims: "1. If an action is brought against a servant or agent of the carrier arising out of damage to which the Convention relates, such servant or agent, if they prove that they acted within the scope of their employment, shall be entitled to avail themselves of the conditions and limits of liability which the carrier itself is entitled to invoke under this Convention . . . 3. Save in respect of the carriage of cargo, the provisions of paragraphs 1 and 2 of this Article shall not apply if it is proved that the damage resulted from an act or omission of the servant or agent done with intent to cause damage or recklessly and with knowledge that damage would probably result".

29 See, e.g., Tomová, Trgiňa and Sedláčková (2015).

the agents and users that are involved in transportation and assumes that EAL research shares the same view.

1.4. Liquidation of damages and opportunity costs in property law

The fourth example is found in the area of *liquidation of damages*: for instance, in cases of damages deriving from the illegitimate use of a property such as a house or land.

The Court observes that:[30]

> [G]iven that the occupation of the property of others is not necessarily a detriment by itself, the [appealed] court[31] rejected the claim on the assumption that the plaintiff neither claimed nor proved: (a) that the usurped property was [a legitimate title to claim damages]; (b) that a damage occurs; (c) that the good was "attractive" in the market of property leases; (d) that advantageous lease proposals were given up. This motivation is in contrast to art. 1226 Italian Civil Code.[32] Indeed, the appealed decision entails the idea that a property cannot have any use besides sale or rental. This idea neglects that any good is likely to also be used directly by its owner, and that direct use has a utility insomuch as it has economic content (the *so-called opportunity cost in economic analysis of law*). In fact, whoever owns a small courtyard used – let us say – as a storage area, theoretically saves the cost of renting a similar space. These are prejudices that clearly cannot be proven in their exact amount and therefore require an equitable liquidation.

The judges recognize that the use of any good involves its own utility. This utility has an economic substance, and they then make reference to the well-known concept *of opportunity cost.*[33] Nevertheless, this reference is neither developed nor explained. The criterion actually applied is equitable in nature as the value of the use and its opportunity cost cannot be calculated in a precise amount. It is worth noting that the judges neglect the vast debate and literature on the models and criteria developed to estimate the opportunity cost of goods, e.g. in cases of irregular occupancy, and they also do not mention that such opportunity cost is subjective.[34]

30 See Court Cass. Civ. Sec. III, judgment 21–9–2015, no. 18494, in database Utet giuridica.

31 Reference is to the court of appeal, which decides the case in the second instance. Such decision of the court of appeal is then appealed, in turn, before the Court of Cassation.

32 Article 1226 Equitable measure of damages: "If damages cannot be proved in their exact amount, they are equitably liquidated by the court".

33 A traditional explanation of opportunity cost is that it is a loss of another opportunity: for instance, in cases of breach of contract (see Cooter and Eisenberg (1985)).

34 See, e.g., Bertrand (2012).

1.5. *Moral damages, rigidity-inelasticity of liquidation criteria and resources of judicial system*

The fifth example regards the reasonable length of civil proceedings, especially concerning the liquidation of *moral (nonpecuniary) damages* caused by their *unreasonable lengths.* The Italian legislation originally laid down the rules on the subject in 2001 and then in 2012,[35] but the case law is nonetheless relevant and generally integrates the legislative regulation. In the judges' opinion:

> [E]ven prior to the introduction of the statutory rules under discussion, the monetisation of the "inconvenience" (*i.e.* non-pecuniary damage) was liquidated. This was done on the bases of a complex evaluation that took into account the content of the claim proposed in the main proceedings, the probability of its success, and the proactive behaviour of the parties . . . in the context of an overall review of the criteria of assessment and liquidation of non-pecuniary damages deriving from the unreasonable length of the proceedings, legislation in 2012 identified the cases where no indemnification was due (art. 2, par. 2-*quinquies*), and, with reference to the quantification of the indemnity, introduced a cap anchored to the economic value of the claim proposed in the main proceedings . . . in this way, on the bases of a previous evaluation, a closer connection was guaranteed between the economic content of the judicial claim and the 'inconvenience' (*i.e.* non-pecuniary damage) that the defendant suffered until the claim was decided. This does not appear unreasonable in the perspective of the *economic analysis of law*, as already stated by this Court in the recalled judgment no. 12937 of 2012.[36]

In this decision held in 2012, the Court of Cassation instead highlights the following "economic argument":[37]

> Consideration should be made of the burden on public finances and hence to the community of citizens that would result from a *rigid and inelastic application of the liquidation criteria* developed by the case-law, which is unable to give relevance to the circumstances of the case. The possibility for any victim of delay – even when the value of the main proceedings is negligible, as often happens, – to ask the Treasury for an indemnity in an amount highly exceeding the value of the true underlying interests – considering the aggregate of tens of thousands of cases – prove unaffordable for the *financial equilibrium of the country* and the Court believes that limiting/minimising the possibility that the resources must be made available in

35 See art. 55, par. 3, Legislative Decree. 22 June 2012, no. 83, converted with modification by Law 7 August 2012, no. 134, according to which: "The extent of the indemnity . . . cannot in any case be higher than the value of the claim or lower than that of law established by the Court".

36 See Court Cass. Civ. Sec. IV-2, judgment 8–7–2016, no. 14048, in database Utet giuridica.

37 See Court Cass. Civ. Sec. II, judgment 24–7–2012, no. 12937, in database Utet giuridica.

> the appropriate budget chapter and that they be timely destined in favour of whomever suffered a serious and important injury due to the slowness in the response of the justice system. The *limitation of available resources* is a parameter that cannot be disregarded by the judge to quantify in concrete terms the equitable indemnity that the system as a whole can recognise.

Therefore, nonpecuniary damages devoted to compensating parties in cases of the unreasonable length of civil proceedings shall be limited to a *maximum* amount related to the *request* at the same proceedings.

Judges here show particular attention to predictability in terms of the expectations of the parties by giving specific relevance to the defendant's expectations concerning the possible economic impact of a negative outcome of the proceedings. The judges based their reasoning on a common-sense belief. In essence, the idea is that the defendant's concerns are correlated to the *petitum* of the plaintiff's claim. The greater the *petitum*, the higher the concern and the relative compensation for the suffering. The latter should be proportionate to the former (i.e. the plaintiff's claim). Moreover, the rationale of the ruling is grounded in a macroeconomic analysis.

Reference to EAL here is made indirectly by recalling a legal precedent. The main reason for fixing a cap is based on the limited resources that public finance can allocate to indemnify people due to the unreasonable length of the judicial process. The reasoning very clearly shows the economic costs of the judicial system, which increase in cases of systemic failure such as in excessive length of proceedings on a broad scale. It is worth noting that, if considered in general terms, the court's reasoning allows for a sacrifice of individual rights due to costs and economic constraints, which must not be ignored in light of the general public interest of the community.

However, the use of terminology borrowed from economics is surprising. I refer to the economic terms *rigid* and *inelastic*, which are normally associated with and used in the analysis of price demand in microeconomics in general as well as in EAL. For instance, rigidity and elasticity are relevant in the analyses of consumer behavior and price policies put in place by firms[38] and in research about the costs of reducing consumption of a good by making its production illegal, such as in the case of narcotics.[39] However, in case law, the concepts of

38 See Nakamuraa and Steinsson (2011), who propose a model to explain the simultaneous existence of a rigid regular price and frequent sales facing firms and consumer habits, the asymmetry of information and time-inconsistency problems. See also Beck and Lein-Rupprecht (2016), who provide an empirical analysis and estimation of price elasticities of demand in three European countries (Belgium, Germany and the Netherlands), considering the degree of demand-side real rigidities and the monetary non-neutrality observed in the data.

39 For instance, Becker, Murphy, and Grossman "show that the more inelastic is either demand or supply for a good, the greater is the increase in social cost from further reducing its production by greater enforcement efforts. So optimal public expenditures . . . depend not only on the difference between the social and private values from consumption, but also on these elasticities. When demand and

rigidity and elasticity do not have proper economic content; their meanings are broader and more similar to their ordinary significances. The rigid and inelastic application of legal rules is in contrast to their equitable application. Therefore, rigidity and elasticity have no relationships to the reactions of agents to changes in the relevant context (changes in prices and/or costs). Rather, they concern the conception of rules and their application by legal authorities; the alternative is between conceiving rules as general and indefeasible – i.e. to be applied without considering unmentioned circumstances – or rather as *prima facie* defeasible rules that can be defeated case by case, depending on equitable criteria.

1.6. Strict liability, **richesse oblige** *doctrine and deep pocket and best risk avoider principles*

The sixth example deals with *strict liability*. This is a legal area where EAL is considered to have taken root and achieved a certain influence. Here the judges recall the well-known studies of EAL on this subject and recognize the contribution of EAL in changing the tort law system.[40] In particular, the judges lay out that EAL contributes to developing a new multifunctional conception of tort law, which gives relevance to other functions such as redistribution and deterrence beyond the function of compensation. Furthermore, EAL also contributes to other criteria of ascription of liability beyond negligence (i.e. fault). The Italian legal tradition is thus completing the shift toward a more complex and modern system of torts, although the role of EAL is not always perceived in the process.[41] In spite of this, economic considerations seem to be erudite *obiter dicta* rather than relevant arguments in Italian jurisprudence.

---

supply are not too elastic, it does not pay to enforce any prohibition unless the social value is negative" (Becker, Murphy and Grossman 2006, 1).

40 See Cass. civ. United Sections, judgment 22–7–2015, n. 15350, in database Utet giuridica, which states that "the current approach of both legal doctrine and case law . . . in its more modern instances conceives of the area of torts as a system of liability that is increasingly objective in nature, directed to achieving a method of allocation of damages in accordance with the principles of the theory of economic analysis of law". The judges here maintain that the central element of the entire system of torts is damages and that torts can be devoted to achieving several aims, such as compensation as well as redistribution in compliance with the principle of solidarity as set forth in article 2 of the Italian Constitution.

41 A remarkable example of this is the overruling in 2017 by the Court of Cassation with reference to punitive damages, which completely disregards EAL literature on torts and the possible punitive function of liability. See Court Cass. Civ. United Sections, judgment 5–7–2017, no. 16601, in database Utet giuridica. According to traditional Italian legal doctrine and case law, these kinds of damages were not admitted, and those foreign judgments whereby this category of damages was awarded were neither recognized nor enforced in Italy because they were contrary to internal public order. The overruling represents a significant change insomuch as it states that tort law has to satisfy many functions beyond compensation, including functions of deterrence and sanction/punishment and, consequently, that punitive damages may be compatible with Italian law if they fulfill three requirements: firstly, determined and expressed legal grounds identified by the same foreign legal system must exist; secondly, punitive damages must be predictable according to the foreign legal system; thirdly, punitive damages must be reasonably quantified, meaning that they cannot be grossly excessive.

The Court of Cassation states as follows:[42]

> Strict liability is not the complete absence or insignificance of the subjective criteria of ascription, but it replaces them with others that are more objective in nature. These criteria perform the same function towards the causality relation that has always been characteristic of subjective criteria of ascription in torts. In strict liability, the criteria to identify ascription belong to the causal sequence, which is potentially infinite . . . The rationale of the allocation of the cost of damages is not the fault, but an objective criterion, which however is not provided by a specific provision of statutory law. It has been individuated in the deep pocket principle in common law systems and in the *richesse oblige* in the French tradition, while the later doctrinal refinement has judged that the rationale shall be found in the principle of exposure to danger or of the risk bearer; that is to say, the cost of the damage shall be allocated on the person who had the possibility of making a cost-benefit analysis, for which such agent should bear the liability – before the damage occurs – insomuch as he is in the best position to avoid it in the most economical way, so that the occurrence of the damage derives from an option chosen by the same agent as alternative to the opposite decision.

Therefore, to explain the concept of strict liability, which is the criterion on which such a form of liability is based, judges turn to the allegedly common-law *deep pocket principle* (Coleman 1976, 262–263; Landes and Posner 1987, 120–121), as well as to the French *richesse oblige* doctrine[43] and the principle of the *best risk avoider* (Coleman 1976, 262–263).[44] Needless to say, the aforementioned principles and doctrines are not identical, and it is confusing to blend them together. It appears the judges wish to show off a knowledge of the relevant studies rather than reflect on them carefully.

42 See Court Cass. Civ. Sec. III, judgment 17–12–2009, no. 26516, in database Utet giuridica.

43 In truth, this doctrine was not proposed or developed in France. At the beginning of the twentieth century, Josef von Unger (*Handeln auf eigene Gefahr: Ein Beitrag zur Lehre vom Schadensersatz*, Jena: Fischer, 1904) urged that liability without fault should take into account the relative financial capacities of the parties; in brief, *richesse oblige* should become a basic principle of the law of torts. As noted, "[t]here is one kind of causation without fault, however, to which the principle of the smallest harm is applied to an ever increasing extent. Beyond rudimentary strict liabilities of incompetent persons and for misdeeds of animals and other dangerous things, the 'negligence' liabilities of both civil law and common law countries have come to aim primarily at an equitable distribution of risk rather than at censuring a wrongdoer or deterring the public. The French *théorie de risque* is perhaps the most significant expression of this shift of emphasis" (Ehrenzweig 1950, 446).

44 "Under a risk spreading argument, accident costs ought to be allocated either to spread them maximally over persons and time or to insure that those individuals best able to bear them do so . . . the risk spreading . . . justifications for a system of liability rules [do not] require . . . fault-based liability rules. . . . That is, to be liable, the party with the deepest pocket need not be the individual responsible for the accident, and the individual best suited to avoid the accident or best able to judge if it ought to be avoided need not be the party at fault in causing it to be liable for its costs" (Coleman 1976, 262–263).

In the Court's opinion, according to the objective criterion, the person who is in the best position to avoid the risk of damages and to minimize the costs of care should be liable. However, it is not clear how the cost-benefit analysis that is implied by this criterion should be carried out. No in-depth economic analysis is required, and strict liability is applied when two situations exist together: when only one party can attend to the risks being allegedly in the best position to avoid damages and when the potential injured party, such as a smoker, could prevent harm to himself by not acting, in the example by not smoking. However, in the end, in light of a strict liability model, the judges assign liability on purely causal grounds. We might debate whether this approach belongs to certain theories found in the relevant literature, such as, for instance, the prominent causation-based liability approach proposed by Epstein (1980). Nonetheless, different theories hold agents to other objective standards of liability which give relevance to other elements such as foreseeability, reasonableness, common-sense maxims and rules of thumb. Some theories hold that "an agent is responsible only for those outcomes of whose risk of occurrence he was or ought to have been aware at the time when he acted. In the language of tort law, he is responsible for those outcomes that were reasonably foreseeable, whether or not he foresaw them in fact" (Perry 1997, 355). Other theories hold that "an agent is responsible for any harmful outcome that he caused. On this account, it is irrelevant that the agent neither foresaw nor could have foreseen the outcome" (Perry 1997, 356). It is, however, remarkable that the subjective/objective opposition evoked by judges is highly ambiguous. On one hand, strict liability does not give relevance to the agent's willingness and intentions, but this does not imply that the ascription of liability to the agent is more objective than if subjective criteria were applied; the subjective criteria based on fault may be more objective (i.e. less discretional) if the subjective elements are certain or clear. On the other hand, any explanation of negligence based on fault as possible knowledge – that is to say, which gives relevance to elements only knowable to somebody – is objective and not subjective in nature. In other words, sometimes allegedly subjective criteria of liability are objectified by standards that do not refer to the actual mental conditions of the people and are based on super-individual conceptions or fictions and presumptions derived from some ideals of a responsible man.

1.7. *Liquidation of damages, unjust enrichment of the injured party and indifference curves*

The seventh example also belongs to the area of damages, where the maxim is routinely repeated that the amount of damages shall be ideally measured with consideration of the "*indifference curve*" of the injured party. In many judgments, the following principle is stated:[45]

45 See e.g. Court Cass. Civ. United Sections, judgment 22–5–2018, no. 12567, and Court Cass. Civ. United Sections, judgment 22–05–2018, no. 12566, both in database Utet giuridica.

> If the harmful act produces, along with an injury, an advantage, the latter must be calculated in reduction with respect to the amount of compensation: in fact, the damage cannot be a source of profit and the measure of compensation cannot be more of the infringed interest or lead to an unjust enrichment of the injured party. This principle is inferable from art. 1223 of the Italian Civil Code, which states that the compensation of damages shall include both the loss suffered by the injured party and the lost profits insofar as they are a direct and immediate consequence of the illicit act. This norm logically implies that the final assessment of the harmful effects also considers the possible advantages that can derive from the effects caused by the illicit act. Otherwise, this means that if the positive effects caused by the harmful act were not considered in the assessment phase of the negative direct and immediate economic consequences, of the illicit act, the injured party could take advantage of an unjust profit, beyond the limits of compensation approved by the legal system (Cass., Sec. 3^, 11 July 1978, no. 3507). In other words, the compensation must cover the entire damage occurred, but it cannot go beyond it. It is prohibited as a source of enrichment of the injured party, who shall be rather placed on the same indifference curve where he/she would be in the event that the harmful act had not occurred.

The quantification should put the party in the same position as he was before being harmed, thus avoiding any possible unjustified advantage. Compensation shall be neither lower nor higher in order to be fair and equitable. Although the express reference to an "indifference curve" is noteworthy and helpful for understanding the knowledge of the judges, this reference is immaterial as it does not seem to add anything substantial to the decision. Even in its absence, the reasoning would remain unchanged and the result invariable: in fact, in all cases, the same outcome is achievable by applying the traditional right to compensation and the prohibition of unfair enrichment. Moreover, reference to the "indifference curve" seems to ignore the open issues in the practical application of such a theory. For instance, EAL scholars have outlined[46] that the indifference curve only responds in principle to the perfect compensation for the destruction of a good, but in cases of unique goods, it is difficult, if not impossible, to infer the subjective value of goods through evidence about the victim's preferences. Besides, in such cases, "in practice courts cannot operate very precisely as it would be too costly to estimate accurate indifference maps . . . Compensation for loss of earnings, which is relatively straightforward calculation, tends to be assessed on more of a case-by-case basis by estimating the capital sum that must be invested to replicate" the victim's expected earnings (Dnes 2018, e-book ch. 6 par. 5). The line of reasoning followed by courts,

46 See Arlen (2013, 442–443), who considers it a consequence of a more general problem concerning the practical application of the preference revelation theory.

whenever they refer to indifference curves or when they apply case-by-case estimations, is basically counterfactual in either case: that is to say, built on an "as if" assumption.

1.8. Right of action, trivial claims and homo œconomicus

The eighth example concerns another famous concept of EAL that judges sometimes evoke: i.e. the notion of *homo œconomicus.* Here, the court debates whether a lawsuit with very low economic value (a few Euros) is admissible under Italian law. The following principle was stated in a case of enforcement where the creditor – after having received the payment of a sum of 17,854.94 Euros – began enforcement procedures claiming the existence of a residual debt of 12 Euros for the interest matured between the notification of the order of payment and the effective payment. Notwithstanding this being an enforcement case,[47] the legal reasoning of the Court seems applicable to all kinds of civil proceedings, as shown by the following excerpt:[48]

> When the subject matter of a litigation is a credit that is exclusively economic in nature and not even indirectly connected to non-economic legally protected interests, the interest to start an enforcement procedure, as well as the interest that must support any claim as to the merit of a declaratory relief, cannot receive legal protection *if the economic amount of the claim is objectively low and hence of such an amount as to make a legal process unjustifiable.* For that reason, even the suspicion of a possible violation of article 24 of the Italian Constitution . . . is unfounded, because – by protecting the right of action – [that constitutional provision] does not certainly exclude that the law might request, in pure economic lawsuits, that the economic value of the claim should overcome a *minimum threshold of relevance, primarily from an economic point of view* . . . As jurisdiction is notoriously a *limited national resource,* surely the law – explicitly or implicitly – may limit the application before a court in cases of economic claims, also taking into consideration that given the limited resources available the number of lawsuits has an impact on the reasonable length of proceedings, which is protected by art. 111 of Italian Constitution and art. 6 of ECHR.

This legal precedent has been disregarded by another section of the Court of Cassation. It was considered limited solely to enforcement proceedings in a subsequent case of declaratory reliefs concerning a claim on the merits. The

47 Under Italian law, enforcement cases follow special rules applicable only to enforcement proceedings. Despite this, the legal reasoning made by the court in the example here considered is not limited to enforcement cases. The same court deems its line of reasoning as general and applicable to claims on the merits in cases of declaratory reliefs.

48 See Court Cass. Civ. Sec. 3, judgment 3–3–2015, no. 4228, in database Utet giuridica.

case concerns a standard contract entered into by a company managing a public service with a user of the same service.

The Judges observed the following:[49]

> [R]egardless of the observation that the value of the dispute . . . could not be considered solely from the user's point of view, but should also be seen from the [public service company's] point of view, [and from this latter point of view, the claim] would be not of the *lowest value* (always based on the evaluation criterion of the *homo economicus*). [However, the precedent quoted earlier is overruled for the following reason:] the issue of the present dispute is clearly traceable to what the legislator has called class action . . . The possibility to start a class action suit has been stated by the legislator without any limitation related to the value of the claim of the single consumer or user, thus it is admissible that the economic value of the identical rights would be of the lowest value if considered singularly. As the class action is not mandatory and the consumer or user is free to individually start a claim, it is manifest that the limitation related to the *economic value of the claim* cannot be applied, also in cases of exercising individual litigation.

Comparing the decisions, the different evaluations concerning the existence of a minimum threshold of relevance in cases of pure economic claims are crystal clear. However, it is interesting to note that both decisions focus on economic considerations and, in particular, are based on macroeconomic rationales. Notwithstanding their *prima facie* inconsistency, they can be justified from two different economic standpoints. On the one hand, the first decision justifies the existence of a minimum economic threshold of relevance on the basis of the limited resources available for the judicial system; in brief, constitutional and international principles allow for the exclusion of the smallest claims in order to more efficiently use the resources available for more relevant claims. On the other hand, the second decision justifies the existence of small claims in cases of litigation that have the same nature as a class action for formal equality reasons: as no threshold exists in class action cases, a threshold for individual claims cannot exist either. In addition, the whole line of reasoning suggests that individual small claims may produce a general benefit for the majority of consumers and users. In this respect, for a better understanding of this judgment, it is important to note that in Italy, class actions are rarely brought by consumers and users while the latter generally begin individual litigations. The rulings issued in each single case, however, easily become *de facto* legal precedents that are binding in other cases. Therefore, if collectively considered, small claims can have a relevant economic impact from the point of view of companies and entrepreneurs. By referring to the well-known *homo œconomicus*, judges aim at putting their position in the best light. In EAL literature, the *homo œconomicus* is the epitome of

49 See Court Cass. Civ. Sec. VI-3, judgment 27–01–2017, no. 2168, in database Utet giuridica.

the infallible rational utility maximizer.[50] Despite this, the quotation seems more an allusion, rather than a quotation adding substantial content to the reasoning. In other words, the concept of *homo œconomicus* – whatever it may be – remains entirely in the subtext and, in the end, does not play any decisive role in the reasoning.

1.9. *Conflict of interest between the agent and the principal and the irrelevance of the analysis of advantages and disadvantages*

The ninth example regards a contract stipulated by the agent in the case of a *conflict of interest* and the remedies available for the principal. On this issue, the Italian judges refer to the studies of EAL but reject their proposals and confirm the traditional principle that the principal has the right to challenge the contract negotiated by the agent, regardless of whether it is beneficial or disadvantageous, as this right is unrelated to the outcome of the contract.

The Court of Cassation states:[51]

> It should be confirmed that the attempts of recent studies based on *economic analysis of law* to subject the annulment of the contract concluded in a conflict of interest it being disadvantageous for the principal are not convincing. This Court has already stated that the fact that the act is advantageous or disadvantageous to the principal is not relevant by itself for the configurability of the conflict of interest between the agent and the principal that makes the contract annullable, if known or knowable by the third party . . . and it is not necessary for the principal to prove to have suffered damage in concrete terms in order to claim the invalidity of the contract.

This approach of the Italian courts rejects the teaching of EAL upon agency problems or principal-agent problems. For readers familiar with the jargon of economists, "an 'agency problem' – in the most general sense of the term – arises whenever the welfare of one party, termed the 'principal', depends upon actions taken by another party, termed the 'agent'. The problem lies in motivating the agent to act in the principal's interest rather than simply in the agent's own interest" (Armour, Hansmann and Kraakman 2009, 3). EAL studies explain that, in almost any contractual relationship where an asymmetry of information exists between the principal and the agent, the latter has an incentive to act opportunistically. However, circumstances may arise which may make a conflict of interest desirable as it provides advantages for the parties. As it has been noted (MacLeod and Yong Tan 2017, 36), "the key issue is about how constraints on the size of the potential conflict affect the form and efficiency of contracts". In such cases, the opportunism risk is the arbitrary

50 See, e.g., Zouboulakis (2014, 1).

51 See Court Cass. Civ. Sec. II, judgment 15–3–2012, no. 4143, in database Utet giuridica.

refusal of inoffensive transgressions by the principal. EAL scholars examine these problems by evaluating whether or not the rules on mandate are justified under a cheapest-cost avoider logic.

1.10. Adverse possession, public powers and external diseconomies

The tenth and final example deals with the notion of "*external diseconomies*" in terms of the negative effects on health and the environment demonstrated by economic studies.[52] Such a notion is mentioned by judges, for instance, in relation to certain statutory provisions which impose taxes intended to disincentivize certain polluting activities[53] or to supplement concession fees – for the benefit of local communities – from utility distributors who exploit natural public resources such as water.[54]

The notion of "external diseconomies" also appears in cases concerning *adverse possession*[55] and *legal distances* between private properties and, in particular, the minimum distances between buildings provided by law. The case law sets a distinction between private and public powers to ensure the fulfillment of legal distances, which are measures that are established in both the private and public interest; the judges affirm the following:[56]

> [T]he construction carried out by the neighbour with a permanent and visible worksite, maintained within legal requirements for over twenty years, gives rise to *adverse possession*; that is to say, the adverse possession and the right to retain property at a distance that is less than the minimum legal one. If not, one would have to allow for the existence in *private relations* of

52 Externalities or external diseconomies have been defined in different ways by scholars. A basic but highly broad definition is proposed by Meade (1973, 15): "An external economy (diseconomy) is an event which confers an appreciable benefit (inflicts an appreciable damage) on some person or persons who were not fully consenting parties in reaching the decision or decisions which led directly or indirectly to the event in question". On the theories of externalities, see, e.g., Cornes and Sandler (1996, 39–68). External diseconomies are one of the main topics of discussion in the debate between the Coasian and the Pigouvian approaches: see, e.g., Buchanan (1969).

53 See Court Cass. Civ. Sec. V, judgment 22–9–2011, no. 19311 in database Utet giuridica, which discusses the application of the special tax concerning the landfilling of solid waste provided by Law 28 December 1995, no. 549, art. 3, par. 24 et seq. In the opinion of judges, the provision is aimed at encouraging a reduction of waste and the recovery of raw materials and energy contained therein. It is an incentive that seeks to balance the external diseconomies caused to society by the production of waste.

54 See Court Cass. Civ. United Sections, judgment 8–8–2005, no. 1660, in database Utet giuridica, which clarifies that this supplementary concession fee satisfies a "solidarity" criterion in the utilization of water resources. In other words, it is a regulatory approach intended to balance, in a redistributive manner in favor of local mountain communities, the external diseconomies caused by the water collection and energy production systems created by utility distributors.

55 It is a possession by a person who has no rights; in Latin it is called *usucapio iuris*.

56 See Court Cass. Civ. Sec. II, judgment 4–4–2018, no. 8227, which refers to and confirms the judicial precedent Court Cass. Civ. Sec. II, judgment 22–2–2010, no. 4240, both in database Utet giuridica.

> perpetual instability and the possibility of private individuals to claim that legal distances be respected at all times . . . In such cases [i.e. where adverse possession occurs], only *public administration* has the power to obtain the fulfilment of the legislative discipline from private properties . . . The worrisome *external diseconomies* (in terms of negative consequences on health and the environment) that scholars of economic analysis of law have found in cases of conventional derogation of legal distances are not legally relevant. It is one issue to infringe the dispositions of public powers, or allow a generalised derogation of legislative provisions, which can cause permanent effects that are detrimental to the protected public interest, and it is another to admit the phenomenon of adverse possession.

In short, on the one hand, judges recognize that constructions carried out at a distance that are less than the minimum provided for by law may cause external diseconomies in terms of negative consequences on health and the environment. They make the assumption that the minimum legal distances have been established by the law, taking into suitable consideration the requirements that guarantee a healthy urban environment. On the other hand, they maintain their traditional view of the prominence of adverse possession and its rationale to guarantee the stability and predictability of private relationships.

Judges seek a fair balance between the opposing needs of public health and the stability of property entitlements. They attempt to do this by recognizing that public administration has the power to intervene through public instruments in cases where adverse possession causes excessive external diseconomies that affect public health. The cases are obviously decided by balancing to potentially contrasting ends and without a specific reference to EAL.

2. Remarks on the case law: conceptions and misconceptions of EAL

The examples outlined earlier distinctly show the general approach of (early twenty-first-century Italian) case law to economic considerations. On the one hand, judges refer to certain reasoning in terms of allocation of economic costs, risk analysis and other ideas that are typical of the EAL movement, including opportunity cost, the indifference curve and external diseconomies. On the other hand, apart from a few exceptions, no real economic analysis is performed, and the occurrences of economic analysis of law in legal cases are irregular and haphazardly arranged.

The following points can be made:

(i) The uses of EAL in so-called "*law in action*" (Roscoe Pound 1910) are part of a generically teleological approach to law. This approach is not specifically linked to a precise approach from any of the schools of thought that have been actively engaged in the EAL movements in the last decades around the world.

(ii) No refined empirical surveys or formal models substantiate the references to EAL.[57] In many cases, the courts briefly touch on both micro- and macroeconomic issues but in the end confirm traditional arguments and disregard the teachings of EAL.
(iii) Economic considerations are generally broad and sometimes akin to commonsense ideas about what is convenient, efficient and costly. In other words, no economic theories, models or calculi are applied or seem to be taken into account.
(iv) References to EAL do not imply a distinctive technique of construction or statutory interpretation.[58] Economic assessments in terms of costs/benefits, incentives etc. are usually embedded in the legal reasoning and combined with many different arguments related to the alleged *ratio legis* and/or the nature of the phenomena, as well as to the literal meaning of legal provisions and so forth.[59] In (Italian) legal practice, no established order or hierarchy exists between normative economic arguments and all other arguments mentioned earlier (Tarello 1980; Pattaro 2016, 132–151). Relying on the case law, the economic arguments – especially those related to EAL – are neither first-level arguments nor conclusive arguments, but rather concurrent arguments that may strengthen the chain of justification.[60] Moreover, references to EAL normally allude to broad cost-effective considerations and do not involve a thorough normative argument based on a precise idea of efficiency.
(v) References to EAL and concepts that typically belong to it or to microeconomics are usually evoked along with substantial considerations. These are then related somehow to such values as solidarity, redistributive and equitable goals or other social consequences. They are not identified in detail through any survey of social reality. Sometimes the EAL approach is assumed as an alternative to others based on justice/equity while, in other cases, EAL seems compatible with such approaches. In both cases, however, concepts and criteria of justice are taken for granted and therefore unclear. Judges allude to social/economic consequences in order to select from a number of different decisions available. As Neil MacCormick points out in his analysis of legal reasoning (Neil MacCormick 1994, 103), decisions must make sense, and this is one of the strongest reasons in favor of the use of the consequentialist arguments in legal practice.

57 In contrast to what occurs in competition law and regulation. Agencies normally prepare surveys to provide evidence to support their interventions. However, this topic goes beyond the scope of the present analysis.

58 However, we may recall the proposal formulated in this direction by Cohen (2009). In the Italian system, there are a significant variety of legal arguments, although neither a defined closed set of them nor an order in their use is generally accepted.

59 Concerning the uses of EAL in the specific field of legal interpretation and reasoning, e.g. Bix (2018); Chiassoni (1992); Cariello (2015) illustrate the possible overlapping between the consequentialist arguments and the other legal arguments as set forth by Italian law.

60 Sometimes "[t]he consequentialist argument could thus serve as a meta rule for determining the hierarchy of the nominally equal-ranking arguments in the adjudicated case" (Mathis 2012, 17).

Accordingly, it should be demonstrated that the potential consequences of a decision are preferable to those deriving from another option. In practice the attempt to provide this demonstration may be very difficult and pave the way for a subjective and evaluative line of reasoning; therefore, preferring certain consequences over others risks being the outcome of a highly discretional appraisal that depends on the undeclared values and preferences of the judges themselves.

(vi) In some cases, references to EAL serves only to embellish the reasoning; judges use them to demonstrate erudition. Although EAL is not generally applied to solving cases and is not a common methodology, it is quite common that judges in the Italian system will display a knowledge of the EAL movement and its ideas.[61] References to EAL are used instrumentally to present an appearance of open-mindedness and to show that the rulings are the result of full-fledged reflective reasoning. As the examples show, the use of EAL terminology is sometimes superficial, limited to scratching the lexical surface, and does not entail a substantial utilization of concepts and theories.

To summarize, references to EAL in (Italian) case law are cursory and appear to be marginal. Furthermore, they are mixed with a jumble of assessments and, as a consequence, standard argumentation based on EAL comes across as a hodgepodge of theoretical and normative assumptions. It is far from being a justification grounded in economic factors, and its use disregards any concern for adjudication based on genuine economic analysis where assumptions are disclosed and the feasibility of models are tested and verified.

3. Consequentialism and values

The economic analysis of law as examined in the previous section appears much more similar to the German *Interessenjurisprudenz* or North American and continental sociological jurisprudence[62] than to EAL as it originated at the University of Chicago and Yale University in the middle of the last century, later spreading throughout many other common law traditions.

In a now-classic article entitled "*L'argomentazione orientata alle conseguenze*", Luigi Mengoni (1994) illustrates that economic assessments and factors are always relevant in case law. His essay still provides a good description of the current state of affairs in this respect. Mengoni (1994) argues that the American EAL has been imported to Italy and applied by lawyers and judges mainly as a broader consequentialist approach intended to give relevance to the interests involved in each case and to the (economic/social) consequences of the

61 From a sociological perspective, we could ask ourselves why some judges show their erudition in economics or tend to manifest some knowledge about EAL. A plausible hypothesis that should be checked empirically is whether the judges' education influences their styles or motivation.

62 See Holmes (1899); Pound (1910).

application of statutory rules. In his opinion, the circumstance that economic considerations are part of legal reasoning depends chiefly on the magnitude and the continuous escalation of conflicts of values that characterize the current pluralistic societies.[63]

Apart from that, there are two other opinions by Mengoni that are shared among jurists (Drakeman 2018, 300–318). First, many jurists believe that, by transforming disputes about values into disputes about the economic and social consequences of rules, it becomes possible to leave the subjective sphere of ethics and to base our decisions on objective criteria open to the control of rationality. A second common belief is that all arguments based on and related to economic and social consequences involve a political responsibility, bringing political and teleological assessments related to concepts of utility and harmfulness into the legal discourse. These two convictions are obviously contradictory.

While the responsibility thesis might be acceptable, it relies openly on the discretionality of the judges, and perhaps for this reason, it is not much appreciated by the courts. The first is misleading on the basis that no dispute on the economic/social consequences of rules in general and their concrete application can be neutral from a moral, political or practical point of view. The point is that the ideas of objectivity and rationality which appear to underlie these arguments are usually confused and inconsistent. Certainly, a control of rationality is possible and practicable within the domains of ethics and economics as well as in the domain of law, but the crux of the matter is which idea of rationality is assumed by the courts in each case.[64]

Many studies on legal consequentialism show that every consequentialist argument is value laden, insofar as it depends on some predetermined criteria that express which consequences are relevant and which are not (Beck 2013, 212; Cserne 2011, 38 and sequ.).[65] This means that the EAL approach that is typical of Italian legal culture and, in particular, the consequentialist argument, may be considered unbiased only if we grant two assumptions concerning the work of judges: (i) the chain of consequences should not be stopped *ad libitum*

63 This is not a suitable context to debate this idea. That being said, I suspect that the issue is too complex to have one single answer.

64 Extensive literature debates the concept of rationality assumed in economics and in law. There are many conceptions related to an ideal of perfect rationality in terms of the maximization of efficiency or utility, but there are also a variety of models of economic-bounded rationality, which are linked with the investigations of behavioral science or neuroscience. In addition, rationality is conceivable as a formal concept that is akin to logic and critical thinking or, rather, a substantive concept related to certain values such as dignity and equality. On this topic, see, e.g., Zouboulakis (2014); Sugden (1991) and Sen (1977). In the Italian literature that discusses the relevance of EAL, see, e.g., Gentili (2013), who calls attention to the differing concepts or conceptions of rationality that can be integrated within the law. In his opinion, the true choice is between an axiological rationality based on justice, equity, equality or other values on one side and another version of economic rationality based on efficiency on the other side.

65 See in particular Cserne (2011, 38 and sequ.), who reflects precisely on what type of consequences matter in legal and EAL doctrines.

or consider purely political valuations, but rather take into account objective verified data such as statistical information, empirical investigations, sociological inquiries etc.; (ii) judges should apply a principle of universalizability in each valuation of consequences and in balancing positive and negative consequences which would follow if every similar case were decided by applying the principle of the decision. If these two conditions are fulfilled, the economic argument would then be transparent and normative. Unfortunately, neither of these assumptions is applied in a satisfactory manner in legal practice. No data is provided to ground economic arguments, and no universalizability is truly applied in making decisions based on such arguments.

Empirical and statistical analyses about the law in action are very rare and do not play a significant role in the legal process. This is true not only in jurisdiction, but even in the context of legislative reforms. The proposals put forward by Calabresi (2016) and Posner (2010, 2013) in their most recent works[66] are the best evidence of current shortfalls in this respect.

As mentioned, the notion of "consequence" as applied in legal reasoning is excessively broad and ambiguous, and its uses and boundaries are generally undetermined. It is not explained in legal discourses that this notion is theory laden:[67] that is to say, its content depends on general assumptions held by individuals and societies. It is also affected by general political theories or policies such as libertarian platitudes, ordo-liberalism, welfarism, neo-institutionalism and socialism, among others. Moreover, while EAL has a definite answer concerning which consequences matter,[68] in case law, notwithstanding references to EAL, neither the relevant consequences nor the methodology and the extent of the fields of empirical surveys are clear-cut, if they in fact exist.[69] We might wonder, for instance, whether the relevant consequences involve the personal and emotional sphere of the persons specifically involved in the case or whether

66 See Calabresi (2016), who supports the idea that stricter interplay and a bilateral relationship should exist between law and economics and behavioral sciences. This kind of normative approach is shared by his well-known opponent, Richard Posner, whose analysis is similarly devoted to making law simpler to understand and evaluate and who aspires to a future of economic analysis of law devoted to developing accurate empirical studies, rather than pure abstract models (Posner 1998, 2010). According to him, judges think (and should think) that "it is very important in dealing with a new case to try to find out what, from a social and economic standpoint, is really involved in the case" (Posner and Cole 1995, 23).

67 For a thorough analysis, see Cserne (2011), who outlines the inherent epistemic and institutional limits of what can be achieved in adjudication.

68 Cserne (2011) explains that the consequence-based arguments purported by EAL are based on economic efficiency. "Orthodox law and economics scholars once argued vigorously that common law judges should and in effect do, decide cases such as to maximize social welfare or 'wealth'. This so-called 'efficiency theory of the common law' is a par excellence consequentialist position both in the sense that it requires judges to base their decisions on consequences, namely their effect on social welfare, and in the sense that it is backed by a consequentialist moral theory, namely wealth maximization" (Cserne 2011, 44).

69 On this issue see, e.g., Cariello (2015, 336).

the reactions and impacts on everybody matters or, finally, if the alleged social consequences and economic effects should be weighed. In this last case – which is typical of law in action – which people and communities should be taken into consideration and which domain of economics bears on the question should be clarified. In such a context, these clarifications are normally neglected as if the concept of society and the domain of economics were both plain and univocal. Contrary to this simplification that produces the illusion of objectivity, the social and economic consequences are, in fact, the most debatable issue in any consequentialist argument.

The final remark, however, is that court decisions using economic considerations and EAL arguments place relevance not on a formal or a calculating rationality, but rather on equity in its ancient sense of the Aristotelian *epieikeia.*[70] In brief, an idiosyncratic criterion of justice related to circumstances and individuals is broadly present in the Italian EAL approach.

In this respect, according to a common view, the economic analysis of law does not encompass any theory of distributive justice. It considers the clear-cut separation between the allocation and distribution of goods as one of its starting points.[71] Allocation is defined as being dedicated to assign goods to everybody efficiently in order to maximize the general utility of a community. However, legal and political mechanisms such as tax and social welfare systems have specific targets and are openly dedicated to the (re)distribution of goods: that is to say, to the assignment of goods to everybody on the basis of a specific concept of justice. This opposition of standards between efficient allocation and just distribution is extremely significant. For the purposes of the present analysis, it is worth noting that judges unreflectively use considerations in terms of efficient allocation together with those related to just distribution. As the examples illustrated earlier show, the references to EAL and the consequentialism that lies behind them in courts are not free from distributive considerations. They also indicate the degree to which judges are concerned with super-individual social needs. In addition, they show that judges do not believe that economics is a value-free science. However, they apparently share and foster the illusion that economic models can directly and univocally shape legal rules/principles or that the latter can perfectly mimic the former.

In this respect, I believe that the ideas of Calabresi (2016), Cooter (1998) and Posner (1979, 2011)[72] concerning the normative role of EAL, its normative and evaluative nature and the importance of a close relation with social sciences

70 For further details, see, e.g., Chroust (1942); Vega (2013).

71 See, e.g., Becker (1979), who complained of a lack of interest in EAL towards just redistribution; in addition, in Italian literature, see Denozza (2016, 87).

72 Posner's opinion about the interplay between the legal method and EAL and other sciences is ambiguous, and some fluctuations occurred in his thinking over the decades. However, his preference looks to be addressed mainly to a close dialogue with empirical and practical researches, and he puts emphasis on the specific feature of legal reasoning and its relationship with common sense (Posner 2017).

and empirical research might help Italian judges improve their consequentialism and make use of EAL. Following the course begun by Oliver Wendell Holmes (1899) and Arthur Corbin (1919), EAL would be a useful tool for enhancing legal methodology for a number of reasons: (i) it takes into account the world as it is (including future uncertainty and historical experience); (ii) it practices rational criticism and methodical analysis; (iii) it helps the observer to be mindful of the relevance of policies and values; (iv) it adds the contribution of a dialogue with empirical-social sciences.

References

Arlen, Jennifer. 2013. *Research Handbook on the Economics of Torts*. Cheltenham: Edward Elgar Publishing.

Armour, John, Henry Hansmann, and Reinier H. Kraakman. 2009. "Agency Problems, Legal Strategies, and Enforcement." *Harvard Law and Economics Research Paper Series No* 644: 1–45.

Baum, Lawrence. 1994. "What Judges Want: Judges' Goals and Judicial Behavior." *Political Research Quarterly* 47(3): 749–768.

Bebchuk, Lucian A. 1987. "The Pressure to Tender: An Analysis and a Proposed Remedy." *Delaware Journal of Corporate Law* 12: 911–949.

Beck, Gunnar. 2013. *The Legal Reasoning of the Court of Justice of the EU*. Oxford: Hart Publishing.

Beck, Günter W., and Sarah M. Lein-Rupprecht. 2016. "Microeconometric Evidence on Demand-Side Real Rigidity and Implications for Monetary Non-Neutrality." *CFS Working Paper Series* 534: 1–42.

Becker, Gary, Kevin Murphy, and Michael Grossman. 2006. "The Market for Illegal Goods: The Case of Drugs." *Journal of Political Economy* 114(1): 38–60.

Becker, Lawrence C. 1979. "Economic Justice: Three Problems." *Ethics* 89(4): 385–393.

Bertrand, Elodie. 2012. "A Key to Coase's Thought: The Notion of Cost." *Centre national de la recherche scientifique, CNRS*: 1–23.

Bix, Brian. 2018. *Economic Approaches to Legal Reasoning and Interpretation*. Cheltenham: Edward Elgar Publishing.

Breyer, Stephen. 2009. "Economic Reasoning and Judicial Review." *The Economic Journal* 119(535): F123–F135.

Buchanan, James M. 1969. "External Diseconomies, Corrective Taxes, and Market Structure." *The American Economic Review* 59(1): 174–177.

Bushlack, Thomas J. 2015. *Politics for a Pilgrim Church: A Thomistic Theory of Civic Virtue*. Grand Rapids and Cambridge: William B. Eerdmans.

Butler, Henry N., and Klick Jonathan, eds. 2018. *History of Law and Economics*. Cheltenham: Edward Elgar Publishing.

Calabresi, Guido. 2016. *The Future of Law & Economics: Essay in Reform and Recollection*. New Haven: Yale University Press.

Carbonell, Flavia. 2011. "Reasoning by Consequences: Applying Different Argumentation Structures to the Analysis of Consequentialist Reasoning in Judicial Decisions." *Cogency* 3(2): 81–104.

Cariello, Vincenzo. 2015. "Osservazioni preliminari sull'argomentazione e sull'interpretazione orientate alle conseguenze e il vincolo del diritto positivo per il giurista." *Rivista del diritto commerciale e del diritto generale delle obbligazioni* 2: 309–343.

Chavas, Jean-Paul. 1994. "Equity Considerations in Economic and Policy Analysis." *American Journal of Agricultural Economics* 76(5): 1022–1033.

Chiassoni, Pierluigi. 1992. *Law and economics: l'analisi economica del diritto negli Stati Uniti.* Torino: Giappichelli.

Chroust, Anton-Hermann. 1942. "Aristotle's Conception of Equity (*Epieikeia*)." *Notre Dame Law Review* 18: 119–128.

Cohen, George M. 2009. "Interpretation and Implied Terms in Contract Law." In Gerrit De Geest (ed.), *Encyclopedia of Law and Economics.* Cheltenham: Edward Elgar Publishing, pp. 125–151.

Coleman, Jules L. 1976. "The Morality of Strict Liability." *William & Mary Law Review* 18: 259–286.

Coleman, Jules L. 1984. "Economics and the Law: A Critical Review of the Foundations of the Economic Approach to Law." *Ethics* 94(4): 649–679.

Coleman, Jules L., Kenneth E. Himma, and Scott Shapiro, eds. 2004. *The Oxford Handbook of Jurisprudence and Philosophy of Law.* Oxford: Oxford University Press.

Cooter, Robert. 1998. "Expressive Law and Economics." *Journal of Legal Studies* 27: 583–608.

Cooter, Robert, and Melvin A. Eisenberg. 1985. "Damages for Breach of Contract." *California Law Review* 73: 1432–1481.

Corbin, Arthur L. 1919. "Legal Analysis and Terminology." *The Yale Law Journal* 29(2): 163–173.

Cornes, Richard, and Todd Sandler. 1996. *The Theory of Externalities, Public Goods and Club Goods.* New York: Cambridge University Press.

Cserne, Peter. 2011. "Consequence-Based Arguments in Legal Reasoning: A Jurisprudential Preface to Law and Economics." In Klaus Mathis (ed.), *Efficiency, Sustainability, and Justice to Future Generations.* Berlin, NY: Springer, pp. 31–54.

D'Agostino, Francesco. 1977. "Appunti per una teoria *dell'Epikeia*." *Rivista di Filosofia e di Teologia* 2: 129–165.

Denozza, Francesco. 2016. "Le situazioni soggettive nelle concezioni strumentali del diritto: un'incursione teorica tra Jhering e l'Economic Analysis of Law." *Notizie di Politeia* XXXII(121): 84–90.

Dnes, Antony W. 2018. *Principles of Law and Economics.* Cheltenham: Edward Elgar Publishing.

Drakeman, Donald L. 2018. "Consequentialism and the Limits of Interpretation: Do the Ends Justify the Meanings?" *Jurisprudence* 9(2): 300–318.

Ehrenzweig, Albert A. 1950. "Assurance Oblige – A Comparative Study." *Law and Contemporary Problems* 15: 445–454.

Epstein, Richard A. 1980. *Theory of Strict Liability: Toward a Reformulation of Tort Law.* San Francisco: Cato Institute.

Farber, Daniel A. 2003. "What (If Anything) Can Economics Say About Equity?" *Michigan Law Review* 101: 1791–1823.

Feteris, Eveline T. 2005. "The Rational Reconstruction of Argumentation Referring to Consequences and Purposes in the Application of Legal Rules." *Argumentation* 19(4): 459–470.

Gentili, Aurelio. 2013. "Il ruolo della razionalità cognitiva nelle invalidità negoziali." *Rivista di diritto civile* 59: 1105–1127.

Gilson, Ronald J., and Jeffrey N. Gordon. 2003. "Controlling Shareholders." *University Pennsylvania Law Review* 152: 785–843.

Hare, Richard M. 1984. "Rights, Utility and Universalization: A Reply to John Mackie." In Raymond G. Frey (ed.), *Utility and Rights.* Minneapolis: University of Minnesota Press, pp. 106–120.

Harrison, John. 1952–1953. "Utilitarianism, Universalizability, and Our Duty to be Just." *Proceedings of the Aristotelian Society*: 105–134.

Hatzis, Aristides N., and Nicholas Mercuro, eds. 2015. *Law and Economics: Philosophical Issues and Fundamental Questions*. London: Routledge.

Holmes, Oliver W. 1899. "Law in Science and Science in Law." *Harvard Law Review* 12(7): 443–463.

Hooker, Brad. 2016. "Rule Consequentialism." In *The Stanford Encyclopedia of Philosophy*. Stanford: Center for the Study of Language and Information (CSLI), Stanford University.

Johnson, Simon, Rafael La Porta, Florencio Lopez-de-Silanes, and Andrei Shleife. 2000. "Tunneling." *The American Economic Review. Papers and Proceedings of the One Hundred Twelfth Annual Meeting of the American Economic Association* 90(2): 22–27.

Kornhauser, Lewis A. 2017. "The Economic Analysis of Law." In *The Stanford Encyclopedia of Philosophy*. Stanford: Center for the Study of Language and Information (CSLI), Stanford University.

Kornhauser, Lewis A., and Richard L. Revesz. 1993. "Settlements Under Joint and Several Liability." *New York University Law Review* 68(3): 427–493.

Kornhauser, Lewis A., and Richard L. Revesz. 2000. "Joint Tortfeasors." *International Review of Law and Economics*: 317–332.

Kornhauser, Lewis A., and Richard L. Revesz. 2009. "Joint and Several Liability." In Gerrit De Geest (ed.), *Tort Law and Economics*. Cheltenham: Edward Elgar Publishing, pp. 109–133.

Landes, William M., and Richard A. Posner. 1987. *The Economic Structure of Tort Law*. Cambridge, MA: Harvard University Press.

Lefebvre, Claude. 1963. "Natural Equity and Canonical Equity." *Natural Law Forum* 8: 122–136.

MacCormick, Neil. 1994. *Legal Reasoning and Legal Theory*. Oxford: Oxford University Press.

Mackie, John L. 1984. "Rights, Utility and Universalization." In Raymond G. Frey (ed.), *Utility and Rights*. Minneapolis: University of Minnesota Press, pp. 86–105.

Macleod, Bentley W., and Teck Yong Tan. 2017. "Opportunism in Principal-Agent Relationships with Subjective Evaluation." www.teckyongtan.site/

Mathis, Klaus, ed. 2014. *Law and Economics in Europe: Foundations and Applications*. Springer: Dordrecht.

Mathis, Klaus. 2012. "Consequentialism in Law." In Klaus Mathis (ed.), *Efficiency, Sustainability, and Justice to Future Generations*. New York: Springer, pp. 3–29.

Mattei, Ugo. 1994. "Efficiency in Legal Transplants: An Essay in Comparative Law and Economics." *International Review of Law and Economics* 14(1): 3–19.

Meade, James E. 1973. *The Theory of Economic Externalities: The Control of Environmental Pollution and Similar Social Costs*. Geneve: Institut Universitaire de Haute Etudes Internationales.

Mengoni, Luigi. 1994. "L'argomentazione orientata alle conseguenze." *Rivista trimestrale di diritto e procedura civile*: 1–18.

Nakamuraa, Emi, and Jon Steinsson. 2011. "Price Setting in Forward-Looking Customer Markets." *Journal of Monetary Economics* 58(3): 220–233.

Ogus, Anthony I. 2001. "The Contribution of Law and Economics Analysis to Legal Transplants." In Jan M. Smits (ed.), *The Contribution of Mixed Legal Systems to European Private Law*. Antwerpen: Intersentia, pp. 27–37.

Pardolesi, Paolo. 2015. *Profili comparatistici di analisi economica del diritto privato*. Cacucci: Bari.

Pardolesi, Roberto. 2003. *I giudici e l'analisi economica del diritto privato*. Il Mulino: Bologna.

Pardolesi, Roberto, and Bruno Tassone. 2005. "I giudici e l'analisi economica del diritto due anni dopo." *Mercato concorrenza regole* 3: 579–600.

Parisi, Francesco. 2005. "Methodological Debates in Law and Economics: The Changing Contours of a Discipline." In Francesco Parisi and Charles K. Rowley (eds.), *The Origins of Law and Economics: Essays by the Founding Fathers*. Cheltenham: Edward Elgar, pp. 33–52.

Pattaro, Enrico. 2016. "Brevi note sull'interpretazione giuridica." In Carla Faralli (ed.), *Argomenti di teoria del diritto*. Torino: Giappichelli, pp. 132–151.

Perry, Stephen R. 1997. "Libertarianism, Entitlement, and Responsibility." *Philosophy & Public Affairs* 26(4): 351–396.

Pettit, Paul. 1987. "Universalizability Without Utilitarianism." *Mind* 96: 74–82.

Polinsky, A. Mitchell. 2011. *An Introduction to Law and Economics*. New York: Wolters Kluwer Law & Business.

Posner, Richard A. 1979. "The Homeric Version of the Minimal State." *Ethics* 90(1): 27–46.

Posner, Richard A. 1998. "Values and Consequences: An Introduction to Economic Analysis of Law." *Coase-Sandor Institute for Law & Economics Working Paper LIII*: 1–13.

Posner, Richard A. 2010. "On the Receipt of the Ronald H. Coase Medal: Uncertainty, the Economic Crisis, and the Future of Law and Economics." *American Law and Economics Review* 12(2): 265–279.

Posner, Richard A. 2011. "Realism About Judges." *Northwestern University Law Review* (105): 577–586.

Posner, Richard A. 2017. "Legal Research and Practical Experience." *University of Chicago Law Review* 84: 239–248.

Posner, Richard A., Epstein Lee, and William M. Landes. 2013. *The Behavior of Federal Judges: A Theoretical and Empirical Study of Rational Choice*. Cambridge, MA: Harvard University Press.

Posner, Richard A., and Jeffrey Cole. 1995. "Economics of Law: An Interview with Judge Posner." *Litigation* 22(1): 23–33, 66–67.

Pound, Roscoe. 1910. "Law in Books and Law in Action." *American Law Review* 44: 12–36.

Richardson, Megan. 1999. "Perspectives on Joint and Several Tortfeasors and Liability for Economic Loss." In Megan Richardson and Gillian K. Hadfield (eds.), *The Second Wave of Law and Economics*. Leichhardt, NSW: The Federation Press, pp. 86–99.

Sanchirico, Chris William. 2001. "The Continuing Debate on Equity and Efficiency in the Law: A Counter-Response to Kaplow and Shavell." *UVA Law School, Law-Economics Research Paper No. 00–19*: 1–28.

Schäfer, Hans-Bernd, and Claus Ott. 2005. *The Economic Analysis of Civil Law*. Cheltenham: Edward Elgar.

Schauer, Frederick. 1999–2000. "Incentives, Reputation, and the Inglorious Determinants of Judicial Behavior." *University of Cincinnati Law Review* 68(3): 615–636.

Schauer, Frederick. 2000. "The Politics and Incentives of Legal Transplantation." *CID Working Papers 44A, Center for International Development at Harvard University*: 1–22.

Sen, Amartya K. 1977. "Rational Fools: A Critique of the Behavioral Foundations of Economic Theory." *Philosophy & Public Affairs* 6(4): 317–344.

Sen, Amartya K. 1987. *On Ethics and Economics*. Oxford: Blackwell.

Sugden, Robert. 1991. "Rational Choice: A Survey of Contributions from Economics and Philosophy." *The Economic Journal* 101(407): 751–785.

Tarello, Giovanni. 1980. *L'intepretazione della legge*. Milano: Giuffrè.

Tomová, Anna, Lukáš Trgiňa, and Alena Sedláčková. 2015. "Ground Handling Business at Non-European Biggest World Airports as a Problem of Market Structures." *Business, Management and Education* 13(2): 321–335.

Tribe, Laurence H. 1985. "Constitutional Calculus: Equal Justice or Economic Efficiency?" *Harvard Law Review* 98: 592–621.

Tucci, Andrea. 2008. *La violazione dell'obbligo di offerta pubblica di acquisto: rimedi e tutele.* Milano: Giuffrè.

Ulen, Thomas S., ed. 2017. *Methodologies of Law and Economics: Encyclopedia of Law and Economics.* Cheltenham: Edward Elgar.

Varian, Hal R. 1974. "Equity, Envy and Efficiency." *Journal of Economic Theory* 9(1): 63–91.

Vega, Jesús. 2013. "Legal Rules and Epieikeia in Aristotle: Post-positivism Rediscovered." In L. Huppes-Cluysenaer and N. Coelho (eds.), *Aristotle and The Philosophy of Law: Theory, Practice and Justice. Ius Gentium: Comparative Perspectives on Law and Justice*, vol. 23. Dordrecht: Springer, pp. 171–201.

Villa, Gianroberto. 2015. "Le idee di Guido Calabresi e la giurisprudenza italiana, in L'analisi economica del diritto a quarant'anni dall'edizione italiana di Costo degli incidenti e responsabilità civile." *Notizie di Politeia* XXXI(120): 93–101.

White, Mark, ed. 2008. *Theoretical Foundations of Law and Economics.* Cambridge: Cambridge University Press.

White, Mark, ed. 2015. *Law and Social Economics: Essays in Ethical Values for Theory, Practice, and Policy.* New York: Palgrave Macmillan.

Zamir, Eyal, and Barak Medina. 2010. *Law, Economics and Morality.* Oxford: Oxford University Press.

Zouboulakis, Michel S. 2014. *The Varieties of Economic Rationality: From Adam Smith to Contemporary Behavioural and Evolutionary Economics.* Abingdon, NY: Routledge.

Case law references

Court Cass. Civ. United Sections, judgment 8–8–2005, no. 1660, in database Utet giuridica.
Court Cass. Civ. United Sections, judgment 8–4–2008, no. 9148, in database Utet giuridica.
Court of Cass. Civ. Sec. III, judgment 17–12–2009, no. 26516, in database Utet giuridica.
Court of Cass. Civ. Sec. II, judgment 22–2–2010, no. 4240, in database Utet giuridica.
Court Cass. Civ. Sec. V, judgment 22–9–2011, no. 19311, in database Utet giuridica.
Court of Cass. Civ. Sec. II, judgment 21–10–2011, no. 21907, in database Utet giuridica.
Court of Cass. Civ. Sec. II, judgment 15–3–2012, no. 4143, in database Utet giuridica.
Court Cass. Civ. Sec. II, judgment 24–7–2012, no. 12937, in database Utet giuridica.
Court of Cass. Civ. Sec. I, judgment 10–8–2012, no. 14392, in database Utet giuridica.
Court Cass. Civ. Sec. 3, judgment 3–3–2015, no. 4228, in database Utet giuridica.
Court Cass. Civ. United Sections, judgment 22–7–2015, no. 15350, in database Utet giuridica.
Court Cass. Civ. Sec. III, judgment 21–9–2015, no. 18494, in database Utet giuridica.
Court Cass. Civ. Sec. I, judgment 4–4–2016, no. 6504, in database Utet giuridica.
Court Cass. Civ. Sec. VI – 2, judgment 8–7–2016, no. 14048, in database Utet giuridica.
Court Cass. Civ. Sec. VI-3, judgment 27–01–2017, no. 2168, in database Utet giuridica.
Court Cass. Civ. United Sections, judgment 5–7–2017 no. 16601, in database Utet giuridica.
Court Cass. Civ. United Sections, judgment 20–9–2017, no. 21850, in database Utet giuridica.
Court Cass. Civ. Sec. II, judgment 4–4–2018, no. 8227, in database Utet giuridica.
Court Cass. Civ. United Sections, judgment 22–5–2018, no. 12567, in database Utet giuridica.
Court Cass. Civ. United Sections, judgment 22–5–2018, no. 12566, in database Utet giuridica.

Index